PRAISE FOR *MINDSET MATTERS*

"Porterfield is a pioneer in expanding access to college. Through powerful and inspiring personal stories, *Mindset Matters* captures why this mission—and the need to teach students how to think rather than what to think—is so important to the future of our country."

—Michael Bloomberg

"The growth mindset can transform obstacles into opportunities. Daniel Porterfield shows how through the stories of incredible men and women he met as president of Franklin & Marshall College. Porterfield's 'growth mindset playbook' makes inspiring reading and should be a call to arms for all who prize learning in the twenty-first century."

—Kenneth B. Mehlman, Trustee,
Franklin & Marshall College

"In advocating for a wide-ranging, holistic college experience, Porterfield provides a compelling counterpoint to a current single-minded focus on job training. When young people—all of them—are encouraged to grow their many talents through active and experiential learning, they flourish, becoming disciplined, creative, compassionate, engaged humans who strengthen our social fabric and sustain our economy. Education that fosters a growth mindset works, and it's on us to figure out how to expand the opportunities and societal benefits it distinctively provides."

—Carol Quillen, former President,
Davidson College

MINDSET
MATTERS

MINDSET
MATTERS

The Power of College to
Activate Lifelong Growth

DANIEL R. PORTERFIELD

JOHNS HOPKINS UNIVERSITY PRESS | *Baltimore*

© 2024 Johns Hopkins University Press
All rights reserved. Published 2024
Printed in the United States of America on acid-free paper

2 4 6 8 9 7 5 3 1

Johns Hopkins University Press
2715 North Charles Street
Baltimore, Maryland 21218
www.press.jhu.edu

Library of Congress Cataloging-in-Publication Data

Names: Porterfield, Daniel R., 1961– author.
Title: Mindset matters : the power of college to activate lifelong
growth / Daniel R. Porterfield.
Description: Baltimore : Johns Hopkins University Press, 2024. | Includes
bibliographical references and index. | Identifiers: LCCN 2023050538 |
ISBN 9781421449289 (hardcover) | ISBN 9781421449296 (ebook)
Subjects: LCSH: Education, Higher—Psychological aspects. | College students—
Psychology. | Learning, Psychology of.
Classification: LCC LB2324 .P67 2024 | DDC 378.1/98—dc23/eng/20231201
LC record available at https://lccn.loc.gov/2023050538

A catalog record for this book is available from the British Library.

*Special discounts are available for bulk purchases of this book. For more information,
please contact Special Sales at specialsales@jh.edu.*

To my family, my mentees, and my colleagues

Fire can only kindle fire. Mind can only awaken mind. . . .
We must be acted upon.

—Frederick Augustus Rauch, 1837

CONTENTS

PREFACE

In 2006, with the publication of *Mindset: The New Psychology of Success*, Carol Dweck introduced twin concepts that have increasing relevance for today's world—and tomorrow's.[1]

One is the notion of the *growth mindset*, which is the belief that we can enhance our core qualities or talents through our efforts, strategies, and education, and with assistance from others. People with growth mindsets have faith in self-improvement. They tend to be goal oriented and optimistic, confident that they can master new challenges because they've done so in the past. Feedback is their friend, errors their opportunities to begin again.

The second notion is the opposite—the *fixed mindset*—which is the assumption that human abilities are largely inelastic. People who hold this view tend to assume that their strengths and weaknesses are set in concrete. In the face of a novel test or task, where mastery is not assured, they may lack confidence in their ability to raise their game. To them, undue effort to improve is a lost cause; more practical is figuring out what they do well and then sticking to that playbook.

While this book will say much more about growth mindsets and how they take hold among undergraduates, I must make one point right away: For today's economy, lifelong self-improvement is more valuable than ever. That's because we have entered a tech-fueled era of escalating dynamism and disruption. Our jobs, our professions, and the kinds of skills needed in the workplace are morphing rapidly for many reasons, including generative artificial intelligence (AI). In periods of societal sea change, with new ideas and new modes of work rolling in like waves, growth mindsets are a critical plus-factor. They enable us to believe, to know, that we can enhance ourselves in response to new opportunities or to meet new expectations, as opposed to feeling stuck or helpless or overwhelmed or set up to fail.

Growth mindsets matter. Fostering them should be one of the aims of education at every level, so that students are constantly developing the will and the skills for each steeper climb, whether as learners, workers, creators, or citizens. People are this nation's greatest natural resource. We need to kindle our students' inner fire—whatever their backgrounds—for futures that are theirs to claim. This means activating them to learn, making sure they know how to learn, and teaching them to love learning, all as acts and facts of who they are and will be for their entire lives. Growth mindsets can be a formidable facet of identity, for in a changing world, all of us, and especially the young, need to be able to change ourselves.

A great college education empowers young people to do just that. I know this firsthand from twenty years of teaching and mentoring about two thousand students at Georgetown University and Franklin & Marshall College. From those relationships, I've seen how a holistic education ignites five forms of the growth mindset: the mindsets to discover, to create, to mentor, to collaborate, and to strive for inherently meaningful growth.

The mindsets for these capabilities are especially relevant right now, as change surges ahead, old assumptions fall away, and new knowledge, inventions, quandaries, pressures, and ways of working come to the fore. In the fast-morphing economies of today and tomorrow, people will need to be able to *discover* insights no one has told them to look for; *create* inventions no one else would have come up with; give and receive *mentoring* with ease; *collaborate* productively on diverse teams; and *strive* joyfully for growth that speaks to what they value. These five growth mindsets empower us to contribute, give meaning to our endeavors, and differentiate human intelligence from the generative artificial kind.

I appreciate that the last decade has brought growing cynicism about the value of college and that public support for it now looks like a balloon running out of air. While some criticisms are off-base, it's certainly on point to claim that college costs too much for too many, which limits the economic diversity of our student bodies and leaves many people with onerous debt that undermines the vaunted "wage premium" associated with a college education.[2] The fiscal model can be fixed, I believe, through a new compact that combines institutional cost-cutting and accountability with government reinvestment in financial aid and new loan policies to help those with debt build savings. If we don't repair the model, more promising young people will likely pass on college, and more investors (families, alums, legislators, businesses, philanthropists) will likely pull back—an outcome that will hurt our economy given that America will need 6.5 to 8.5 million *more* college graduates in 2030 than we have today, according to two recent studies.[3] We need to rebuild confidence in the value of college—based on clear-eyed vision, not nostalgia.

To do so, I think it helps to look closely at the real learning of real students today. That's why I have written a book that delves into the experiences of more than thirty undergraduates I worked with when serving as F&M's president, from 2011 to 2018. Through their stories, I will show how college activates growth mindsets, why that matters today, and what more educators and students alike can do to enhance this strength and power of the holistic undergraduate experience.

Admittedly, Franklin & Marshall is only one institution in a higher education sector that contains thousands of colleges and universities with varying missions and resources. But it is an illuminating example, because its core purpose is to cultivate the growth of about 2,000 to 2,400 eighteen-to-twenty-three-year-olds per year, which it does with a modest endowment per student that is about ten times smaller than those of fellow liberal arts colleges such as Amherst, Williams, Pomona, and Swarthmore. Today, some critics make the sweeping claim that undergraduates who are thirsty for animating experiences will now find our campuses to be parched deserts. Yes, some institutions, and some state legislatures, have allowed nourishing resources to dry up in the sand. But I'm confident that the profound ways that I saw F&M's educators and ecosystem support student learning growth are also prevalent at many institutions, even the larger ones. My purpose here is to showcase the power and value of promoting growth mindsets and to encourage schools of any type to explore the benefits of this approach in ways that fit their missions and students.

Igniting growth in undergraduates is work worth doing. When activated in one individual, the five mindsets promote success at work, participatory citizenship, and personal fulfillment. When activated in millions, they provide society with a critical mass of citizens who will perpetually learn, innovate, mentor, collaborate, and strive for meaning—all of which our country needs now at scale, and higher education can help provide.

MINDSET
MATTERS

INTRODUCTION

The young dream and the old teach, and in that slow process comes a tomorrow that we who are older may never know but will have helped to shape in the minds and hearts of our students.

—TIMOTHY S. HEALY, SJ

GRADUATIONS ARE SUBLIME.

I should know. From 2011 to 2018, as president of Franklin & Marshall College, I had the best view from the commencement platform.

It stirred me to look upon fifty rows of black-robed students, eyes gleaming beneath their mortar boards, and to confer their bachelor's degrees before their families and professors. There and everywhere, graduation feels vast and very American, evoking tradition and progress, the vision of a school's founders and the hopes of a rising generation. F&M was first established in 1787 as

Franklin College. It was named for Benjamin Franklin, who viewed the education of the people as the lifeblood of a democracy. Commencement brings those ideals into focus. We honor the college's long role in history, ours to steward and extend if but for a time, to ensure that learning serves liberty for the good of the whole.

Equally affecting, however, was when the ceremony became more intimate, as each graduate crossed the platform to the whoops and hollers of classmates and little islands of loved ones in an adoring crowd.

Mary Kate Whitmoyer . . .

Amber Wong . . .

Anastasia Woods . . .

Because I knew telling aspects of many students' stories—starting points and sacrifices, decisions and difficulties—I found beauty in this procession of the proud. What an honor it was to present the diplomas, one by one. Every exchange carried a charge—smiles and seriousness, jubilation, purpose, perhaps regret. For some, the split second of claiming their long-labored-for degree will be a touchstone for the rest of their lives.

The American model of residential higher education, which emphasizes holistic development, is still envied around the world; yet here at home the chorus of detractors is growing louder, and public confidence in higher education has been eroding steadily since the mid-2010s.[1] Some critics call college a left-wing indoctrination factory where cancel culture runs amok. Others say it's an elitist prestige machine only good for locking privilege into place. To still others, it's an engine of corporate conformity, a coddler of the fragile, a debt-spawning racket, or an overpriced irrelevance.

And then there are the claims that truth, reason, research, facts, faculty expertise, impartiality, dialogue, and respectful disagreement no longer have currency on campus. We're now seeing from numerous state legislatures an unprecedented rush of illiberal bills and laws prohibiting the teaching of "divisive" concepts involving race, gender, and sexuality in public institutions.[2]

While reforms are surely needed, most of these criticisms ignore the ways that a quality undergraduate education genuinely helps millions of young people every year. That's an important miss, to say the least. After all, as observed by journalist David Leonhardt, "College graduates earn much more on average; are less likely to endure unemployment; are more likely to marry; are healthier; live longer; and express greater satisfaction with their lives. These gaps have generally grown in recent decades."[3] In 2023, the Lumina Foundation and Gallup assessed the evidence linking postsecondary education to positive life outcomes. Their study found that, beyond enhancing employment and earnings, additional years of study also correlate to better health, greater civic and social engagement, heightened self-confidence about achieving goals, and a stronger feeling of professional satisfaction.[4] Many other evidence-based evaluations have painted the same overall picture.

The reality is that gutting and giving up on college will hurt our young people and our country. Every society needs systems to help late adolescents transition into the relative independence of early adulthood with both a base of knowledge and skills and, critically, the capacity for lifelong learning and growth. The latter is especially important today not only because we live in a global knowledge and innovation economy but also because the rate and reach of change in key aspects of our lives is escalating rapidly, especially due to transformational technologies. Our jobs and ways of working are changing. Our population is changing, as people live longer, birth rates slow, and America becomes more diverse. Our information sources and cultures are changing. Our climate and ecosystems are changing. Our scientific knowledge, medical technologies, defense systems, privacy, political norms, energy sources, and financial and commercial systems are all morphing swiftly, for good and for ill. The stunning arrival of generative artificial intelligence in everyday life will only intensify this trend.

The plain fact is that, in today's shapeshifting economy, those who can't deal with dynamism will miss out on new opportunities and fall faster and further behind. College can and must help young people prepare for lives and careers where, in warp speed cycles, what was once new becomes normal, old, and then out-dated. "Adapting" to change can mean many things, including holding fast to core values that tell us who we are, but overall, being able to grow is essential. To meet the challenges of unrelenting change, people need to be able to learn and develop constantly, alone and in teams—as an act of will, as an act of habit, as an act of identity, as an act of resilience, as an act of citizenship. For that, we need a *growth mindset*—which, to paraphrase psychologist Carol Dweck, is the experience-based belief that one can learn and change.[5] No belief is more empowering as we negotiate the choices and challenges of life, the undoings and the new openings, because with a growth mindset, we think, we know—*from experience*—that we can define and drive our own development.

In this book, I describe five interrelated forms of the growth mindset that college fosters extremely well: the mindsets to dis-cover, to create, to give and receive mentoring, to collaborate, and to strive for growth that reflects and realizes one's values. These capabilities are particularly important in these flux-filled times, when we are constantly confronted with new knowledge, technologies, economies, and ethical questions. Growth mindsets matter for the one and the many, the individual and the society. A holistic college education demonstrably activates these mindsets in eighteen-to-twenty-three-year-olds—and can do so even more effectively in the future if colleges prioritize undergraduate learning with intentionality and creativity. This is the fundamental argument of this book.

*

It's sometimes said that college works by assembling a class of talented undergraduates and then getting out of their way so they can educate one another. In practice, that would actually be a rather empty pedagogy. Aspiring young people want and need adult educators to *get in their way*, all four years, at every turn and chapter. That's how we nurture the will and skill for growth—a reaching spirit—through thoughtful instruction and active learning, teachers and students making meaning together. I admire the way the founding president of Marshall College, Frederick Rauch, expressed this idea in his 1837 inauguration speech: "Fire can only kindle fire. Mind can only awaken mind. . . . We must be acted upon."[6]

Kindle fire. This is what all true educators are committed to doing—helping their students to find and form and know and grow and use their gifts, for their good and the greater good. It's a sacred relationship, that of teachers and learners. For me, the throughline across seven and a half years at F&M and, before that, fourteen years at Georgetown University, was the chance to "act upon" my students as a mentor—whether by scribbling on their essays, or coaching them before fellowship interviews, or dropping hints while hanging out at a ballgame, or looking to help after hearing a hope or a fear or a question or a plan. Such person-to-person encounters are the essence of education.

I loved seeing firsthand how a college education helps young people take self-chosen steps to explore and develop. With its array of intellectual resources, including four years of diverse and progressively advanced classes, college kindles students' fire to learn, yes, but also to learn to learn and to revere learning. It allows them to extend themselves, alone and in groups, with intention and by osmosis, and broadens their perspectives and sense of independence. It provides a stimulating, immersive setting in which students create indelible memories while gaining insight into their strengths, preferences, purposes, and values. And then there are the beloved bonds—the best friends and mentors, the future spouses and children—all coming from a single place and space and time. Is any college flawless? Of course not. Is our higher ed system? No, obviously, significant reforms are needed, especially in terms of cost to students and families. But have untold millions grown and benefited from our holistic residential model? That is an indisputable fact, despite today's dismissals and attacks.

Originally, I envisioned this book as an exploration of how students create meaning in college. To gather ideas, I reached out to thoughtful recent graduates I knew well, like Akbar Hossain, Markera Jones, and Sheldon Ruby, whose tenacious American journeys close the final chapter. I imagined inspiring readers through these portraits and the purity with which undergraduates of all backgrounds say yes to opportunity and an American dream in which a college education plays its starring role. In these pages, you will learn about more than thirty of these impressive young people, through stories that make the case for college in human terms.

As I talked about the value of college with these recent F&M alums, I began to notice patterns. None of them focused on end results like honors, credentials, or starting salaries. Rather, they spoke of learning *journeys*—years and processes of actively sampling, seeking, testing, discovering, connecting, creating, overcoming, giving, loving, aspiring, and emerging—aided by mentors and friends. All told me about panoramas of personal growth they couldn't have foreseen starting out. They recounted hard work, high callings, deep friendships, peak experiences, impactful professors, indelible epiphanies, new goals, new cares, new ideas, new joys and pains, new selves. Not that this growth was easy or inevitable. Some described feeling lost or alone or unseen or unwelcome or unsuccessful at times. Some had regrets. Some rued their naïveté starting out. For many, however, converting pain into new triumphs of the self was the marrow of the experience. College was a multiyear process of self-creation and self-emergence, a becoming that was true and still unfolding, activated because they applied themselves in a place rich with stimulating people and happenings and resources and ideas. An opportunity ecosystem.[7]

From these conversations, I came to see that many graduates enter their early adult lives believing, *because they have done so in college*, that they will be able to keep growing as new prospects emerge. It's such a motivating insight—"I can meet the challenges of change." So, I decided to organize this book to allow readers to see up close the kinds of campus experiences and relationships that help young people develop this self-confidence. Their belief that they can learn across their lifetimes is what, through decades of research, Dweck has incisively identified as the *growth mindset*.

What is a mindset? According to Dweck, it's "the view you adopt for yourself" that "profoundly affects the way you lead your life," a self-perception that one consistently lives into and acts upon.[8] While in theory there may be countless mindsets, the growth mindset she identified stands out because it helps explain why some people regularly succeed at hard tasks, which is that they act on the belief that they can learn and improve. Its opposite is the *fixed mindset*, which is that there's an innate cap to one's abilities.[9] Thus, the student with a growth mindset understands that, if she applies herself, she can learn Chinese, despite not knowing one word or character, and signs up for a class; the one with the fixed mindset thinks Chinese would be hopeless because she's not that good at languages, and perhaps dreads risking a mediocre grade, and so lets the opportunity pass, and others as well. With that, Dweck emphasizes that a "pure" growth mindset does not exist, and that "everyone is actually a mixture of fixed and growth mindsets, and that mixture constantly evolves with experience."[10]

Educators certainly influence that evolution—although not always for the better. Sadly, we all know of individuals who were told by teachers not to waste time on impossibilities (for them) like science (Jane Goodall), social advocacy (Helen Keller), ballet (Misty Copeland), or law (Malcolm X). This is educational malpractice. "Don't judge. Teach. It's a learning process," Dweck reminds us.[11] With humanistic optimism, educators should feed their students' growth hopes by providing: (1) well-sequenced learning opportunities, (2) actionable feedback on their work, (3) useful mentoring about how to learn, and (4) moral support to keep trying. Because, when a person develops a growth mindset, whether she is ten years old or fifty, she understands that she can enhance her capabilities by exercising them, which makes us more optimistic and daring. Her choices become more hopeful. The future beckons. Starting over is no setback because one's gifts are elastic. Knowing this fortifies people for arduous tasks—the ones that stretch and test and hurt—which adulthood offers in abundance. Dweck puts it this way: "The *growth mindset* is based on the belief that your basic qualities are things you can cultivate through your efforts, your strategies, and help from others. Although people may differ in every which way—in their initial talents and aptitudes, interests, or temperaments—everyone can change and grow through application and experience."[12]

From twenty years of mentoring college students, I know this to be true. With all their uniqueness and differences of "initial talents and aptitudes," I have seen thousands of undergraduates both grow and come to know themselves as growers. The process unfolds in assorted ways, but we can discern patterns of learning when we know students and college cultures well. Informed by my relationships and my years on campus, in this book I describe the growth mindsets that I have seen take hold most often and why these mindsets matter, show through stories how it happens, and make recommendations for how colleges can empower students for lifelong learning even more effectively.

Critically, growth mindsets emerge from the experience of *actually growing*, not just motivational messaging. That is to say that actually creating helps launch a creator's mindset, actually collaborating helps forge a collaborator's mindset, and so on. It's pushing through obstacles and knowing that you can do so again that begets growth mindsets. These mindsets may be tacit or explicit; they may be stronger or weaker; they may be differently useful in certain contexts; the range of growth they fuel may be greater or less. The bottom line: Mindsets help drive our choices and actions; as we adopt and live them, Dweck suggests, they become a part of our agency and identity. They become ours.

How do they form? In general, from two kinds of experience: We assume growth mindsets *both* by our own choices *and* through the influences of others. On the one hand, we can be assisted by outside forces, whether by individuals like faculty, supervisors, parents, and peers, or by the stimulating cultures of an academic major or a student club or the campus itself. On the other hand (and I see this as the pivotal factor), we can activate growth mindsets ourselves in the ways we make sense of and act from our prior learning, values, desires, and strengths. Our own agency is essential. As the philosopher Agnes Callard writes of aspiration (which I regard as one's yearning for growth):

> An aspirant's value-transition is her own work, which means that she is a certain kind of cause: a cause of herself.
>
> This is not to deny that the aspirant receives help. Major value-acquisitions reflect the influence of one's environment, especially the people in it. Parents, teachers, and lovers have transformative effects on the people they parent, teach, and love. But they cannot, at least typically, have these effects on someone unless she participates in the process. They assist, rather than substitute for, the activities of the agent herself.[13]

To be clear, growth mindsets are not skills like collecting data or writing well, but they do take hold when we systematically learn or improve our skills. Nor are they intellectual habits, like testing assumptions or backing up arguments with evidence, but, again, the processes of absorbing such habits feeds them. Rather, growth mindsets are attitudes people form about themselves—the suppleness of their capabilities, the breadth of their experiences, the might of their will—that, once lodged, consistently inform their actions and choices. While some research suggests that a single well-placed intervention can enhance self-efficacy and promote growth mindsets,[14] my emphasis here is on the layering of edifying experiences *through four years* in a personalized, relationship- and learning-rich campus ecosystem.

As this book shows, it's positive and motivating for eighteen-to-twenty-three-year-olds moving toward maturity to take on the growth mindsets for discovery, creativity, mentorship, collaborating, and striving. Each equips people to continuously use and grow their assets in ways that are both inherently gratifying and instrumentally useful for adult lives full of change and challenge. They make us more agile and aspirational, more resilient and resourceful—and the earlier they form, the better. In an era of rising depression, disconnection, and burnout among young people,[15] we can and should become more intentional about igniting these mindsets. Think of the young people in your life: You know that you want them to develop an ever-regenerating capacity for growth and greatness as they enter futures theirs to create and not fear.

Consider Julia Ramsey, who formed a striver's mindset (which I'll define below) over five and a half years at F&M. Before college, at Wilmington Charter School in Delaware, Julia had earned stellar grades while dealing gamely with the painful genetic condition Ehlers-Danlos syndrome (EDS), which involves a defect in one's connective tissue. Hellbent on not allowing EDS to slow her entry to college, during her senior year she pushed her doctors to give her a cranio-cervical fusion that required placing a metal plate and bone grafts in her neck. Nothing would stop her.

For college, her plan was to do and be everything, and first semester, while making fast friends and joining the Chamber Singers, she earned a 3.93 GPA, reinforcing that take-the-hill ethic. Sophomore year she won a role in a musical and pledged with a sorority—until EDS came roaring back. First her muscles ached, and her head felt heavy as an anvil. Then she'd pass out for twelve hours only to wake up even fuzzier and more lethargic. The student health center had no answers as all her energy drained away. Although she resisted taking a leave of absence and falling behind her self-imposed standards, doing so became inevitable.

Spending the next nine months at home brought no relief, and a deep undiagnosed depression set in. Blaming herself for her predicament, she resolved to return to campus in January 2014 with the do-it-all ferocity she considered her superpower. But that proved futile. While rehearsing for a play, she collapsed backstage and had to withdraw again—for the spring semester and, at a minimum, the full 2014–15 academic year.

What should have been her sophomore and junior years became a prolonged saga of pain, anger, boredom, and anguish. Some days the most she could do was brush her teeth. She and her parents tried everything to get this malady under control, seeking out the best doctors, grasping for new therapies, but nothing helped. Ailing and idle, constantly depleted from new drugs, with her nervous system going haywire, Julia felt imprisoned within herself.

Understandably, she resented this assault on her body and her plans, and struggled with shame, but didn't yet have the tools to deal with depression. Doing Sudoku puzzles in doctors' offices wasn't the F&M education she'd envisioned. As the semesters passed, it stung to see on social media how friends from freshman year were choosing majors and studying abroad and moving ahead in life. It was ROMO, not FOMO—the *reality* of missing out. But she couldn't vanquish this force that sapped her powers. Why this? Why her?

Julia's path forward began with a shift of perspective. Isolated and listless, feeling utterly deprived, she began to yearn for different things, simpler things, that she could create from these fleeting years of youth. Wellness. Friendships. Community. Exploration. She sensed that the only way to pursue these newly valued goods in college would be to deal with EDS rather than defeating it, and then to pace herself accordingly. One of her doctors advised that if she could do twenty things just 5 percent better that would lift her trajectory—guidance that led her to make dozens of changes of medication, sleep, diet, self-care, and light activity. "Simply doing things that were good for me," she came to see, "helped me to feel productive and get going."

It took a living nightmare, but she broke through a mental wall of castigating herself as a should-be achiever with a blank resume. Instead, she started to envision a whole person with life and learning to strive for and sustain if only she could accept EDS rather than trying to exorcise it. Her aha moment was that "when the plan goes differently is when you discover who you truly are so be open when time reveals a different set of priorities."

In the fall of 2015, as her first-year friends began their senior year, she came back to campus ready both for learning and for balance. She sought out computer science professor Erin Talvitie as a mentor and fell for the camaraderie, methods, and logic of the field. She joined the campus interfaith community, enjoying discussions about spirituality with new friends from around the world. She made time for morning walks and reflection. Her goals weren't lower; they were longer and centered on her values. A big difference, she told me, "was that I now had more clear priorities. It wasn't about achieving all A's anymore, and I cared a lot less what people thought of me." This is one for the five mindsets—the striver's mindset, which entails seriously pursuing growth or change based upon one's deeply held values, whether enduring or emergent, and with a mature yearning for authenticity.

So, in Julia's case, striving meant slowing down—not ramping up—savoring her surroundings, listening to her body, and finding traction in small steps setting up the next maybe bigger bounds. Second semester, Talvitie nominated her for a research assistantship with his colleague Christina Weaver, whose work centered on computational approaches to Alzheimer's and Huntington's diseases. Even though Weaver realized that a relapse could put

Julia out of commission and stall the research, she admired this sincere and resilient young woman, and so, mentor and mentee both took a leap.

Weaver had created an accurate but computationally exhaustive mathematical model to represent real neurons in the frontal cortex of mice. Julia's project was to help implement a much simpler model using a coding language called NEURON and then test how well it could model the same real mice neurons—which turned out to be not well at all. The model she created was much faster than Weaver's original but poor at matching real data.

In the old days, this result might have felt like a failure, but, with her gelling striver's mindset, Julia saw it as grist for life lessons: "I learned I can be completely self-disciplined if I need to be, but that working alone is not my ideal work setting," she once reflected. "I also learned that I thrive on completely understanding the problem at hand, and struggle when I must try and fit the one piece I understand into something larger. And I learned how to communicate these feelings and frustrations, and now when I encounter similar struggles in classes or work experiences, I can recognize and address them."

There's a virtuous cycle here: Julia's striving fed the mindset that then fueled more striving, like a plant growing faster in the direction of the sun. As a result, the next fall she became a peer mentor on themes ranging from diverse identities to "invisible disabilities." She also accepted Professor Weaver's invitation to attend the annual Grace Hopper Celebration of Women in Computing conference in Houston. Joining fifteen thousand women passionate about this male-majority field raised her vision to another level—she could do this, she was needed, and she would not be alone.

Senior year was strong, steady, and joyful. She loved how the results in computer science all came down to her; she either could or couldn't find the solution to a problem, but it was on her. Her striver's mindset and the exigencies of her field were now one and the same, giving her the sense that "my choices are up to me."

Which brings us to the 2018 graduation exercises, when Julia opened her hand to take hold of the diploma for which she'd fought and cried and changed. I will never forget the inner light with which she glowed. Yes, she acquired coding skills and earned a job offer, which had monetary and moral value, but there was more: In college, from the fires of adversity, she forged an actionable, values-based attitude toward life. She internalized how to sustain growth not despite Ehlers-Danlos syndrome but because of it— helped by F&M's supportive educators and culture. Julia's learned response to EDS became a strength and a marker of identity, an ability and not a disability, a mindset for striving to carry into any vista opening before her. As she explained in a speech to new students, "My original vision of college didn't happen—something even better did. My identity feels truer now than at any other point in my life."[16]

I witnessed such flourishing every semester among undergraduates of sundry backgrounds, identities, and interests, and I look forward to seeing what more they do and how they develop.[17] The heartfelt desire to grow and give among the students I've mentored evokes the wisdom of my college English professor, Timothy Healy, SJ, who served as Georgetown University's president in the 1970s and 1980s. A Jesuit priest, Fr. Healy often told his mentees that the true purpose of college was to prepare us for the adult responsibilities of work, parenting, and citizenship. Like Cardinal Newman, whom he quoted often, he believed that a liberal education "brings the mind into form" and bolsters "human knowledge and human reason to contend against those giants, the passion and the pride of man."[18] Such humanistic cultivation would ready the young for the wide, quickening world beyond the campus gates, a landscape of competition and consequence and change, where healing and justice exist in too short supply. That's where we were needed, he emphasized—oriented toward the greater good, with a quality education helping us to apply ourselves.

Is today any different as humanity faces defining threats like rising seas, democracy's decline, and big tech taking over our lives? These dilemmas will not resolve themselves. As argued by Richard K. Miller, the founding president of Olin College of Engineering, "The world has never depended more on science, collaboration, and good will—all of which must be learned by the young."[19] With that, as the philosopher Danielle Allen claims, our pluralistic democratic society requires social actors with the cultivated "participatory readiness" to co-create "the political institutions that will themselves pull toward social equality and economic fairness."[20] For both of these imperatives, America requires an ever-renewing reservoir of ever-growing young citizens, and for that it needs college.

In this book, I explicate patterns of student growth to encourage readers to intensify the very best of holistic undergraduate learning, which many educators want to do.[21] While there's much more to learn about the power of college to boost growth mindsets and lifelong learning, institutions can take positive steps right now. *What's imperative is for individuals to have opportunities to find and freely direct their growth.* The fact is that growth mindsets can be inspired but not imposed. They are not the result of developmental determinism. Rather, as we saw with Julia, when students take the lead in their learning, supported by educators, not only will they grow, but also they will believe that they have grown and value being growers, and believe they can do so again—priceless assets in the long making of a life.

No doubt, college may also promote other mindsets, but, as I listened to my mentees, discovery, creation, mentorship, collaboration, and striving stood out for a few reasons.[22] First, as we'll see, these mindsets are fostered by the core cultures and activities of a residential campus. Second, they all strengthen *intrinsically* resonant feelings of agency, identity, growth, authenticity, and purpose, crucial to the forming identities of young adults. Third, they're also *instrumentally* valuable with automation and artificial intelligence surging, which demands the agility to learn constantly, think creatively, adapt confidently, and work in teams. Finally, they may contribute to *ethical* thinking and action, in that they foster social benefits like cooperation, new knowledge, new inventions, and new art. Now, let's look at each one.

Mindset One: Discovery

This is the mindset that tells us that we can interpret and understand our reality, often filled with ambiguities, and create new ideas or findings, in contrast to being passive consumers of information. It responds to and reinforces the astonishing natural curiosity that we see in children. It pushes us to hunt down knowledge for ourselves rather than being spoon-fed by others. It leads us to challenge inherited notions and invites each generation to build upon, and correct, the contributions of the distant to recent past. In the soaring words of James Baldwin, who viewed artists as the quintessential discoverers:

> The artist cannot allow any consideration to supersede his responsibility to reveal all that he can possibly discover concerning the mystery of the human being. Society must accept some things as real; but he must always know that visible reality hides a deeper one, and that all our action and achievement rest on things unseen. A society must assume that it is stable, but the artist must know, and he must

let us know, that there is nothing stable under heaven. One cannot possibly build a school, teach a child, or drive a car without taking some things for granted. The artist cannot and must not take anything for granted, but must drive to the heart of every answer and expose the question the answer hides.[23]

Discoverers repeatedly show the verve to take up the next problem or job or field with mastery in mind. That's how they're oriented, which is why employers adore them.[24] They constantly, restlessly probe. They work to close the gap between what they do and don't know, drawing energy from difficulty. They use their imagination to connect ideas, integrate thought with experience, and make sense of their surroundings. They build banks of knowledge and skills they can draw from when needed. They read signals of change and can adapt to the shifting frontiers of thought or professional expertise. After love, the capacity to discover may be the greatest strength we humans have, in this age and every age. It has particular value in our protean knowledge economy that requires intellectual dexterity and problem-solving in all fields. Without discoverers, how will America invent tomorrow's cures, compete in a flattened world, help cool our heating planet, and deploy AI for human good?

Because no two people are the same, four years of college fosters discovery differently, case by case. One factor that's consistent, however, is the pivotal influence of mentors who prioritize teaching— cultivating, correcting, prodding, training, and rewarding undergraduates. Good ones reinforce searching in salutary ways, helping students learn and not just cheerleading; poor ones can leave their mentees feeling helpless or overwhelmed or demeaned, even if they're saying the right things. As Ken Bain has written, impactful teachers create a "natural critical learning environment":

"Natural" because what matters most is for students to tackle questions and tasks they naturally find of interest, make decisions, defend their choices, sometimes come up short, receive feedback on their efforts, and try again. "Critical" because by thinking critically, students learn to reason from evidence and to examine the quality of their reasoning, to make improvements while thinking, and to ask probing and insightful questions. This is, by far, the most important principle—the one on which all others are based and which commands the greatest explanation.[25]

Here's one story I like. A mentee of mine asked an F&M professor what it would take to get an A on an assignment.

"I don't know," the professor replied.

"How can that be?" she asked. "You're the one who gives the grades."

"That's right. To get an A, your paper needs to teach me something that I don't already know. . . . Come talk when you're ready."

The professor is telling her that academic excellence requires her to produce original thought beyond effective memorization. He's conveying that curiosity and discovery are values of the college (that's what earns A's) and that he, the scholar, is also a continuous learner. In chapter 1, I will show some of the ways that an undergraduate education moves students to be and see themselves as discoverers, helping them, in and after college, to create or co-create the learning that they seek and need. Faculty play a central role in this process, as research suggests that students achieve more when working with professors who believe that intelligence is malleable rather than fixed.[26] Looking forward, it's essential that our colleges and universities expect and support teaching excellence from all faculty and ensure that undergraduates have access to permanent full-time faculty, especially early in their education, a tall task given the overreliance on part-time, short-term adjunct faculty at too many institutions.

Mindset Two: Creativity

This is the mindset to make one's own product, to fill a void or meet a need, to add color to one's environs, to stamp a tattoo on society that says, "I was here." Such ingenuity flourishes in youth cultures where students labor long nights to create a painting or a club or a cause. On campus and beyond, invention is both a private calling to touch and tap an inner source and a public commons where human beings meet to make the world in which we wish to live. The mindset to create adds value, drives progress, and enables exchange. It has both practical and moral worth, stemming from the generative and expressive instincts of our species. Creativity preserves and creates culture and identity, as for the author Reyna Grande, who turned to writing in college "to give meaning to my experiences . . . [as] an act of survival" and to "hold on to my native country and keep it from floating into the mists of my memory."[27] It leads to feelings of flow and fulfillment, purpose, pride—even exhilaration. As creators and innovators, we build upon one another's work with offerings we hope will move others to make their marks too.

Creativity is the engine and the output of a vibrant campus. Why? Partly it's the dynamism, an "enriched environment" of energy and ideas, with libraries bustling like train stations, with proposals being pitched, with controversies swirling, with deadlines looming, with the daily diet of questions and collaboration and feedback and hope.[28] Partly it's the academic invitations, guided by faculty, to create original products like a thesis or a business plan or a sculpture. Partly it's the ethos of research and scholarship, all about creating new knowledge. And partly it's the pulsing heart of the young to make or speak or solve, *sui generis*, now or never, because they crave it and they can. "Inexperience erases fear," the legendary choreographer Twyla Tharp has written, which combined with thirst and talent, makes undergraduate maker cultures so dynamic: "Inexperience provides us with a childlike fearlessness that is the polar opposite of the alleged wisdom that age confers on us, the 'wisdom' telling us some goals are foolish, a waste of time, invitations to disaster. In its purest form, inexperience erases fear. You do not know what is and is not possible and therefore everything is possible."[29]

Take Alec Hersh, who jumped in fast as a first-year, auditioning for a play. This brought him into the campus arts community—full of passionate peers who were writing scripts and choreographing dances and chipping in on each other's projects. The active ingredient was energy—rousing, ricocheting energy. Fired up by this spirited creative culture, Alec decided to write his own play based on the family histories of John F. Kennedy and Teddy Roosevelt. After a critique from a drama professor, he revised his script and recruited a student cast. Drawing upon the example of a second professor, he taught himself to direct, from coaching the actors to lighting to sound to the set to staging. It all came to fruition when *Domestic Animals* played five times in F&M's Green Room Theatre. The production was intense, demanding, and thrilling—with epiphanies that will live on for Alec and the cast.

In chapter 2 I bring us inside Alec's experience to see what he learned from the creative process and how his urge to make was influenced by a community trauma when he was younger. And then we'll look at three students who drew from F&M's culture to make business ventures, a *pro-speech* protest, and an art exhibition, each of which involved working iteratively to solve tough chal-lenges. The stories demonstrate how student ingenuity, engaged peers, faculty mentoring, campus culture, and the right resources combine to nourish the mindset to create.

Mindset Three: Mentorship

This is the mindset both to give and receive mentoring, which is about helping others realize their purposes by sharing useful knowledge or skills or perspectives or footholds into opportunity. At its core, the best mentoring is relational and ethical, conveying respect for mentees, their need for assistance, and the activity they are pursuing. Mentoring can involve validating the mentee, or providing warmth in a storm, or brokering a new relationship, or setting high standards. As the journalist Gwen Ifill once said, "a good mentor . . . gives you a sense of everything that's possible for you, not only with their own example, but also with their faith in you."[30] Overall, it's a cyclical form of citizenship, as those who seek and use mentoring often pay it forward to the next wave com-ing up behind, thus growing further through the giving.

This cycle of mentorship is a hallmark of undergraduate cul-tures. That's because the annual rhythms of college life, where new students enter and returners advance, require upper-level students to pass down know-how about what it takes to run an event or do a job or excel in a class or negotiate with the adminis-tration. It's a worthy type of servant leadership—generous, pro-active, practical, empathetic, relational, and reciprocal.

One student who activated the mindset to mentor was Darrius Moore, a super-social New Yorker who genuinely and sincerely made time for anyone. As a freshman, he gravitated toward the senior Lorenzo Daughtry-Chambers. It wasn't just that he followed him into the African Drumming Society and Intelligent Men Purposefully Accomplishing College Together (I.M.P.A.C.T.), a high-octane club that created community among men of color. Literally, if they were in the same room, he would go stand by Lorenzo's side, glowing with pride. He knew he could rely on Lorenzo and the other I.M.P.A.C.T. brothers, as "they took me under their wings and showed me the ropes, directly and indirectly."

Sophomore year, as he was no longer a newbie, Darrius churned over how to define himself on campus. That year, I saw him make a decisive choice. He was working as an advisor in F&M College Prep, our summer program for top high school students. Something about those hopeful kids brought out his caring soul and 1000-watt personality. He could get reticent sixteen-year-olds dancing the Wobble and restless ones settled down for homework. Whether they were rural Pennsylvanians, immigrants from California, or city-enthusiasts like himself, he always knew what to say and how to say it and what to reveal. The students adored him just as he'd adored Lorenzo. Watching him give from within, I sensed that it wasn't Darrius alone doing the mentoring; to me, he was channeling his father and the other role models and educators he'd had growing up in Brooklyn—a living tradition of Black kinship and love.

This way of relating felt good and right. It both drew upon his values and deepened his growth, for the act of mentoring led him to think more deeply about what he could and couldn't accomplish in such a role:

It was difficult to realize that we had to send some of these students back to the hardships they faced at home. All I wanted to do was save them. I remember crying on the last day realizing that I could not . . . and that my job was not to save them. I could not accomplish that in three weeks for any single student. My job was to play a role in their journey. Sometimes you just have to play your part, leave a nugget of wisdom or show one act of goodwill to impact the journey of another.

He came into junior year eager to mentor again, which led him to stand for president of I.M.P.A.C.T. This gave him a platform from which to show green freshmen that they could be and feel authentic as F&M men of color and "stake our claim on the campus." Almost overnight he grew into the stature that the role required. One evening, for example, I saw him end a meeting early so that the brothers could attend a workshop on healthy relationships organized by a women's group. *Time to show up, fellas*, he cried out with a smile, prompting twenty first-year men to rush out behind him, joining him in joining others.

As a senior, Darrius mentored his peers during a running campus discussion about equipping our police officers with sidearms. He came to every town hall meeting well-prepared, having reviewed the information circulated beforehand. He asked productive questions and stayed behind to hear from anyone who wanted to talk. He befriended some officers and walked the grounds with them. I think he was conscious of how his example set a tone for others, from students to educators to safety officers, although he probably didn't realize how strongly he helped us sustain a civil debate on a red-hot issue, which some say our colleges can no longer do. I say that such conversations do happen regularly, usually beyond the view of outsiders, because student-mentors like Darrius show that hard topics can be talked and thought about.

On campus, mentoring is one part care, one part listening, one part probing, one part artistry, one part modeling, and one part holding back. Giving and growing as a mentor in a culture that prized mentorship made Darrius want to do it more often and better—leading him, after graduation, to choose to work with college-bound teenagers. Now he can express a personal philosophy of mentoring that involves leading "by action, by work ethic, and by deeds, not just words." For him, mentoring is a mindset because "you have to choose to pour into people with knowledge, feedback, advice, lessons, and wisdom." Chapter 3 looks inside several relationships to show how college elevates this "pouring into people" as a way of thinking, giving, partnering, growing, and being.

Mindset Four: Collaboration

This is the mindset to "co-labor" with partners to scale higher heights than individuals can reach alone. It responds to the human longing to connect with others in pursuit of a unifying vision. The mindset to collaborate helps us supplement the natural limits of individual time or perspective with what Keith Sawyer calls "group genius,"[31] leading to new insights, solutions, products, or experiences. When we effectively tap others' knowledge, skills, strengths, and humanity, we improve not just how we solve problems but also how we frame them—which increases our ability to learn and work productively.

In the terrain of adult endeavor, whether in research, business, government, diplomacy, public health, education, or national defense, teamwork is ubiquitous, and the most serious trials demand that people collaborate. Think of the civil rights movement or the blockbuster triumphs of Apollo 11 and 13 or the high-speed development of the COVID-19 vaccine. Strong, inclusive teams bring more perspectives, aggregated brainpower, complementary capabilities, moral unity, and public legitimacy. Pluralistic teamwork can be both a driver of democracy and evidence of its existence.

The daily operations of a college demand constant collaboration and partnership. Each day, most students work cooperatively toward shared purposes in classes, jobs, clubs, labs, casts, dorms, and teams. All this helps them learn the hows and whys of goal setting, trust, compromise, and much more. Campus collaborations don't always work, of course, for reasons ranging from immaturity and uneven commitment to conflict avoidance and groupthink, but failures lead to learning too. As 2018 graduate Bendjhi Villiers once said in a speech, "The collaborative network challenges us to be better and do better. It reminds us that excuses aren't enough. It invites us to grab every hand that reaches out to us and to return back more than what was given."[32]

No other environment gives eighteen-to-twenty-three-year-olds such a complement of team experiences, including in classes.[33] There's power in peer endeavor—in both practice and performance—whether it's putting out a newspaper or revisiting the meta-question of a seminar or competing for a championship. The students are doing it themselves, and they're doing it together. Much of the value comes down to mutuality—shared care for a goal, for each person's role, for the result, and eventually, for each other. All this stimulates a collaborator's mindset, which we'll examine in chapter 4.

Mindset Five: Striving

As we saw with Julia Ramsey, this is the mindset to reach for more learning, more impact, and more excellence *as an expression of new or emerging personal values.* Examples might be the junior who moves from coping with a parent's death to creating a grief support group or the sophomore who's so enthralled with liberal arts approaches that she pivots with her mind on fire from pre-med to public health. Strivers are a lifeforce for any campus—and any society. They believe in broadening. They leap into openings and tap the resources around them. They're directed "not at satisfying wants but rather at generating them."[34] They persevere when the road gets rocky. They pursue new possibilities with elan and a spirit of interior freedom. Growth is their goal, powered by their values. In the words of the double refugee from the Nazis and the Soviets who grew up to become the 64th US Secretary of State, and much more, Madeleine Albright, "I was taught to strive not because there were any guarantees of success but because the act of striving is in itself the only way to keep faith with life."[35]

Our colleges encourage striving in myriad ways. The classes call on students to challenge themselves. The faculty exemplify the inner quest to find the next insight. Many alumni model the ideal of a personal calling. Each semester presents new invitations to surprise oneself into growth through service, contemplation, spirituality, boundary-crossing dialogue, and so much more—and strivers are partial to raising their hands. Campuses are places of idealism and aspiration—and these students set the tone with their openness and initiative. Typically, they're the ones others seek to include and emulate.

Strivers have a distinctive resource—it's their values-charged restlessness for meaning and "the more"—although, often, that's a force the young need to figure out how to harness, like Julia did. After all, it's an occupational hazard of undergraduates to take on too much or jet among commitments or neglect the mean between extremes. Strivers need to learn how to transition to new interests, reflect purposefully, balance their commitments, and avoid dabbling. Often, their question isn't *whether* to strive but, given who they are, what to strive for and how to sustain striving. All this comes with experience and mentoring—which college life offers in buckets over the course of eight choice-filled semesters.

A quintessential striver is Aicha Camara, an immigrant from West Africa, who received her F&M diploma in May 2016. On the commencement stage she gave me a beaming hug and then waved like a movie star to the crowd. An hour after the ceremony I saw her standing behind a building, leaning on a friend and sobbing uncontrollably in her cap and gown.

I knew why. Her path to the bachelor's degree echoed iconic American stories like Anzia Yezierska's 1922 novel, *Bread Givers*, in which a gifted Jewish immigrant girl must outwit her religiously orthodox father to enjoy new world freedoms like schooling and work. Aicha's life started with a typical childhood in Guinea, but a series of blows radically bent the rails of her future. Her mother died young, leaving her bereft and emotionally alone. Then her father remarried and moved to New York City with his second wife. He sent Aicha to live with relatives in the Ivory Coast for a year while the family got settled and then brought her to America when she was thirteen.

There was much to adjust to, of course, for this teenager on the brink of womanhood. She had to navigate the unfamiliar size and mores of New York while taking on childcare duties at home. Even though she made prodigious progress, learning English felt like an unending torment. Making sense of the ways her Guinean culture touched or clashed with the city's countless cultures seemed overwhelming but soon enough became fascinating.

Fortunately, she ended up at Manhattan's High School of Economics and Finance, a small school that emphasized leadership—

an ideal fit, as she was contemplating the purpose of her life. Her journey, grueling as it had been, gave her the benefits of perspective—multicultural, integrative, gendered, and new. The school promoted rigorous learning for an ever-changing economy and society. Molded in a cauldron of migration and adversity, Aicha latched onto this unapologetically ambitious vision. She seized every prospect for learning and experience—which placed her in conflict with her father, who valued schooling mainly as book learning to equip her to hold a job that would help support him and the family.

Once she told me that she and her father had "two distinct 'American dreams' for me. For a while, I was able to fulfill both. But as time passed it became almost impossible to feed his and mine at the same time." As a result, their small Bronx apartment became a battleground of worldviews, especially about college. He wanted her to stay in his home and study locally before marrying a man of his choosing; she wanted to go away to school, make her own choices, and find herself. A well-behaved *Maninka* woman, he'd complain, would not defy his edicts. She would go into her room and cry about her fate before summoning the resolve to keep striving all the same, for education was the portal to survival. Their two-year power struggle culminated with a Battle Royale concerning the deposit to hold her place at F&M—when, to his credit, he relented and wordlessly left a check on her backpack before going to work.

Aicha came to F&M with soaring aspiration. She'd fought her father's worldview—and perhaps influenced it—for the chance to grow. Now she could take her shot. Right away she stood out with her craving for intellectual exchange in class and in our weekly Common Hour lectures, where she'd invariably pose the first question in front of the whole school. No wonder the faculty admired her, especially government professor Susan Dicklitch-Nelson, to whom she opened up in a crucial early seminar on refugees. She yearned for depth in her relationships and relished the merging of perspectives from which new ideas are born.

By sophomore year her accomplishments began to stack up. Selection as a house advisor. Academic honors. A Rouse Scholarship for outstanding achievement. A paid internship with Viacom in New York City. However, she felt it unwise to even mention any of this at home for fear of provoking her father with the doors swinging open for her. Aicha was the disobedient daughter, the bad seed becoming "too American." So what, for example, that she won a prestigious summer fellowship to study public policy at the University of Michigan? That would just extract her from the household and make her more likely to want to go to graduate school, so he didn't want to hear about it.

In theory, walking away from home to pursue her path was an option, but she didn't want to lose contact with her siblings and her heritage. Why couldn't she have it all—her freedom, her learning, her family, her faith, and her cultural identity? At home, these loyalties squeezed her tight, but she resolved to bear it for as long as necessary for her father to come around.

On the other hand, at school, these values were not a vice but many roads converging in a circle. For Aicha, and for many students navigating cultures without and within, every day and every hour of college life was a running dialogue of self and soul. For example, being a house advisor required her to lead workshops with first-year students on alcohol use, seeking and giving sexual consent, and bystander intervention—all of which were, initially, beyond her comfort zone by several ZIP codes. For two years she led the Muslim Students Association, requiring her to bridge the variations of culture and religious practice among the members. And, near graduation, she shared with me that one of the greatest benefits of her college education was the chance to become friends with fellow students from countless countries and cultures—enriching her understanding of both herself and the world.

At commencement, on top of her academic honors as a government major, Aicha received F&M's leadership prize named for the World War II hero Dick Winters ('41). As Dweck might say, it's clear that what Aicha believed about herself influenced the defining choices she made.[36] Although Franklin & Marshall didn't endow this remarkable woman with her striver's mindset, the school shaped and braced it with plentiful opportunity, mentors, and moral support. Her life destiny is to manage the stresses from her dual identity as an aspiring new American and a proud *Maninka* woman. College fed this quest and her inner incantation never to sell herself short—a crucial resource for all the Aicha Camaras out there scrapping for the lives they desire.

That's the striver's mindset that prompted her after graduation, while working for Bloomberg Philanthropies, to compete for and win a coveted George J. Mitchell Scholarship to study at Trinity College, University of Dublin. Her field? Gender and women's studies, where she examined the intersection of culture and religion in Islam, the next step in her unending quest for a fully lived life. And in the years since her college graduation, Aicha's father has become more accepting of who she is and continues to become.

It's heartening to know young people like Aicha, Alec, Darrius, and Julia for whom college fed their soulful longings. All claimed their learning and their futures, knowing when they graduated that they could keep growing and giving as young adults. Each is human evidence of the value of college. In the chapters ahead, I'll introduce more earnest learners of their ilk. But first, three thoughts on why colleges should place even greater emphasis on growth mindsets:

First, fostering growth mindsets realizes education's primary aim—to develop talent

Talent is the holistic set of assets and potentialities we can tap to pursue our purposes, deal well with difficulties, and add value to the world. While talent may include one's cognitive or physical resources at any given moment or for a particular task or goal, it also includes the so-called meta-cognitive or character qualities like optimism, motivation, awareness of how to learn, self-control, independence, emotional awareness, perseverance, curiosity, and agility.[37] Surely, a growth mindset is a relevant *talent* for any task or goal that requires actual growth.

For example, imagine a young person's long-term goal is to lead a financial services company. Over the varied chapters of her career, all these mindsets will be durable assets. She'll need to stay ahead of the curve in her field through constant discovery. She'll need to create her own distinctive contributions. She'll need to collaborate effectively and get and give mentoring. And she'll need to sustain her growth trajectory across many years and many pitfalls, easier to do with vitality if the effort required runs through her values rather than around them.

The five growth mindsets can "future-proof" people against the kind of professional irrelevance experienced by those who can't or don't want to keep up with change. They're *germane* to the choices and challenges in work and life. They're *integrative*, uniting baseline capabilities, skills, experiences, and values from school, work, and cocurricular and social milieus. They're *accretive*, strengthening with use.

Critically, they're also *authentic* to the individual—the whole person—for, having emerged from one's unique attributes, actions, values, and purposes, and from the narrative of one's life, they may become an element of self-proclaimed identity. *I am a mentor*, Darrius Moore might have thought as he grasped the ethical impacts of his mentoring. *I am a striver*, Julia Ramsey might have internalized as she acted on her new aspiration to breathe in the everyday joys in life. Each version of the growth mindset presumes that the individual is the primary agent of her experience. Creators value and choose creating. Collaborators value and choose collaborating. Strivers value and choose striving. In helping young people choose, form, and hold these mindsets, we're helping them understand that they can act in and on their environment, which leads to a second reason for this focus.

Second, the mindsets for discovery, creating, mentorship, collaboration, and striving are invaluable resources in today's fast-morphing world

In 2008, Claudia Goldin and Lawrence Katz published a magisterial book claiming that America rose to economic ascendency in the twentieth century because, as technology changed significantly, America's historic investment in education placed us "in the best position to invent, be entrepreneurial, and produce goods and services using advanced technology."[38] Now the pace of change is turbocharged—in technology, in science, in economics, in the biosphere, in communications, in diplomacy, in culture, in the waves of true and false information crashing upon us.[39] Technology is reshaping every field in every country and culture. In this "second machine age" or "fourth industrial revolution," it's often said that most professions that can be automated will be—from accountants to tellers to truck drivers to radiologists.[40] For sure, advances in science and technology, including generative artificial intelligence, will bring wondrous benefits to humanity, or to some humans, but constant upheaval will also be dangerous to freedom, justice, equity, and social cohesion. In the brave new world rising like waves before us, adaptive *human* learning and *human* sensibility and *human* collaboration must play even stronger roles— and that requires education.[41]

Those with growth mindsets will be well-prepared to adapt to change and to thrive—and to help solve defining problems like bettering the economy for all, containing the climate crisis, and dealing with America's divides in hair-trigger times. These aren't dangers that we can tackle discretely or delegate to another era. Nor are the cognitive strengths needed for epic challenges best inculcated through impersonal instruction and rote memorization.

This is why it's essential to foster growth mindsets among young people. The economy and society of their future will demand lifelong growth from them. Undergraduate education can and must meet this need, for the now and the next, which leads to the third reason for this focus.

Third, by understanding how college students form growth mindsets, we can build upon what's working and improve what's not

Throughout this book, I make suggestions about how colleges can design even more impactful learning experiences and opportunity ecosystems for growth mindsets. Certainly, more research, more ideas, more discussion, and more voices are needed on the following themes:

A. Strengthening student agency. If we value these mindsets, we need to constantly ask how we can help undergraduates from every starting point to become the authors of their own educations. Too often, well-meaning educators or advocates ask what we can *do* for students. That matters, of course, *but it's critical to equip students to do and create for themselves.* As Eduardo Briceño argues, "To grow and succeed, we must develop the belief that we can change, as well as the competence for how to change. These two elements work hand in hand and reinforce each other."[42] What environments, relationships, messages, modes of learning, and battery of learning strategies will help young people enjoy hard challenges and enact their own growth?[43] How can we assess what works and what doesn't? And how can we include more students in creating the creative approaches that are needed?

B. Equipping mentors and advisors. As Daniel Chambliss and Christopher Takacs argue in *How College Works*, "Personal relationships are often *the central mechanism and daily motivators* of the student experience. . . . Faculty-student interactions both inside and outside the classroom have dramatic effects on student learning."[44] Nothing readies the young to grow like being seen and engaged personally, especially by professors, which I refer to as the "pedagogy of involvement" and will discuss in chapter 1. Coaches, supervisors, counselors, advisors, chaplains, librarians, financial aid staff, and others on campus also unlock talent. Can we give more students more truly formative relationships and learning experiences with faculty and staff?[45] Can we prepare mentors better— sharing new findings from learning science, showing new ways to promote active learning, challenging ourselves to walk empathetically in our students' shoes and understand better the places from which they started?[46] How can professors make college learning more holistic and personalized, more supportive of growth mindsets, and better determine what works and what may not?[47]

C. Supporting students. Institutions need to make sure students have the basics for learning, such as financial aid and baseline access to food, shelter, health care, safety, and the money to get by. Sadly, however, new research shows that more than 70 percent of undergraduates have unmet financial needs, reflecting a gap between their school's financial aid award and the actual costs of attending college that worsens for lower-income students.[48] Mental health is also a growing concern, of course, and more students have needs than ever before, but as we saw with Julia Ramsey, when we work through psychological difficulties, we often plant the seeds for thriving growth mindsets. Also critical are intellectual freedom, civility in campus dialogue, equity of opportunity, belonging, and personal accountability. How can all the resources of an institution, including all staff and faculty, be aligned to promote student agency and success? And, what barriers to full participation must colleges try to knock down, especially for students from under-seen, under-visited, under-valued, and thus under-included communities?[49]

D. Fostering students' moral and ethical development. For as long as we have had colleges, some educators have argued that higher learning can and should facilitate moral and ethical formation. However, it's like untying the Gordian knot to decide precisely which virtues and values should be emphasized—if any. For two reasons, the notion of growth mindsets may offer a new avenue into this discussion. First, this focus reminds educators that each student has her own distinctive talent and agency to build and use, and thus is an end in herself, with equal dignity to all others; from this perspective, the ethical role of teachers is to individualize education and accompany students in their efforts *to become their desired selves*. Second, these growth mindsets may orient students for ethical citizenship by enhancing prosocial behavior like creating discoveries, sharing knowledge, helping others, and working together.

E. Strengthening our campuses as learning ecosystems. We know from decades of research that students of all ages learn holistically—and that social and emotional maturity provide a sturdy bedrock upon which to add layers of academic knowledge.[50] These insights suggest that we should regard the *full campus and total college experience* as catalysts for growth and empowering life outcomes. Richard A. Detweiler's recent survey of 1,000 generationally diverse college graduates speaks to the value of this "ecological" framework. His research associates the *context* of liberal arts education (even more than the *content*) with positive adult outcomes like leadership, altruism, life learning, cultural involvement, success, and fulfillment.[51] What more can we do to spur or structure growth through resources like campus jobs, mentoring, peer leadership roles, community service, living-learning communities, and off-campus engagement, much of which is led by staff? How can we innovate with and evaluate more cocurricular, project-based, team-enabled, and experiential models of learning? In what ways do our overarching campus cultures and traditions bolster the five mindsets—or inhibit them? And can we design new research methods to assess what makes a difference and why?

F. Learning from diverse models of college. As mentioned in the preface, my perspectives on student growth come from twenty years of experience at Franklin & Marshall College and Georgetown University. However, while the traditional residential campus is my starting point for exploring how college fosters growth mindsets, other models may be equally influential for students and society. We should assess, for example, how commuter schools, larger universities, two-year colleges, online programs, and technical training programs can and do activate growth mindsets. Likewise, we need to explore distinctive mindsets promoted by historically Black colleges and universities (HBCUs), women's colleges, and schools serving tribal, Latino, or immigrant communities. What about religious and military institutions, and higher education systems around the world?

G. Constructing the student body. In the mid-2010s, F&M became nationally known for our multipronged Next Generation talent strategy. This was our comprehensive initiative to enhance the academic profile of the student body by almost tripling our enrollment of first-generation, low-income students, many of whom identified as rural, Black, Latino, and/or immigrant.[52] To do so, we tripled our investment in need-based student aid—meeting the full financial need of all domestic students while also using aid to attract splendid international students of modest means. The talent strategy produced an enormous influx of outstanding students, including from the south and west, where the youth population is growing and F&M had previously had little reach. Increasing need-based aid also was a prudent financial strategy, as it reduced our overreliance on attracting students from the small percentage of American families (8–10 percent, and shrinking) wealthy enough to pay the full cost of a four-year private education. It helped that both of my board chairs, Larry Bonchek and Sue Washburn, had been the first in their families to attend college and thus lived learning like a humanistic faith.

We started with the knowledge that each year tens of thousands of low- and moderate-income students do not apply to any of the top colleges they're qualified to attend, mainly because they haven't been encouraged and recruited.[53] Then we made a few experience-informed assumptions about which qualities of talent would most empower students for success in our particular undergraduate program. For example, because of F&M's demanding curriculum, we decided to look for curiosity and strong grades in a college prep program (our internal studies found that standardized test scores did not predict high or low student achievement at F&M). Since our faculty prized academic rigor and eschewed grade inflation, we emphasized an iron work ethic and resilience in pursuit of one's goals. And, because smaller colleges need and reward students who get involved outside of class, we decided to favor applicants who showed the initiative to chase after learning opportunities.[54] Admittedly, we embarked on this approach somewhat intuitively, but in the process we quickly learned a great deal from impactful educators at the schools, networks, and access programs that sent us motivated young people such as Aicha Camara and many others in these pages.

One might say that we were recruiting students with inchoate growth mindsets, although we didn't start with that vocabulary. Nor were we informed at that time about Angela Duckworth's pathbreaking work on "grit."[55] We just knew that we were looking for hungry teenagers with the *talents* of aspiration, persistence, industriousness, curiosity, initiative, and purposefulness about college—and that many lower-income communities would have such young people in abundance. The Next Generation talent strategy was a living and long-term partnership of the students and the school, not a one-off project. Powered by their own strengths, and supported by F&M, our cohorts of lower-income, first-generation students typically performed at or above the mean on metrics like grades, honors, fellowships, graduation rates, and postgraduate employment. They were less likely to drink heavily and misbehave. They helped us improve school policies and services, from financial aid to advising to student health, and so much more. Individually, most of the students gave their all, engaged their professors, mentored others, made meaning, and propelled themselves into ongoing growth. With more donations or federal funding for financial aid, we could have enrolled even more lower-income stars, but it is a limiting reality that F&M and virtually all colleges depend on tuition dollars to cover the annual cost of running the school. This is the major reason why upper-income students have such an advantage in competitive admissions; institutions need tuition revenue to pay the bills.[56]

From Washington University in St. Louis to Georgia State University and from Pomona College to the University of Maryland, Baltimore County, numerous schools have implemented their own versions of F&M's approach, which entails investing in financial aid and viewing talent holistically. In a front-page story in 2014, *The Washington Post* called F&M's approach a "recruiting revolution"[57]—but I would argue that the real change was the *evolution* in our understanding of how to define, find, educate, and launch talent, which is central to the missions of all colleges and universities. This initiative helped us appreciate that the readiness to drive one's growth is talent. With the US Supreme Court's 2023 ruling limiting race-conscious (but not class-conscious) practices in college admissions, F&M's experience may offer a *talent-based* framework for expanding the inclusivity of selective and elite institutions, provided they can figure out how to make do with less tuition revenue.

*

These are the kinds of questions that this book surfaces—not because higher education is an abject failure, as some say, but because there's much to appreciate, and because young Americans want, deserve, and need an education that will help them live fully and adaptively. The mindsets for discovery, creation, mentorship, collaboration, and striving are especially empowering as one's life gets more complex. And sometimes all five fire up together—a marvelous outcome—as with F&M graduate Andrea Smith.

Growing up in Las Vegas, she was one brave child. After her parents split up, and her mother left the state, she stayed with her father—but then he took off, leaving her alone. Andrea had just finished fifth grade. For part of that summer, she lived by herself, pretending nothing had changed, until her former swim coach figured it out and took her in to live with her family. Later she would earn a scholarship to a private day school where she leaned on her new friends and her love for learning. Talk about resilience. Through the long nights and lonely years of adolescence she held on with the grittiest of grips—living with families from school, watching every step, accepting help, never making waves, and clinging to hope.

Andrea was a survivor. By senior year, that mindset brought her to the front gates of college. But which one? Susan Walker, an admission dean with a keen eye for potential, started recruiting her at a college fair in her hometown. That spring, however, holding an offer from the University of Nevada, Las Vegas, she turned down F&M. It just made more sense to stay close to her support network; she'd never even set foot in Pennsylvania. But Walker saw her gifts and wouldn't give up. In May, when the college began enrolling students from the waitlist, she began chipping away at Andrea's resistance. After all, at F&M, she'd be known right away. Thanks to the school's talent strategy, she'd get full financial aid. She could pursue research and even research design with professors. It was all right there for her, and it would cost very little. She'd *earned* this, Walker told her.

Andrea ended the call and teared up. It was a real boost to be wanted, but still, the choice seemed impossible. Big versus small. New versus familiar. Friends versus strangers. Making lists of pros and cons didn't clear the fog, so she put her future in fate's hands . . . and *flipped a coin*. It came up heads—and so she came to F&M.

At the beginning, predictably, she felt like an outsider. She was shy and seemingly unlike everyone else. Why was she there? Was it worth the cost? What kind of job would it lead to? At the time, she didn't yet realize how a college education could turn her survivor's mentality into something even more formidable.

So, what made the difference? Along with Andrea's determination and ardor for learning, it was caring adults on the faculty. Professor Michael Penn showed warmth and respect, which made her feel valued. Likewise, in a first-year chemistry class that gave her fits, Professor Kate Plass helped her build key study skills while also taking the time to connect her to the financial aid office when she had a crisis. Both educators led her to see that F&M "was a place where I could grow and challenge myself while being supported by my faculty, peers, and college staff."

Others engaged with her on course material in ways that opened new avenues of thought: For example, the music professor Sylvia Alajaji showed her how to recognize when personal biases might be influencing her ideas. Krista Casler in psychology helped her grasp that "how you treat and talk to children becomes the voice in their head—the script they adopt about who they are and what they can achieve."

As a result, Andrea began playing a new script in her head too. "What was important to these professors was not the grade I received in their classes, nor that I adopted their beliefs or ways of thinking, but rather that I developed a new way of approaching the world and solving problems." Much of that "new way" came from the respect they conveyed about her identity, which they saw as relevant for creating new knowledge—and certainly no reason for shame.

In high school, education was about proving she'd memorized information her teachers gave her. In college, the faculty invited her to create her own ideas and "to imagine the impact I could have on the world." No longer would she just answer questions; now she needed to investigate "which questions have already been asked, who was asking them, who/what was impacted by the findings, and where gaps in knowledge remain." The faculty could teach her techniques, but they expected her to dig for discovery and believed she could. They challenged her to expect more of herself and, in short, "made my identity central to the learning process," fortifying her to push back against imposter syndrome. While the professors came from different fields and used diverse teaching methods, they all worked from a tacit "pedagogy of involvement" that I'll discuss in chapter 1. These caring college educators led her to begin to know herself as an active learner honing her mind for self-spawned thought.

Junior year, Professor Joshua Rottman invited her to coordinate a new cluster of child development research projects. He was impressed by the initiative with which she turned empty rooms into superior lab spaces, built up a participant database, designed a website, and involved community members. It also required collaboration with faculty, peers, children, and families. Here, she began to grasp and enjoy her capacity to work as a teammate and a team leader, stepping up to solve problems instead of awaiting instructions.

The next year, Professor Penn, who'd seen the improvement in her research and computational skills, suggested she design a senior thesis. She and a classmate chose to explore a topic she knew from life, housing insecurity among college students. The project gave her "ownership over my education," meaning that she could pursue her interests and proudly share "voices in higher education that are often unheard." It taught her "that my identity is central to my learning, that learning connects to the problems that I want to solve, and that I am capable of playing a role in solving these problems."

Across the arc of her education, Andrea grew into a curious intellectual, self-motivated and other-centered, living to give and be her best. College nourished her thinking, her desire, her sense of self. It taught her how to use her mind and the good she could do with it:

> When I began my studies at F&M, I was primarily concerned about whether or not I belonged in college, if it was worth the cost, how to get by financially, and what kind of job I might gain upon graduating. I didn't recognize that what I would learn in college would be what would change my life—it seems so obvious now! College is about learning—not just about the world, but about yourself.

With that lofty self-knowledge—the beliefs that she *could* learn, that she knew *how* to learn, and that she knew *why* she wanted more learning[58]—Andrea extended her hand in 2016 to receive her diploma. She'd come to F&M on a hunch, knowing little of what to want, but ready to trust and try. How precarious her life had been just four, eight, twelve years before—and now she was educated and in love with learning. No one can know what life she might have launched without the almost providential influences of Michael Penn and Kate Plass. One thing I did know, however, looking into her eyes at commencement: Powered by her education, Andrea Smith now pilots her life.

She'll never flip a coin again.

After graduation, eager to apply her passion for education, Andrea took a two-year job as a college advisor in a rural Pennsylvania school. Most of the students were like she had been—good kids, positive, cooperative, and responsible. It moved her to rouse *their* hopes and dreams by pointing out pathways for good learning and good jobs and good lives. As she sees it:

You don't have to be related to someone to let them know that you believe in them. You don't have to be related to someone to treat them like family. If a young person feels like they have someone who believes in them—if they feel like they have somewhere they belong—there will always be a spark—something in them that tells them, "You can do it."

And it is okay to accept help. It doesn't always need to come from your parents. There are lots of people out there who care about you, and if you show that you care too, you will go places.

The more Andrea mentored, the more she wanted to discover about theories of learning and education policy. This led her to Ann Arbor for a master's in education and to her current work advising Carnegie Mellon undergraduates. Now in her mid-twenties, she's clearly a striver—always reaching, always alert to her values, always looking to expand her awareness of how best to help others. But she's not *only* a striver. Four years of college also activated this introverted teenage survivor's abilities to create, mentor, collaborate, and discover. Her education was a series of experimentations and self-willed breakthroughs and new outlooks on self and life, supported by involved faculty, pursued within a total learning culture in which most peers were challenging themselves too—all creating together what 2020 graduate Robert Maze once called "something that is even more than a college."

In 2018, as I began organizing these ideas, I would reflect on whether my orientation was too affirming, given the mounting disparagements of higher education. But then I'd remember that I've seen the impact of college in real people's lives a thousand times over. Rigorous research and national studies have documented these impacts.[59] During the worst of the pandemic, undergraduates across the country clamored for college—in person. Yes, the fiscal and payment models must be fixed, and doing so will be arduous, but it will be worth the effort because the campus-based learning model has enhanced innumerable lives across the generations and, with renewal, will improve our national prospects. That's because as we enter an era of dizzying and dazzling change, we need:

- *Discoverers* who can find answers to questions no one has thought to ask and bring light to darkness no one has dared to explore;
- *Creators* who can ignite change or innovate from it;
- *Mentors* who can share knowledge, values, and growth mindsets;
- *Collaborators* who can build or improve teams by bringing talents together; and
- *Strivers* who embrace an ethos of self-propelled, values-grounded growth and adaptability.

This book shows the power of a strong undergraduate education to activate these mindsets. If college is threatened today, with much to lament, it is worth saving and strengthening because of our country's crying needs and democratic values. Our founders and every generation after them had faith that education liberates the citizen to think freely, fully, and boldly, which helps one and all. In particular, Benjamin Franklin believed that "the good education of youth . . . [is] the surest foundation of the happiness both of private families and of commonwealth."[60] His premise: When societies invest in their people, they go on to invest in society, a virtuous and pluralistic circle.[61] And he believed that a strong intellect and a character defined by self-improvement would allow Americans to work, invent, adapt, care, cure, move, lead, and keep a republic.[62] With that, he also knew that apprentices need mentors—in trades, in arts, in science, in statecraft.

In this model, teaching is a form of citizenship. We who educate help the young take hold of their minds, goals, and civic selves. We ask and prod and instill and advise; we share what we know and how we think and how we learn; we guide them to be active in their pursuits—and then we must let go on commencement day, with a wish or a prayer, to watch them step past us, primed for further growth, toward their adult lives and callings.

To show this process more closely, chapter one will explore how four students from varying backgrounds forged mindsets for discovery. Their talent bodes well for the future of America.

Introduction: Questions for Discussion

1. How do you understand Carol Dweck's concepts of fixed and growth mindsets? Why does the author believe that growth mindsets are a powerful resource for today's undergraduates, especially in this era of accelerating economic and technological change?

2. The introduction describes five growth mindsets—for discovery, creation, mentorship, collaboration, and striving—and gives examples of students who ignited one or more of them in college. How would you define and contrast these mindsets? Can you rank them in importance? And which one are you most interested in learning more about?

3. What is it about the residential college experience that leads the author to argue that college can be highly effective at activating the five mindsets? Do you believe that the size of an institution may influence how well an institution might do this?

4. Do you think there are additional growth mindsets that this model of college fosters well? And do other college models ignite these or other mindsets effectively?

5. The author writes that, to form growth mindsets, students must lead their learning and drive their development. At the same time, he says that the institution must provide a personalized, learning-rich ecosystem. How do you evaluate this balance of responsibilities between the individual learner and the college?

6. The introduction describes the fulfilling undergraduate experiences of Julia, Darrius, Aicha, and Andrea. Do you identify with any of these students, and, if so, why?

7. Higher education is being criticized from many quarters, as the author acknowledges. Which criticisms do you agree with? Why do you think the author has written this book?

1

THE MINDSET FOR
DISCOVERY

> But perhaps knowledge is not a thing simply obtained so
> much as a pattern of undoing. Our education at its best were
> times when we allowed ourselves to feel disoriented because
> that disorientation served as a site of growth.
>
> —MORGAN KINCADE

MOVE-IN DAY IS AN AMERICAN TRADITION. It starts early, with fat-packed SUVs rolling up to the residence halls, swarmed by cheering students in matching tees. The vibe is festive—balloons and bagels, music and mascots, fall sports teams ready to lend their muscle. Squads of helpers empty out the vehicles in the minute it takes a dazed mom or dad to shake hands with the undergraduate boss running the show.

Some new students arrive heavy with dread, wondering how they'll adjust, while others ooze cool or confidence. About one in three shows up alone, in taxis or airport shuttles, overloaded with suitcases. Inside the residence halls, the families become pit crews, dressing beds, filling closets, and firing up the Wi-Fi. When the roommates first meet, the conversations seem forced, with relatives hovering like strangers at a wedding.

For the parents, about to let go, there's love and sadness, pride and worry. They've worked and saved and sacrificed for their children to cross this threshold, and now the long-sought moment is at hand. It's poignant to witness the goodbyes, some tearful, some stoic—and then college begins.

After three days of icebreakers and orientations, Franklin & Marshall College formally inducts the first-years into the academic community at the annual New Student Convocation. To start the ceremony, the dean of admission introduces the class, extolling its strength, personality, and global reach. Then a stream of speakers invokes the college's history and values and invites the class to take the wheel of their experience right now. Toward the end of the ceremony, the students receive chords braided in the colors of their College Houses and pledge honesty in all they say and do.

Convocation is a preamble and a provocation, telling these teenagers, as growth beckons, "We want you, we see you, we will teach you, and we will help you, but *you* must drive your learning. *You have the power to create the education that you seek.*" It's an insight that can reroute a life. In this place and time, with these professors and peers, *you* can become the leader of your learning, the generator of your growth—as long as you claim and act upon this self-understanding.

When classes start and they begin to try out this notion—*I can and will lead my learning*—undergraduates enter into the mindset for discovery. I like how the current F&M president, Barbara Altmann, a renowned scholar of medieval French literature, has described an independent study in college that stirred her with "questions big enough, penetrating enough, interesting enough, challenging enough, to think about every day, with endless curiosity and passion."[1] For individuals, the discoverer's mindset allows us to use our intellectual talent and grow as we go. For societies, this mindset is the great engine of progress—from cell research to climate solutions to space travel. Discovery is intrinsic to our species. It's ours.

That said, the mindset for it must be prompted, prepped, directed, and ethically informed, which is a vital role for college. What does *activating* a discoverer's mindset look like?

- Helping students build a foundation of baseline knowledge and usable learning skills.

- Teaching them scholarly methods like how to frame a thesis, revisit an assumption, interrogate one's own biases, reset after errors, or gauge the limits of a claim.

- Inculcating the values of discovery—freedom of thought, impartiality, reason, rigor, doubt, dialogue, evidence, precision, resilience, and through it all, the timeless oath of integrity.

- Acculturating them to critical thinking, which John Dewey defined as "the active, persistent, and careful consideration of any belief or supposed form of knowledge in the light of the grounds that support it and the further conclusions to which it tends."[2]

- And finally, to activate mindsets for discovery, teachers need to structure and sequence learning so that students come to *know and feel* that they are learning skills or substance step by step by step by step by step, like new bicyclers being coached and cared for, until that magical moment when they can pedal alone and go where they choose.

Four years of such intellectual formation prepares students to think freely and thrive in today's tech-paced global knowledge economy, with its widening gyres of good and bad digitized information. As discoverers, they can sort through complexities—in work or graduate school, alone or in teams—and put puzzle pieces into patterns others don't know to look for. They can separate fact from fantasy and proof from pretend. They can pivot when stumped and find new angles into old problems. They can keep pace with disruption in their jobs and fields. They can ask and imagine and connect. They can draw upon diverse ways of knowing and know when they don't know. They can subject their own convictions to interrogation and improve their thinking through the productive friction of civil disagreement. In some cases, they may be able to construct the new paradigms of thought to help others understand their work, their roles, their lives, or their time.

To stoke the flame for discovery, faculty matter profoundly, because they design the courses and construct the exercises and lay out the lessons through which students actively make findings—yes, small ones at first, like the meaning of a couplet, the reason for a street name, or the limits of translation—all building to the meta-discovery that they can control how they use their minds. We often hear graduates say that a professor "taught them how to think," which usually means they mentored them to ask the better questions that bring about the bigger revelations. An example: The journalist who told me that a professor trained her to ask of any text, *What is at stake here?* Another: The charter school founder who learned a life truth when a mentor taught him that while data often bring new knowledge, deeper understanding comes from *knowing how data were produced.* These are the moments when passive thinking melts away, as we'll see in this chapter. The distinction? Passive learners answer; discoverers ask. Passive learners settle; discoverers persist. Passive learners follow; discoverers lead. Passive learners seek approval; discoverers seek insight. At their core, discoverers enter into the unknown with a growth mindset. Says Dweck, "In the fixed mindset, everything is about the outcome. If you fail—or if you're not the best—it's all been wasted. The growth mindset allows people to value what they're doing *regardless of the outcome*. They're tackling problems, charting new courses, working on important issues. Maybe they haven't found the cure for cancer, but the search was deeply meaningful."[3]

There's gold in this move from anti-friction to active learning, from fixed mindset to growth mindset. We should want this for all people, for their flourishing and for society's. As we make our way through life, there's always more to find, or to connect, or to take in, on the edge of what we know or think we know or wish we knew; in that restless searching for the new or the next, we find dimensions of ourselves we hadn't known to look for. What activates this mindset? How does college spur and serve active learning and discovery, and what more can we ask our institutions to do, understanding that their missions and resources vary?

This chapter addresses these questions by tracking the intellectual development of four undergraduates—Morgan Kincade, Eddie Alsina, Wyatt Fabian, and Charisma Lambert—at decisive stages of their education. From their experiences, three key points stand out: (1) College often fosters active learning and ignites the mindset for discovery right away, in a student's first year; (2) for many undergraduates, the discoverer's mindset takes hold as they advance through the curriculum; and (3) the emergence of this mindset, wondrously, may help students overcome personal hardships and develop a liberating sense of purpose and meaning. At the end of the chapter, I'll suggest ways to fuel this mindset and why doing so matters for the world beyond the campus gates.

As we'll see, it is striking when young people embrace their innate ability to explore, uncover, connect, learn, and expand. For Morgan and Eddie, the mindset for discovery emerged steadily from their earliest days in college, like a bulb growing brighter, while for Wyatt and Charisma it was more like the flipping of a switch after a pivotal realization. All four benefited from a tacit "pedagogy of involvement" embraced by many F&M faculty, which is the facilitation of *active learning* on an *individualized* basis by educators who are *directly involved* in their students' growth. Such personalized mentoring may be the most impactful way to hasten growth in eighteen-to-twenty-three-year-olds, whether for discovery or the other mindsets discussed here.[4] As Benjamin Franklin is reputed to have said, "Tell me and I forget. Teach me and I know. *Involve me and I learn.*"

Point One: College Often Sparks Discovery Right Away, in a Student's First Year

I met Morgan shortly after move-in day and Eddie the December before, right after his admission to F&M through a Posse Foundation program for outstanding students interested in the fields of science, technology, engineering, and math (STEM). Both told me that they had opted for a liberal arts college because they hoped to grapple with challenging concepts across diverse fields like humanities, sciences, languages, and the arts. While she was the more reserved at age eighteen, and he the more outgoing, both walked into this new world primed to meet and think and learn. I noticed how they gravitated toward conversation and tended to linger at gatherings for as long as others had something to say. To paraphrase Agnes Callard, Eddie and Morgan seemed ready to immerse themselves in the "point of view" they hoped to acquire—in this case, that of the engaged learner.[5] F&M didn't make them curious—they arrived that way—but the college met them in their readiness, right away.

The youngest of four children in a middle-income family from Valhalla, New York, Morgan loved reading and, from her work with an influential high school teacher, knew that learning was a strong suit. Deeply introverted, in those initial seminar meetings she would listen and think intensely without saying much. The first faculty member to "involve" her in learning was anthropology professor Misty Bastian, a straight-talking iconoclast who'd begun her career in the military. At each office hour session, Morgan would offer up musings that might seem silly in class, like, for example, her question about law—namely, *Why do we have it?* Bastian was more than willing to engage, showing that "concepts that had seemed more straightforward could now be explored as if they were splintered or scattered at the foundation." Although this reticent first-year wasn't yet comfortable speaking in front of peers, that was OK, because her irreverent professor seemed just fine kicking around ideas one-to-one in the late-afternoon light. Such professors believe, like Wordsworth, "What we have loved, / Others will love, and we may teach them how."[6]

An early paper earned a fine grade, but Bastian told her she needed to assert her points more firmly and probe the questions that intrigued her. No one had ever critiqued her work like that. Bastian also impressed upon her that "good writing is essential because clarity of writing indicates clarity of thought"—a maxim that Morgan went on to apply throughout college. Most of all, through Bastian's insistent prodding—What is your point? Why do you believe that?—she grasped that in college, faculty want and value rigorous discussion. That led her to seek out many more instructors across the ensuing semesters.

Starting out with a faculty mentor like Bastian calls incoming students into the stirring new terrain of mind-to-mind dialogue and self-propelled learning—especially valuable for those who may be shy or self-conscious about asserting themselves. In a thoughtful article, JT Torres, the director of the Center for Teaching and Learning at Quinnipiac University, challenges educators to ask four questions: Do your students feel safe enough to take intellectual risks? Do you consider false starts and failure a valuable part of academic experience and learning? Do you respond to students' work and ideas with the goals of affirming and challenging them? And, Do you give students the chance to digest, interpret, and apply the feedback you provide?[7] If the answers are yes, then the professor is conveying that she values and believes in her students' ability to learn, and will be their partner in that profound endeavor—an invitation that can become an inspiration.

The first professor to "involve" Eddie was Rob Jinks, a focused, white-coated geneticist who analyzed mutations in Amish and Mennonite children that lead to devastating conditions like retinal degeneration, maple syrup urine disease, and Crigler-Najjar syndrome. They'd met during a ten-day summer orientation for Eddie's STEM Posse cohort. In the fall, Jinks called out to him from a moving car to invite him to join his research program. After learning the basics of lab safety, the freshman helped on a special project—the investigation of a rare gene mutation associated with a form of intellectual disability in children. The professor asked him to scan the scholarly literature to try to understand the gene's role and what might be happening in its mutation, showing him the importance of mapping the terrain of established knowledge.[8] He also taught him to clone a protein—all before he'd finished his first college science course.

Eddie appreciated Professor Jinks as an energy source that jump-started his F&M career. "It showed me that he saw me as a fellow researcher," a fellow learner, he told me. "It showed me that I, a first-gen child of immigrants, had a place here. It also showed me that it would be OK to make mistakes, that the research experience was in part for my learning as well as for whatever findings I might help make." Jinks modeled the mindset of a discoverer while encouraging this eighteen-year-old to join a community of explorers. Learning in college, he grasped, would be different than in high school—and he was wanted and welcome. Could there be a better set of messages for a striving new student to hear from a scholar he respected?

These are the kind of mentoring moments that summon teenagers to claim and shape their education. That first semester, Eddie and Morgan were still making new friends and experimenting with how to study at the college pace. They were still feeling out campus social life and what to do on weekends. The overtures from Bastian and Jinks—the pedagogy of involvement—gave them the heady feeling of arrival.[9] This was the place for which they'd been preparing all those years. The professors became their "allies in learning"[10] and beckoned them like apprentices, right away. They invited them to observe how scholars frame and conduct inquiry and set them up for the even more in-depth mentoring that could be theirs as the highway of original thought opened before them.

These outreaches also helped them accept the need to keep applying themselves, and ask for help, during the intricate processes of learning (and unlearning) how to learn. For instance, Eddie's fast start in Jinks's lab didn't change the fact that his early science classes were quite taxing. His first neuroscience course "kicked

[his] butt, because it required *showing* the thinking process"—not just getting the correct answer. And when he did that well in basic chemistry and organic chemistry, "the courses pushed well beyond rote memory for a synthesis of the various factors in play." Those initial classes also taught him that high-level science was about offering, testing, and refining hypotheses, "a process defined by facts, not feelings." Our brains may hurt like bones when they stretch, but the byproduct of pushing forward is the battle-forged certainty that we can lift our learning. Fortunately, Eddie had already internalized a growth mindset from excellent precollege teachers and didn't view his early test scores as signs of his limits but rather as useful measures of how much more he could discover—including about himself. We should celebrate such perspective and resiliency—for discovery and, well, for most things in life.

I love that scene from Frederick Douglass's 1845 autobiography in which he hears his owner admit that learning would "spoil" him as a slave, making him unfit, discontent, and unmanageable.[11] Thus, he saw in a flash that he must take charge of his learning. His humanity required it. From that epiphany, Douglass devoted himself to endless discovery, which freed him first from the white supremacist logic of slavery and then led to his escape and the valiant life of leadership and opposition to racism that we celebrate today. Yes, this is an exceptional story—but we cannot forget that tomorrow's Frederick Douglasses are out there right now in every type of school and college, open to epiphany, and we should try to see and support them.

In fact, no one can simply *bestow* an education on someone else. It's not a present or a product or a credential, but the result of an individual's will to learn. Many young people realize in college, as my mentee Carolina Giraldo once said, "My education is determined by me." Others may grasp this fact even before college in an AP class or through science fairs or a mentor's example. For some it comes later in life. But, whenever it happens, we must engage young people when they show that urge to seize their learning.

So, what helps activate discovery mindsets at the very outset of a college education when students are especially open and receptive? I'd like to highlight four practices, all of which are elements of the "onboarding" process, which occurs when students consistently hear, "This is what *college* is about, this is what *our college* is *distinctively* about."[12]

First, faculty should make special efforts to forge personalized intellectual connections with new students. At F&M, government professor Stephen Medvic invited new transfer student Jamie Davidow to talk with him after her first paper on the pros and cons of net neutrality; loving that repartee, for the rest of the semester, Jamie would hurry to Medvic's office after her morning rowing practices so they could discuss the course topics and work on her writing. When Julia Ramsey returned to college after two years, computer scientist Erin Talvitie became a welcome ally, coaching her through challenging material, never implying judgment when she seemed stumped. The lines outside her office became a community of fellow learners, exactly what Julia needed. In both cases, when a young person raised her hand, professors responded with encouragement. For new students, personalized instruction boosts learning, of course, but just as meaningful is how it shows students that their instructors care about them, which Joshua R. Eyler calls "the single most important strategy we can use to help our students succeed in our courses."[13]

Second, as students begin college, faculty should ensure that their classes acculturate them to dialogue and active learning. Megan Lipset once told me about the contagious spirit of exchange in a class in which every first-year student had a voice.

At the end of each meeting, the conversation would continue—echoing across the quad and spilling into the dining hall. Professor Alison Kibler's course was a catalyst for thought, not a container. It gave the first-years a feeling that together, through strapping dialogue on difficult topics, they could fuel and focus each other. Megan so enjoyed asking, searching, and discovering with her classmates, some of whom later became friends, that she prioritized taking discussion-based courses in future semesters. Besides learning how to learn, she was learning how she *wanted* to learn. Today, educators worry a great deal about America's worsening problem, which extends far beyond campus, of people silencing themselves for fear of being criticized or canceled by peers.[14] Classes like Kibler's make it meaningful for students to think and probe and disagree, together.

It's also possible to hook undergraduates right away on active learning and discovery, as I saw many times at F&M.[15] History professor Doug Anthony has first-years create visual presentations of racial stereotypes in everyday culture, from advertising to sports logos to news photos, which also accustoms them to discussing sensitive material. Architectural historian Kostis Kourelis sends his students into Lancaster to find examples of classical building styles. Environmental science professor Suzanna Richter requires her first-years to bring to class a garbage bag containing any nonbiodegradable trash they generate in a week. Anthony, Kourelis, and Richter are master teachers who infiltrate their students' sensibilities to summon from the fissures of their brains that geyser-like force we call imagination. They structure and deliver their classes to give first-years the keys to their own minds. This style of teaching is not easy; research shows that some students prefer the passive lecture environment to these more demanding active learning classrooms.[16] But the payoff is clear. As Beth Mc-

Murtrie reports, "a 2014 meta-analysis of 225 studies of STEM courses . . . found that active learning increased grades and reduced failure rates, compared with lecture-style teaching."[17]

I especially appreciated classes taught by chemistry professor Rick Moog, who co-created an evidence-based peer-learning method called Process Oriented Guided Inquiry Learning, or PO-GIL.[18] Throughout the semester, Moog rarely if ever teaches by lecturing. Rather, he places students in small groups to tackle problem sets using a manual he authored. Their role is to figure out answers collaboratively, and his role is to lend a hand when a team gets stuck. Cameron Rutledge, a 2016 F&M graduate, told me that Moog's method "set the foundation for my collegiate learning experience inside and outside the classroom, instilling in me the importance of teamwork, awareness, and adjustment to group dynamics, trusting one's team, and constant communication." The process helped him overcome his fear of a field that had vexed him in high school, and he went on to major in chemistry, on his path to Temple University Medical School.

Third, after whetting students' appetite for research and discovery as early as possible, colleges need to keep feeding it. At F&M, more than one hundred students stay on campus over the summer for funded research internships. After his first year, for example, rather going back home to work, Eddie stayed in Lancaster supporting Rob Jinks's program to identify genetic mutations in Amish children. Ten weeks working full time in a lab gave him an immersive experience in chasing down new knowledge. He learned enough to be able to make a presentation at the school's research fair the following fall on a gene mutation that seemed to lead to intellectual disability at birth. Carrying out projects like this one and presenting on them can set the trajectory of an education, showing undergraduates that they can drive discovery and not just study it.

Finally, to establish inquiry and discovery as preeminent values, colleges should emphasize active learning across many aspects of the undergraduate experience. To do this, mindset scholar Mary Murphy argues that educators need to ask, "How do we change systems, cultures, policies and norms that move people between fixed and growth mind-sets."[19] The answer is to emphasize the importance of discovery not just in classrooms but also in new-student orientation, academic integrity standards, student research opportunities, residential life, student activities, the career center, the part-time jobs, and the campus events and ceremonies—in the fullness of a college's culture.

Doing so requires a shared vision, collaboration across the institution, and financial resources. Not easy, of course, but highly inviting for campus innovators. At F&M, three highly all-campus reforms strengthened intellectual life and the culture of discovery. First, in 2010, the faculty and staff collaborated to create a weekly Common Hour lecture series. Every Thursday at 11:30 a.m., upwards of seven hundred students, faculty, and staff would gather in the gym to hear speakers such as theoretical physicist Brian Greene, technologist Jaron Lanier, Teach For America founder Wendy Kopp, and writers Richard Blanco, Suzan-Lori Parks, and Lynn Nottage. It takes a village to host twenty-four large lectures a year. A committee must find the speakers and manage the series. The athletic department must give up the gym for half a day each week. Funds must be secured for the audio-visual system and grab-and-go lunches. Most important, everyone must agree that no classes, meetings, rehearsals, or practices will be scheduled during the Common Hour. The payoff is that the entire school gets a scintillating weekly reminder about the centrality of dialogue and discovery.

Second, in 2012–13, the full faculty collaborated on a new core curriculum called Connections that included two first-year classes designed both to emphasize discovery and to build the academic skills of close reading, precise writing, civil debate, use of evidence, and critical analysis. The seminars cover cross-disciplinary themes such as digital cities, the business of food, mortality and meaning, and living the examined life—all suggesting the value of "connecting" ideas and ways of knowing. Critically, most of the courses are taught by full-time faculty who'll be at F&M for years and careers, and thus remaining available to their mentees during and after college. This is no small commitment. Unfortunately, at many institutions, the introductory curriculum is taught by short-term adjunct faculty and managed by teaching assistants who will not likely be able to sustain mentoring relationships after a course ends. Curricular reform may not be easy, but to spur discovery mindsets we need to make sure that students start their college careers with engaging classes taught by professors who want to get to know them and sequence their academic skill development. That fosters the will, skill, and spirit for discovery.

The third major reform was instituted in 2005, when then-president John Fry teamed up with faculty and student life educators to convert a traditional and tired dormitory system into a College House model. As a result, F&M now places incoming students in one of five residential communities, each of which has a faculty don and staff dean, welcoming meeting and study spaces, and distinctive house crests, colors, and traditions. This model encourages intellectual life right where students live through seminars, discussions, dinner meetings, films, and awards ceremonies. As we'll see in chapter 4, each house has a unique model of student government designed to promote involvement, collaboration, and pride of place. Bringing together academic and residential learning, and the faculty and staff dedicated to both, it was a gutsy, transformational change.

Point Two: For Many Undergraduates, the Discoverers' Mindset Takes Hold as They Advance in Their Studies

With two engrossing semesters under their belts, Eddie and Morgan returned to campus as supercharged sophomores. Learning was theirs to create, with faculty mentors to find. Nothing was predetermined or pre-scripted. Many of their friends were also active and passionate discoverers. If there was a single takeaway from year one, it was that F&M believed that students could carve out their own paths of discovery, self-guided but never alone. That invitation defined their next three years.

Sophomore year, Morgan dove headlong into the classic liberal arts core curriculum in science, history, literature, and religion. She also involved herself in religious life, combining Christian and interfaith worship with attendance at Shabbat dinners and discussions of the Muslim Students Association. She especially liked integrating ideas and experience—and religious studies professor SherAli Tareen helped her see that multidisciplinary scholarship would allow her to do that in class too.

One can't understand Islam, he showed her, and deconstruct falsehoods about its tenets without also having knowledge of world history, Arabic language, and international relations. She heard this as an invitation to carry ideas from one class into another, suggesting she could join "a conversation with others in many fields on a given topic, seeing how people were reformulating a proposition." Learning wasn't simply what she did in class; it was what she did *among* classes. If there were connections to be made, for example, from one seminar on ancient Islam and another on Middle East conflicts, those insights were uniquely hers to seek and find. She was not receiving an education so much as making one.

For Morgan, education became "about looking around and coming up for answers on my own"—not because all knowledge exists and is simply there to be found, but rather because we live within a kaleidoscope of contending propositions. With this growing intellectual adventurousness, she chose to study in Paris and Jordan during junior year. She knew that leaving the comfort and culture of home would spark intellectual fire. When she got to Amman and moved in with a gracious host family, she decided to do something novel—a blog of her impressions and ideas, to prompt her thinking and give her family and friends a window into her encounters. I remember the searching quality of her entries, the writerly tone and mood. It was impressive, brave, and hers alone.

The blog gave this self-described introvert a voice, a product, and an audience—leading her, as senior year approached, to try something still more ambitious—an honors thesis in contemporary Islamic studies. Because Professor Tareen was on sabbatical that year, she worked with Annette Aronowicz, an expert in Jewish studies known also for her scholarship on understandings of the spiritual and the secular. Her methods were exacting. In their sessions, the professor always expected the young scholar to speak first—to initiate inquiry rather than replying to it, which made Morgan uncomfortable. For her thesis, she argued that the hostile reactions of French academics to the scholarship of Tariq Ramadan came from their anxieties about his work as a boundary-breaking intellectual. Most demanding was how Aronowicz required, before writing, that the student sit with her ideas for longer than Morgan wished . . . because deep thought, labor at the mind's limits, could not be rushed.

The thesis won a prize, but what mattered more was the experience of producing her own original scholarship, the realization that she could do so again, and the satisfaction of earning the respect of an eminent scholar. As Eyler observes, when mentors help under-graduates design research projects and create new knowledge, they learn more "than if we ask them to build knowledge in environments that are void of conceptual frameworks or artificial in design."[20] The best part of such learning is how it lets students see and feel their inherent capacity to discover—theirs to apply again and again. The experience of discovery makes the mindset for it.

Looking back, Morgan entered college introverted but open to branching out. When it was daunting at first to express her ideas before others, the faculty helped her confirm that she was where she needed to be. From her first class with Misty Bastian until her last day of college when she received the Williamson Medal as the outstanding student in her class, she was always aided by invested professors and staff who saw and heard *her*. They made time. They modeled mental acuity. They invited her to speak. They coached and challenged her as she learned. They worked with her ideas and spoke to her mind-to-equal-mind. They invested in *her* innate capacity to learn, which they believed in with the force of faith. Such involvement enables students, as Agnes Callard writes of her own undergraduate mentor, "to hold myself up to the set of standards that I was just beginning to recognize as my own."[21]

At each step, faculty mentorship gave Morgan new ways to use her mind, readying her to spend two years after graduation teaching and traveling in France and Jordan before graduate school in religious studies at the University of Chicago. By actively delving into learning, despite the discomfort, and by being met at every growth point by professors who valued her, she formed a personal and actionable view of discovery that gave her confidence. Four years after those first labored meetings in Misty Bastian's office, when her mouth trailed her racing mind, she was selected by the faculty to give the commencement speech, where she expressed her philosophy of learning: "Opening space for new questions can be frustrating and even disorienting. But perhaps knowledge is not a thing simply obtained so much as a pattern of undoing. Our education at its best were times when we allowed ourselves to feel disoriented because that disorientation served as a site of growth."[22]

Today, Morgan's intellectual flourishing looks inevitable, but surely it was not. The faculty were there for her, and the college valued her values. At a larger or less personalized school, she might not have been seen or challenged. But at F&M, with each more advanced learning experience, this shy and sincere human being became more self-assured in her ability to work with subtle ideas and say what she wanted, which gave her pleasure and purpose and meaning. I especially love the way that she came to understand her introversion as a *strength* for turning disorientation into discovery—a shift she attributes to workshops and the mentoring of staff in the college's Office of Student and Post-Graduate Development. We often use the word "transformation" when trying to know and name the value of college. Sometimes what "transforms," however, is neither the person nor her values but rather her understanding of what she can do with her mind and talent. That's why I'm partial to the word *activating*. It implies that the role of college is less to "change" people than to help them develop and become.

Eddie, who would spring into any conversation as if by instinct, also grew his intellectual strengths and identity across the last three years of college. The Posse program gave him an ideal four-year mentor in chemistry professor Ken Hess, who advised him early that "it was OK to be like a kid in a candy store and sample many things his first two years of college" because doing so would lead to self-knowledge that would guide his later choices of direction.[23] Acting on this wisdom, he took courses in film and environmental studies, expecting to expand even if he didn't yet know how. Fortunately, he could build relationships with those professors, too—like Ellie Rice, whose education seminar allowed him to share his passion for science with fifth graders at a local school, sparking scintillating questions about brain science and the fate-making force of growth mindsets in children. Senior year, he even made an experimental short film. He also extended himself outside of class, founding a campus chapter of the service program Rotaract, serving as a residential advisor, and engaging high schoolers as a tour guide. All these growth moments piled up on one another, and reinforced each other, giving him the same feeling that powered Morgan to so many discoveries: *This is where I'm meant to be.*

In his sophomore year, F&M's stimulating ecosystem also helped Eddie form a radically new proposition: Maybe he would enjoy using science not only with partners in a lab *but also with people in the world.* After all, he was thriving on his relationships with friends and profs. There was so much to do and learn and give *with others.* This intoxicated him—like love, it changed everything. But how to live his love of science in everyday life? As a first foray, he chose an integrative neuroscience major focusing on both biology and behavior—not either/or. This inclusive major felt right, as it would let him keep exploring the brain/mind connection in clinical, research, and social settings.

Junior year, Eddie created two divergent discovery experiences in science. First, he secured a Howard Hughes Medical Institute summer internship that placed him on a University of Colorado Boulder team investigating heart enlargement in mice, rats, and pythons. Then he spent a semester in Denmark counseling low-income senior citizens who were, obviously, quite different from him. Although one experience involved bench research and the other living beings, both were cutting edge and consequential. In both, growth felt great.

Predictably, graduation brought him to a fork in his road: It was time to go farther, but in which direction? It was a definitional choice. He came to college aspiring to a career in discovery in the domain of the cell, and took giant strides toward that goal, but from his active pursuit of learning he also grew intrigued by how the brain works in everyday life. After four years he revered science more than ever—while also knowing himself and the many uses of science better than ever.

Keeping all options open, he applied to doctoral programs in both neurological science and clinical psychology. Then he consulted with friends and mentors, trying to discern his strengths and his calling. In the end he chose a path that eight semesters earlier had no coordinates on his mental map—a PhD program in clinical psychology and behavioral medicine at the University of Maryland, Baltimore County. Today, having just completed his doctorate with a focus on physical and neurocognitive health, he has found joyful purpose living the life of his mind for the lives of others and the world.

Eddie and Morgan flourished as undergraduates because so many professors viewed, valued, and mentored them *as discoverers*. Teaching for discovery is about leading young people into the widening outer rings of their minds so they can learn to go even further on their own. I saw this happen for Jack Madden, who came to F&M loving physics the way an artist loves form. The summer before junior year, he received a Hackman grant for summer research with physics professor Fronefield Crawford. Using high-powered F&M computers to process data from the Parkes radio telescope in Australia, Jack probed the Milky Way in search of dense, rapidly rotating neutron stars known as pulsars. Improbably, he found one—160,000 light years from earth—becoming one of one hundred people in history to do so. This discovery, and the curriculum and mentoring that enabled it, gave Jack the self-assurance that he could do something like that again. A month after graduation, his mother composed a letter thanking F&M for helping her precious son to be and become himself, to claim his abilities, and to build the academic muscle for his next lift, a PhD in physics at Cornell University. There are many more examples, from Karli DeRego's research on Indigenous and colonial interactions in Guam, to Mihika Miranda scuba diving to find coins and objects from the Roman empire at the edge of the Mediterranean Sea, to an undergraduate team that helped unearth in Tuscany a fragment of a clay pot with the world's oldest known depiction of childbirth. Every semester, at our research fairs and thesis presentations, I watched a parade of undergraduates report on their findings and their future projects, and the mentoring of their professors, with sunny pride in their lived experience of discovery.

In a celebrated 1986 speech to new students, the president of Yale University, A. Bartlett Giamatti, poetically described a liberal education as a "voyage of exploration in freedom" and a "splendid opening out of the self as you use the mind to explore the mind." He went on to say, "But each of you will experience your education uniquely—charting and ordering and dwelling in the land of your own intellect and sensibility, discovering powers you had only dreamed of and mysteries you had not imagined and reaches you had not thought that thought could reach."[24]

This is the growth that Eddie and Morgan made for themselves, assisted by faculty and the college's pronounced intellectual culture. At F&M, Morgan learned to synthesize ideas across borders of culture, religion, and language—using introversion and disorientation not as conditions to escape but as assets for thought. Eddie discovered new "powers" and "mysteries" through science and research—in ways both planned and unplanned—by "dwelling" in non-science fields, work, travel, and reflection. Whether it was a new class or a senior thesis, study-away or community service at home, every time they tasted growth they salivated for more. They powered their learning—loving it, believing in it, owning it—through which they built and bolstered the mindset for discovery that they carried forward into graduate study.

That's invaluable, because the work of their lives will require the work of their minds, and, for that future, these two will never be finished products.

Point Three: Some Undergraduates Develop a Liberating Sense of Purpose and Meaning through the Discoverers' Mindset

Not every student comes to college geared up for purposeful learning like Morgan and Eddie, or, as we'll read later, Brian Rivera and Andrew Foley. Some need to learn to apply themselves. Some worked so doggedly to get into a selective institution that they're now onboard to coast. Some carry the consumer's expectation that college will curate their education. Some simply don't value the learning process or aren't disciplined enough to apply themselves consistently. Some, like Julia Ramsey, must contend with serious health needs or sources of heartache. A few may think they already know everything. Some have other priorities, from sports to social life to taking care of family.

When we enroll students, it becomes our duty to help them break through any blocks so they can more freely explore the myriad paths of promise before and within them. The Jesuits refer to this commitment as "engaging students *where they are.*" It's a morally respectful and empathetic way to teach, inviting educators to step into their mentees' shoes and try to understand what would put spring in their step. The payoff can be liberating—helping the young to claim their minds and lives—but the student must want this and work for it.

Which brings us to Wyatt Fabian and Charisma Lambert. Early in college, they dealt bravely with emotional pain; supported by involved educators, both claimed their identities and learned life lessons by using the power of their minds to interpret the world.

At The Hill School in Pottstown, Pennsylvania, Wyatt was a cerebral student and a superb soccer player. Built like a linebacker and blessed with standout field vision and judgment, he fulfilled a longtime goal to compete at the Division I level when he signed with a school in the Patriot League. A man of few words, he earned universal respect from teachers and students alike for his stoic demeanor and humility.

However, in the summer before college, he faced an unspeakable heartbreak when his mother and aunt died in a car crash. Shocked and devasted, he talked about taking a gap year with his father, Chuck, only to decide that the better way to work through the grief was to keep on track with his plans and start his college soccer career.

When practice began in early August, he had to make lots of adjustments—to a new coach and system, older teammates, and a faster and more skilled game. Wyatt got the hang of it, but his head and heart weren't fully there. That became the case in class too. He felt cut off from his lifelong enthusiasms for the sport and for studies. It was like sleepwalking, except when waves of loss and depression would crash down on him.

His new institution seemed empty and impersonal compared to The Hill School, with its shared purpose and close teacher-student relationships. As the semester progressed, going to practice became like punching the clock at a job. He knew he still loved the sport and wanted to play, but in his hierarchy of values, soccer alone couldn't touch family, education, and emotional fulfillment. He was attending an excellent college, Wyatt is the first to say, but he just didn't take to it that year and went home for the summer sensing he might need a plan B.

In August that became a conviction. He needed to grab the wheel of his education. Aided by his high school coach, Wyatt contacted a few Division III program leaders, including Franklin & Marshall's Dan Wagner, to see if a late-summer transfer was even feasible. During his first visit to F&M, he had a lively conversation about classes and life with two future teammates. Indeed, *too* lively, because he forgot to take in the campus he was touring, and so he needed to come back the next week.

He also felt drawn to Coach Wagner's emphasis on character and on being a first-rate teammate on and off the field, which we will explore further in chapter 4 on the mindset for collaboration. Inspired by his faith, Wagner mentored his players as unique human beings in formation. He ruminated about how to draw out the potential in each one, and not just on the field, challenging them through readings about leadership, discussions with alums, and tours of the Gettysburg battlefields. Every three years, Wagner would bring the team to South Africa to lead youth clinics and learn about life in the sprawling township of Khayelitsha, where he'd helped create a gorgeous synthetic turf field that has become a community hub.

It was the soccer program's culture that won over Wyatt. He came to F&M because he wanted a fresh shot at a total undergraduate experience. That said, he still had to learn the program's style of play, which was high-speed, and when practice started, he immediately found out that one year in Division I didn't mean he'd be a D-III superstar. Wagner recalled how things started: "Wyatt was always looking for feedback, craving relationship. I told him the first week that he was doing fine, but he was only our tenth best player. He agreed. It was at that point I knew he could be special as he didn't have the D-I chip on his shoulder. One year later, he was an All-American."

Wyatt also needed to adjust academically. Initially, he planned to major in business, but the first classes didn't speak to him. So, he dug out his high school transcript and reflected on the courses in which he did well—French, history, world cultures, government—and then decided simply to take what he liked and see where it led. From that choice, an exciting turn occurred in Professor Ben Mc-Cree's class on Tudor England. It was the first time he had to dig in and do research with primary materials. He was looking at statistics related to plagues, drawn from online archives, trying to decipher its secrets. The independence felt intoxicating: "When you look at the events of history through the eyes of the most famous author, or through an unrecorded person, it's up to *you* to interpret what's going on and make connections," he shared with me. "Two of the most highly educated people in world can read a source and have completely different opinions based on it. *I loved that.*"

He also felt awakened by the historian Richard Reitan, who taught his students to analyze a text with the objective of identifying its "lens." By this, he meant an implicit or projected way of knowing the world that is idiosyncratic to the writer or her era. This way of thinking moves the student from trying to accurately identify what a text *says* (which is critical) to the next level of discovery, more theoretical, which is what the text may *show*. The professor expected him to unspool the assumptions in any reading, drawing upon knowledge of the historical context but also *using his own intuitions.* "The skill of dissecting and determining the author's worldview also allows you to build a deeper knowledge base," he told me, praising Reitan's discovery-oriented approach. In the study of Eastern cultures, for example, by scrutinizing a work's biases and blind spots, "you can see better how the West sees the East. That teaches us that we cannot base our complete understanding of the East off Western perceptions." That's what the pedagogy of involvement and critical thinking look like in practice.

Wyatt's budding desire to direct his learning also energized him to dive into languages—taking French, Spanish, and Russian, despite his heavy soccer schedule. When I asked why he assigned himself so much extra work with all these classes, he replied:

> When I was deciding how to approach college sophomore year, I asked myself what I loved besides playing soccer. And one thing, which grew out of soccer, was that I love to travel and want to do that my whole life. My middle school and high school both emphasized getting out of the US and growing. From traveling, I knew that you only get a one-dimensional view if you can't understand what people are saying.

He also responded to the sequential logic of language learning. Like an athlete practicing footwork until it becomes second nature, he loved focusing first on learning sentence structures and verb tenses, setting him up to layer on vocabulary over time. It was all up to him, which he relished. The nightly studying and in-class drills, unit after unit, kept him engaged and progressing, even though the process required perpetually getting a lot of answers wrong. As with athletics, he felt that "the best way to learn the language is to keep failing; if you are learning, it *should* be difficult."

The academic regimen required him to commit to daily and weekly goals that would position him for a more far-reaching goal: lifelong learning. Because "we are trapped in our English understanding of the world," we have to want and work to expand our perspective. Perhaps Wyatt's insight came from the loss of his mother and aunt. Or from changing colleges with a thirst for more. Whatever the reason, he willed himself to squeeze every drop of meaning from his education. "When else but now," he said to me, "can I get help from professors creating the foundations" for the life of continuous discovery he envisioned.

Through language classes and the mentoring of historians, college equipped him to construct his own lens for understanding our multicultural, interdependent world—and yet even as he oriented himself to try to view other cultures as if from within, through their history and their languages, he also gained a healthy humility about the challenge of doing so. His mindset was to resist settled propositions and continuously engage questions of culture with an open mind. That he did this while grieving makes his journey even more illuminating. Wyatt's education reminds us that a discovery mindset can help people heal, providing layers of searching, learning, and meaning around an absence of the heart so that at least the hole doesn't seem so big. His strengths made him stronger. His growing mind became a medicine.

In fact, many undergraduates show up with a fractured or fragile emotional base. It might be family trials, cultural loss, or generational trauma. Such hardships can hinder learning—but they don't have to. Sometimes learning helps us cope or hope or mend, busying our brains in ways that bring relief, perspective, and joy. With every discovery, we discover ourselves anew. Learning shows us, even if we are powerless to change the past, that we can be powerful in creating our futures.

Here's another story to bring this idea to life. Hailing from New-ark, New Jersey, Charisma Lambert came to college as a survivor of family tragedy, having lost both of her parents as a child. The cliff she had to climb was not grief per se but the haunting worry that, as a woman of color who was born into poverty, she might never really fit in and find her place at F&M.

As we know from the research of Anthony Jack and others, when underrepresented students feel like outsiders, their aca-demic performance can suffer.[25] It makes sense. Feeling like an ex-ile or a ghost on campus can erode one's self-assurance and lead to withdrawal—and any given day may be defined by a new signal of non-belonging. It can come from the lack of familiarity with the hidden curriculum of college or terms used in class or labs. It can come from other students' pricey clothes, cars, or cameras in a photography class. It can come from offhand comments signaling privilege or prejudice. It can come from the air of familiarity with which confident students swap stories or find preset cliques. It can come from a first failed quiz or the crashing of an outdated laptop.

This problem has existed for as long as lower-income students have been climbing the college ladder, as we know from moving accounts like Tara Westover's *Educated* and Ron Suskind's *A Hope in the Unseen*.[26] Almost a century ago, Anzia Yezierska wrote in *Hungry Hearts*, "At last I came to college. I rushed for it with the outstretched arms of youth's aching hunger to give and take of life's deepest, and highest, and I came against the solid wall of the well-fed, well-dressed world—the frigid whitewashed wall of cleanliness. . . . And what did I get for it? A crushed spirit, a bro-ken heart, a stinging sense of poverty that I never felt before."[27]

Some educators cling to the notion that we can prevent "crushed spirits" with mandatory new-student orientation workshops or re-quired inclusion-themed courses, but that's too simplistic. Imagine coming from a segregated American community where the average working adult makes less than $20,000 a year and then being surrounded by well-to-do students who have never spoken with anyone like you. Then imagine feeling unschooled in college rites of passage that your classmates have down pat. And then imagine you don't know how to excel in your courses . . . and have too much open time . . . and feel that fellow students are looking through you . . . and fear of letting down your people at home . . . and worry about failing in both worlds . . . and start to blame yourself . . . and then you have the epiphany that, in fact, your college has a short and flawed history of students like you even being there.

Such pains can undo students' belief that they're where they should be. As I heard Georgetown University president Jack De-Gioia say when announcing a new LGBTQ initiative, it's exceedingly difficult to take the risk of growth, of putting yourself out there, if you doubt that you're in a place that knows and wants you. Belonging and trust go hand-in-hand, but trust is complex—slow-growing as a bond but sinkable like a stock.

Which brings us back to Charisma, who I first met in our summer enrichment program, F&M College Prep. Designed in 2011 to prevent "undermatching," which occurs when qualified low-income students do not apply to or attend top institutions, this three-week program allowed rising high school seniors to live together, learn from professors, and get an early taste of college life. She was seventeen that summer. I remember talking to her one evening as we walked to the campus gym. She was an arrow pointed toward education. All she wanted was to go to college to explore ideas and meet new people. I sensed how much love and strength she drew from her family and the Black community of Newark.

Six feet tall, poised, active, and sensitive to others, she already carried herself like a confident undergraduate. A few days after our talk, I visited her class with sociology professor Katherine Mc-Clelland. She and Karolina Heleno, another star Prepster, were having great fun debating the question of whether one group has to lose power for others to gain it. They were beaming as they played with their minds—and they genuinely excited our faculty, most of whom had never taught high schoolers.

The following fall I visited Charisma's school, which had sent two outstanding students to F&M the year before. North Star Academy is one of those dreamlands, like Chicago's Cristo Rey Jesuit High School and KIPP NYC, that shows schooling for some as it could be for all. Clad in their blue uniforms and squeezing in our reunion between classes, Charisma and the other Prepsters were stoutly standing up to college application mania and the AP grind. A few months later, when she texted me that she would be taking her talents to Lancaster, I was overjoyed. With a rare mix of brains, drive, maturity, and kindness, along with a lifetime of struggle and success, she was a superb recruit and, no question, North Star would make sure she was ready.

Which she was . . . though, from the start, she clung to her F&M College Prep friends Melanie, Ruth, and Anastasia, from Arkansas, Chicago, and New Orleans, respectively. It threw all four to come back to the campus where they'd absolutely reigned the summer before only to find it teeming with well-off students. In some classes, she was the only Black student in the room. Had the community she felt in College Prep been just a dream?

A first dilemma concerned Calculus II and III. Although her strong AP score placed her in the advanced level, with each class meeting she felt the water rising closer to her chin. Another issue was that she didn't really know how to study—a typical first-year problem, but that was no consolation. Was she really well-enough prepared? She wasn't herself here, or maybe here just wasn't for her. As the months passed, with a routine and a widening circle of new friends from the community of color, she felt less like an anomaly in this uber-white world. Especially helpful were weekly meetings at the Black Student Union (BSU) and with a cohort of ten first-generation students, mentored by a heterodox economics professor and two sophomores, Alex Welbeck and Cristina Diez. "The only person you are competing against is yourself," advised Cristina, a perceptive mentor we will meet in chapter 4. "This experience is all about how much you can learn."

During winter break, Charisma sat with this advice and tried to compose a balanced picture of her first semester. Things started rough, for sure, but she saw much to appreciate. Although she dropped calculus, her grades were fine. She enjoyed a final assignment in one class that allowed her to analyze India Arie's song "I Am Not My Hair." Still, F&M wasn't sticky just yet. The default culture of the campus felt distant. Was this what college would be the whole time, as an outsider looking in? She pondered transferring to a school where she might feel more comfortable—and it was then that she heard the wise teaching of the aunt who'd raised her while also working two jobs as a transit driver for students and adults with disabilities: "When you try to run away from something, you may run *into* what you're running from."

It was true, and she knew it with the force of revelation. If she felt uncomfortable with the ways racial identity played out on campus, the distance and divides, the subtle hierarchies, she could transfer and then face the exact same factors at Drew or Princeton or NYU, or she could stay and help make the changes she wanted to see. She could be a *great* college student—she always had been. She could grow. There were plenty of resources at F&M. The financial aid package was strong. She did have supportive friends. And she found inspiration in another quarter over winter break, watching her curious five-year-old cousin whom she loved with her heart's every cell. She longed to be his role model, his image of Black excellence.

So, at this turning point, she leaned into F&M. The first step was to pick a class that looked fascinating—Race Movies—and go ask Professor Joe Clark to let her in off the waitlist. The course began with *Do the Right Thing*. Right away, she embraced Clark's practice of letting the students direct much of the discussion. It lifted her to be able to bring in observations drawn from her life. Clearly, Clark had created one of those "natural critical learning environments" that challenge students "to compare, apply, evaluate, analyze, and synthesize, but never only to listen and remember."[28] Sometimes, he'd proactively introduce themes like structural racism out of a concern that students of color shouldn't be the ones left to bring up the most sensitive topics. He was sharing authority for his classroom's culture, rather than arrogating or abdicating it. That balance felt so respectful to Charisma—like their minds were on the same wavelength, in the class but also above it, as fellow theorists on how race could and should be considered in a class of this composition—and it persuaded her to find more profs like him. Most activating, she felt a moral thirst for illuminating content and liberating ways of knowing right there for her to imbibe.

Second semester, she also started speaking up at BSU meetings, after having bit her tongue all fall. She idolized seniors Cayla Young and Isaiah Cromwell, and when they welcomed her comments, she bubbled over with ideas. "Finding a home in the BSU," she told me, "helped me find my voice overall. After speaking in a meeting, I remember thinking, 'Instead of sitting in class silent, maybe I should say something.'"

Clark's class lit the lamp, and now she wanted more light. The turning point had become a tipping point. She started picking courses with equity themes—like public policy, urban education, and American studies—courses that could help her work consciously after college toward a vision of shared prosperity for the Black community. With that, she also looked for professors known for partnering with their students to make the classroom sing. Joe Clark, Alison Kibler, Carla Willard, and Katherine McClelland brought out her best, for they all "created the environment where our education was *literally ours*." Each professor expected students to start class ready to "express yourself and learn," and all were in equal measure tough graders and eager for student feedback. One of just a few African American faculty members, Willard was unusually giving, often checking on Charisma and others with the warmth of family—while also connecting her to research internships, like one with Kibler on the desegregation of public swimming pools in Central Pennsylvania in the 1950s and 1960s.

Some may ask if all professors need to go the extra mile like Willard. No . . . and yes. That is to say, teaching is a daily expression of identity, and educators won't do well trying to sustain a fake self. But it is also a professional act, which means that, as a group, the faculty needs to reach out to and reel in every student—especially those from under-represented groups—and so everyone has a role to play. All who teach also should make a steady, nondefensive effort to be a continuous learner about the dynamics of identities and culture among the young, which change much faster than the makeup of a faculty, and to avoid projecting any deadening lack of confidence in students' ability to learn. I would add, it's clear that white professors such as Clark, McClelland, Kibler, and Hess can be highly effective teachers and mentors of students whose backgrounds differ from their own. Doing this well is a calling and an honor—and a responsibility of all. As Andrew Delbanco writes, "an American college is only true to itself when it opens its doors to all—rich, middling, and poor—who have the capacity to embrace the precious chance to think and reflect before life engulfs them. If we are serious about democracy, that means everyone."[29]

For Charisma, who prized this "precious chance to think and reflect," each new opportunity might surface doubts—but she would steadfastly push ahead remembering all that she'd achieved so far. Outside of class she showed growing initiative too. She tutored at Ross Elementary School, served as copresident of the group S.I.S.T.E.R.S., and cofounded the organization First Generation Diplomats with two rural Pennsylvanians, Sheldon Ruby and Jasmin Wright. Sophomore and junior years, with all this meaning making, her creative energy compounded. The curricular and cocurricular reinforced one another, both prompting more curiosity and active learning.

With senior year approaching, she took two intrepid steps fueled by her attraction to discovery. First, she secured a highly competitive Public Policy & International Affairs fellowship that sent her to Carnegie Mellon for summer study in economics and public policy. This program placed her in graduate-level classes with other top undergraduates (including her first-gen classmate Thanh Nguyen), which showed her that she was every bit their equal. The courses were advanced, so sometimes she needed to relearn material that she had not fully mastered at F&M, especially in statistics. "It was very intense and very rewarding," she told me, "because it showed me I could do it" after fighting against the subject during her sophomore year. "The summer class allowed me to relearn it all—it gave me the mindset that you can try again and get it." That's a gift that never stops giving.

Just four days after finishing these two grueling months of academic growth, she burst into another open field by embarking on a rigorous study-away program focusing on human rights. That fall she traveled to South Africa, India, and Brazil, pinching herself with each mind-boggling discovery about humanity or culture or law. Academically, it let her compare global approaches to education, gender equity, and health care with the United States no longer positioned as the norm. For the first time, she began to think of cities as units within which to enact social repair and social change—helping her design a final paper on how, around the world, just like at home, anti-Black beliefs have undergirded countless decisions of urban design.

It is astonishing how much this young woman blossomed once she claimed her place and power by seeking to gain academic insights about the factors that cause inequity in the Black community, *her* community. She became active, energized, and relentless. Other students gravitated toward her, brightening in her presence. Professors looked to her for in-seminar leadership. She made herself into the picture of flourishing, and it started all because she did what she came for—she embraced learning. Her commitment to forging her one college path began with neither self-assurance nor a focused goal but rather and better with a full embrace of Black pride and her aunt's wisdom. No running away, never.

Accompanied by faculty, and true to her ancestry and her younger cousin and herself, this strong Black woman accepted that the education she could pursue at F&M would be far more valuable than seeking out comfort somewhere else, because it would be *hers*. Her most electrifying discovery was that the injustices into which she was born could be thought about, understood, and changed. Charisma's education proves the proposition that advanced learning can help us link past *with* present toward a better beloved future in which Black and Brown children won't have to beat back stereotypes and beat down barriers to become their best selves. I love how she realized that she would deepen her authenticity, not lose it, by building her capacity to make intellectual contributions she valued. Toward that vision, after college Charisma served as a Teach For America educator in Baltimore and Newark, giving back to the community that has loved her, before pursuing a master's degree in public policy. bell hooks once wrote, "to be truly visionary we have to root our imagination in our concrete reality while simultaneously imagining possibilities beyond that reality."[30] The mindset for discovery helps students from marginalized backgrounds to do just that in unique and personally significant ways. Donnell Bailey, a 2017 alumnus who has worked since graduation in education reform, had a mind blast that sent him back to the library many nights on end when a sociology reading taught him that what he called his "poverty-stricken" neighborhood was in fact a "poverty-*structured* neighborhood." His rural Pennsylvania classmate Michelle Bailey (no relation) overcame early feelings of inadequacy to thrive in class, expressing herself through creative writing and graduating magna cum laude. After a Fulbright year in Taiwan, she returned to rural Pennsylvania to counsel students on college, and now she's pursuing a PhD in education. Nadia Johnson, who we will learn about in chapter 5, spread her intellectual wings after realizing that sociology and women's studies offered fascinating sightlines into her own life and would help her to give back in morally fulfilling ways. Remember these examples when you read about Alejandra Zavala's art exhibition in the next chapter.

I do not believe it's the proper role of mentors and educators to tell young people how to live their lives or what to study; but I do believe we must try to help all students become alert to and motivated by their inherent abilities to create learning and knowledge, always and endlessly. When we spark this belief among students from "poverty-structured" communities, the ignored and the marginalized, we will increase the likelihood that tomorrow's thinkers and doers will emerge out of today's inequities and exclusions, and redeeming the past will help redress them. Some of those discoverers will take up this charge as scholars, determined, like the legendary John Hope Franklin, "to use [their] history and ingenuity, [their] resources and talents, to combat the forces that isolate [them] and [their] people and, like the true patriot that [they are], to contribute to the solution of the problems that all Americans face in common."[31] That's Charisma Lambert.

The night before her 2018 graduation, the Black Student Union held a ceremony for families, with Charisma as the speaker. She talked about how the community and its ideals provide a sense of family that enhances everything one might pursue at F&M. The next day, her commencement speaker was New Jersey Senator Cory Booker, who'd been the mayor of Newark during her school years. There he'd taken on entrenched powers, stressed community safety, and backed new public charter schools, including North Star Academy itself—all while living in community with the people he pledged to serve. Introduced to Charisma backstage, he quickly grasped the moment. Their meeting had an air of destiny—a big-visioned public man coming face-to-face with a now-grown child of the city whose life prospects his support for education had helped to lift.

Robed and ready, honored by her peers and blessed by her senator, beloved by her family and on fire to go teach, one thing was clear: With the education she created, and the mindset to discover, Charisma Lambert belonged.

Looking Forward: What the Mindset for Discovery Offers and How to Promote It

It's moving to remember that Morgan, Eddie, Wyatt, and Charisma converged on Franklin & Marshall from distinct byways and carrying their own hopes and doubts and burdens. Invited from the New Student Convocation onward to seek and ask and find and change, to spark minds with the faculty, they said yes and then found professors to see and push and know them, as they came and might become. Each developed the confidence to wrestle with complex ideas, to dwell in uncertainty, and to come out in the other side of deep thought with a new perspective or idea they could defend, whether about science or religion or language or racism. They all arrived with a yearning for Giamatti's "splendid opening out of the self" and left loving learning as life. These four young Americans are remarkable, but they're also representative: of the talents among the young, and of their promise, and of the incalculable advances of the mind that come from active learning and the pedagogy of involvement.

At commencement, I knew their diplomas augured lasting learning and not its end, and that the growth mindsets they and we set off would be a gift to the world and a wonder. As a person, it saddened me to see them leave, because I would miss them, but as an educator, I couldn't have been happier. Morgan, Eddie, Wyatt, and Charisma weren't leaving college so much as taking it with them—because, thanks to the education they created, they now owned a mindset for discovery, with these ways of thinking:

The drive to build ever-bigger foundations of future knowledge;

The grit to persevere when learning is laborious;

The agility to sift when unreliable information arrives in torrents;

The imagination to interweave ideas or fields;

The hunger for dialogue as a catalyst for breakthrough thinking;

The willingness to re-think assumptions;

The poise to integrate thought and experience;

The curiosity to go deeper;

The acceptance of disorientation as a doorway to discovery;

The independence to put forward one's own interpretations;

The inclination to locate mentors;

The reflectiveness to evaluate on one's own learning processes and gauge areas of needed new growth;

The desire to apply oneself fully;

The thirst to like and live with questions;

The craving to uncover answers and truths and new possibilities;

And, most of all, the resourcefulness to engage a new book or problem or field or question or trend with nothing but your own intellectual faculties—and to know that you can succeed, over and over, time after time, that you can find what must be looked for—because you are a discoverer.

I don't think there's too much mystery to why Morgan, Eddie, Wyatt, Charisma, and so many like them forged mindsets for discovery in college. In the main, doing so came straight from their own strengths, brains, families, and precollege teachers. With that, it grew from the core nutrients of the F&M ecosystem: Devoted professors who engaged with students early and at every stage of an education with the pronounced belief that they could learn, high-impact classroom practices requiring active learning, hands-on research and research design opportunities, and a campus culture that prized learning and discovery both as ends in themselves and as ethical means to make a better world.

How best to promote a discoverer's mindset among all or most undergraduates? *The most important action is to consistently rein-*

force that they must lead their learning. That is our students' power, no matter what, which educators must champion and enhance. I have taught students who were deaf, blind, or paraplegic. I have taught students whose parents were killed or deported, whose families disowned them, or who grew up homeless. I have taught students recovering from brain injuries or addiction. I have taught students enduring prisons built to keep them down. And in every case, I have seen that learning begets more learning, that discovery gives people both interior freedom and some power over their circumstances. When students find themselves stuck or highly constrained, and thus deserve our care, we do them no favor when we offer only consolations without the support to create the growth that they seek.

With that belief in our students' ability to learn, we also must invest in the resources for discovery—full-time faculty positions, student financial aid, research internships, and high-impact learning experiences. Workshops to help faculty both learn about and activate growth mindsets are highly valuable, as research shows that college classes utilizing growth-signaling practices and messages "can have a positive impact on learning, motivation, and engagement."[32] Expensive? Yes, quality costs money— although many teaching innovations that lead to active learning do not require massive spending.[33] A bad bet? Hardly. Given the value of igniting the minds of the young, for one and all, for today and tomorrow, for prosperity and democracy and national strength, high-impact education at every level is still our most cost-efficient investment.

Can new virtual classrooms and new uses of artificial intelligence help colleges to activate growth mindsets more effectively and efficiently? No doubt, if used well. By coping with COVID-19, colleges have learned a great deal, and many educators are now exploring the potential uses and abuses of AI. As technologies improve, faculty innovate, educators collaborate, digital divides close, and new assessment tools emerge, education will improve. Already, students are using AI to personalize their learning and power their explorations. Some now envision the wider use of holistic e-portfolios that document skills and credentials gained in college.[34] More and more, they will be able to take galvanizing virtual courses not offered on their campus. We should neither fear nor fetishize such change. That said, if our concern is to kindle the fire for discovery (and other growth mindsets) in our future leaders, if excellence in the holistic formation of young adults is a national need, then we must invest in opportunity-rich campuses that spur students to design and drive their learning, aided by mentors. New technologies can support, without supplanting, this approach.

As the historian Steven Mintz writes, the top priority of our institutions should be "Teaching that's engaging, inspiring, thought-provoking and genuinely helpful," by which he means responsive to the potential and real needs of each undergraduate.[35] Developmentally, young people thrive from quality relationships with educators—in-person and mind-to-mind, forged in the crucible of free inquiry and growth. We saw this with the four undergraduates profiled in this chapter, each of whom was aided and activated by caring professors and staff in a personalized four-year process through which they absorbed the search for insight as a calling, a strength, a freedom, and a dimension of their identities. That is the power of the pedagogy of involvement and what it can deliver.

To catalyze original thinkers and lifelong learners, we must expose college students to the minds, methods, motivations, and standards of faculty-discoverers, while expecting and supporting teaching excellence at every stage of the faculty career, starting with the training future professors receive in graduate school.

We must nourish the sensibility that moves from observation or inquiry to a heat-seeking search for knowledge combined with a dispassionate honesty about findings.

We must work to lower the social and emotional barriers to intellectual flourishing that some students must deal with as they move toward adult life.

We must inculcate the moral value of thinking through concepts that may seem off-base, disagreeable, or unpopular, and of chasing down truth to its farthest frontiers, even though we may not like what we find.

And we must help students experience the timeless rush of making a new known out of the synapses of their working minds.

There are many reasons for doing so. We need the Eddie Alsinas and Charisma Lamberts of *every* generation to make findings that will help improve people's lives. Our economy needs job-discoverers. Our businesses want strategy-discoverers. Our science and tech fields demand ethics-discoverers. Our health cries for wellness-discoverers; our education, for learning-discoverers. It's a perilous age, with change raging like an endless storm, and we need discoverers in every boat. Our democracy requires citizen-discoverers, our diplomacy requires coexistence-discoverers, our planet requires sustainability-discoverers, and our humanity requires wisdom-discoverers.

Another reason is moral. A good society helps its young people know and grow their intrinsic abilities, rather than leaving them stranded on the island of what-could-have-been. We get just one short life. We are in it to be and use what is best in our humanity—love, service, faith, freedom, creativity, and yes, discovery. These are not things to waste. They are elements of our human dignity going back to times and places the records of history don't even reach. If we believe in dignity, intrinsic to our species, equal within all, then we must fuel and fan the fire for discovery in our young, in this time and all times, so that each rising generation can awaken to its humanity and know and see and be its best with the time it has. We cultivate discovery in the young because they are human, and because we are too.

Chapter 1: Questions for Discussion

1. How do you understand the mindset for discovery? Why does the author believe that it is a powerful resource for individuals and society?

2. What are some of the intellectual skills students need to develop so that, after college, they know how to learn and discover independently?

3. What major challenges or questions did Morgan, Eddie, Wyatt, and Charisma face as they formed their mindsets for discovery? Who or what helped them? Do you identify with any of them, and if so, why?

4. Throughout the chapter, the author praises the work of many professors. What are some of the techniques they used to help their students develop into discoverers? What other actions or practices can be impactful?

5. Each of the students profiled was able to take part in research as a part of their studies. Why is that valuable? What more can be done to give more students such opportunities?

6. The chapter celebrates "active learning" and "the pedagogy of involvement." How would you define these concepts and their benefits? Do they have any drawbacks? What factors may prevent educators from employing them?

7. The author claims that the larger culture and ecosystem of a campus can encourage intellectual life among students. Do you agree with this? What can be done at the institutional level to promote learning and discovery?

2

THE MINDSET FOR
CREATION

When I dare to be powerful—to use my strength in the
service of my vision, then it becomes less and less important
whether I am afraid.

—AUDRE LORDE

IT'S SAID THAT SANSKRIT has ninety-six words for love, but we
may need twice that many to name the myriad forms of energy
flowing on a college campus.

There's the burst when classes change—students hustling after
their professors, or cooking up plans while crossing paths, or
rushing to print a paper. There's the quickening of debate inside a
seminar room and the camaraderie of teammates limbering up
before practice.

You feel it in the chatter and clatter in the dining hall, before a
swift mass exodus to the evening's activities, while a few tables
linger longer in friendship.

You hear it late into the night—the crackling of keyboards in the coffee shop, a cappella snapping from a stairwell, the upbeat din on the social floor of the library.

You see it in profiles of concentration—intent thinkers decamped in study carrels, or a couple talking seriously on a bench, two minds merging to make a memory and maybe more.

In physics, energy is defined as the capacity for doing work, and on campus that work often creates something new, from artwork to social startups to research. What sparks the making? Maybe it's an assignment from a class or the capstone of a major. Maybe it's an inner muse or a role model, a probing dialogue, or a problem on campus. Maybe it's the enriched ecosystem itself with elevating spaces and so many young minds and bodies in motion—writing and revising, planning and doing, acting and reacting and connecting. Creation is always in the air.

Fostering this mindset, whether in college or elsewhere, improves our lives. Creativity gives us art, advances, fresh thinking, products, jobs, trade, cures, pleasure, meaning, and love. It promotes exchange, partnerships, and community. It gives us solutions. It gives us progress. It gives us lofty feelings of wonder and possibility and power. With creativity, we help shape the world that we've found, reaching for more while knowing and showing who we are.

For many students, the mindset to make takes flight in college. How does it happen? I think it comes down to this: Residential campuses are highly creative cultures, with prompts and resources and mentors and collaborators abounding 24/7. There are problems to solve, gaps to fill, services to provide, and audiences to engage. Innovation is always in high demand. When students invest themselves in creating a product, work of art, or a new club, they are also investing in their growth. Making gives them new skills, new pleasure, new experiences, new epiphanies, new self-knowledge—insights that lead students to believe, "I can create, I like creating, I am a creator." As we'll see in this chapter, four insights stand out: The ideas that, by tapping their talent and bringing something original into the world, students: (1) forge meaningful relationships, (2) develop their voice in the service of their commitments, (3) boost their critical thinking and problem-solving skills, and (4) claim their power and their agency. These are revelations that can last a lifetime.

Point One: Creators Forge Meaningful Relationships

Alec Hersh, who we met in the introduction, chose F&M in 2015 wanting to be "a big fish in a small pond right away, without delay." With high school experience in musical theater, set design, and lighting, he promptly tried out for a role in *Hair* at the urging of theatre professor Carol Davis, who cast him in a supporting part. The arts community felt welcoming and not at all competitive. At least three productions were holding auditions that fall. Film had just become a major. There was an improv club; open mic nights; faculty-led dance, voice, and music programs; a new spoken word club; and the popular jazz-rap fusion group Culture Blue. So many people were making and doing—and firing up one another.

Alec became friends right away with James Ngo, a sophomore reveling in the creator's life, who had broken out the year before when he played a balletic Puck in *A Midsummer's Night Dream*. Now he was singing for the a cappella group The Poor Richards, rehearsing for *Hair*, and writing his own musical about a rollercoaster ride of college partying and coming out. For James, F&M was a 24/7 workshop for art and expression, setting an example that led Alec to start dreaming about what he could add to the campus.

College classes were better than high school as well, and Alec quickly fell for the access to faculty and talk-rich seminars. One fast influence was theatre professor Rachel Anderson-Rabern, who cast him for the spring production of *One Man, Two Guvnors*. He marveled at how his new teachers would ask questions to elicit students' ideas. Every day overflowed with reading, rehearsing, and conversation. At night, he and James would swap thoughts about art and invention, what they loved and why. He felt alert and connected in this greenhouse of creativity.

So, what would *he* add? What would he create?

He leaned toward blending his interests like history, writing, and theater. One beacon was the red-hot musical *Hamilton* by the young Wesleyan graduate Lin-Manuel Miranda. Alec loved the audacity of a hip-hop refresh of colonial history with a Black and Brown cast. The language was captivating, the conflicts were eternal, and the characters were just familiar enough to be reimagined. Perhaps American history could also give him wet clay from which to sculpt.

As his first semester wound down, he went fishing for ideas in the college library, where he found a new biography of Rosemary Kennedy, the sister of the president, whose father arranged for her to have a ruinous lobotomy because of her sharp mood swings and seizures.[1] It was surprising to learn that this daughter of American royalty was hidden away like an abomination—and that few in his generation even knew about it. He could work with this, he thought. He knows a good tale and a smart plot. With research, he certainly could present Rosemary's story as a play, cast students, and bring it to an F&M stage. Why not him? And why not now?

For two months that spring, while rehearsing for Anderson-Rabern's production, he began drafting scenes of the Kennedy family and its conflicts. Then he introduced himself to theatre professor Brian Silberman, a playwright, who generously read the text only to send him back to the drawing board, suggesting that the play would need another facet to complement the Kennedy saga. Although that wasn't what he wanted to hear, Alec accepted that he didn't know everything and spent the summer pondering a second storyline.

When sophomore year started, he dove back into the stacks and landed upon the figure of Teddy Roosevelt, the roughrider president who served from 1901 to 1909. He learned that, on the same dark day in 1884, at age twenty-five, he'd lost his wife, Alice, and his mother, Mittie. There must have been a tortured soul beneath that big-stick swagger, he surmised. Curious about Roosevelt's early life, he found out that the college actually had a fund for student research. Perfect. Three paragraphs later he had the grant and a plan to visit the Kennedy Library and Sagamore Hill, Roosevelt's longtime home on Oyster Bay Island.

These mid-semester visits made history more human. Aided by expert librarians, he got the sense that Teddy must have carried grief throughout his public life, perhaps like JFK. This gave him all the material he needed. Now fully invested, he began writing in an intense state of flow, and over winter break, he drafted a second act depicting Teddy's tragedy and cut down some of the Kennedy scenes.[2]

When school started in January, he believed that *Domestic Animals* was ready for production. After securing the Green Room Theatre for four days in April, he put out the word that he'd be auditioning for twelve actors to play roles in both stories. A short time later, with the cast selected, he launched the rehearsals and began puzzling over staging, lights, sets, and costumes. Somehow, he felt calm in this tempest of details and deadlines, pulling it all together in a mere eight weeks.

I attended one of the five performances and was moved by the play and the production. Though inexperienced, the actors were clearly committed to the production and each other. The conflicts faced by the Kennedys and the Roosevelts kept the plot moving, and the parallels among the two domestic tragedies felt suggestive. The audience of about fifty people was clearly transfixed by the image of the future titans of American history fretting and raging and suffering on stage.

Two years later, I asked some of the actors what they took away from this all-student experience. Syed Saquib, who played a prince and a doctor, recalled struggling to deliver his lines: "Alec said, 'The reason why is that you are trying to *impersonate* these people. Just say it the way it feels right, because what is right is what you see in the character.' So, I made the doctor a kind of a mad scientist, and it worked."

Will Kay, then a first-year student who hadn't acted since tenth grade, played Joe Kennedy in the first act and Roosevelt in the second. He'd auditioned on a lark, egged on by a friend. It elated him to join this brave cast of novices. Isn't that the point of theater, he said to me, "*Anyone can do it.*" He recalled how one pivot point set a new course for his entire education: "It was my first reading of a soliloquy where Teddy Roosevelt relives the anguish of his wife's death. Alec told me to read the script one time and then just improv, so I did. It was just me and Alec alone in the dark theater. I gave all my emotion to it and went for it."

I heard so much pride in Will's voice: "When I finished Alec said to me, 'You are *never* looking at that script again.' That was so big for me. I reflect on that moment all the time. This is what liberal arts education is all about. You are in a set paradigm: *Now make it your own.*"

Which he did for the next three years. Will went on to serve in student government, perform in *The Elephant Man,* and design an independent study on contradictions in American Christianity. Without this early epiphany, Will might not have taken charge of his education as quickly—just as Alec might not have envisioned himself as a creator but for those midnight parleys with James Ngo. Makers spawn makers—that's what transpires in college—and mentors matter too.

For Alec, *the* mentor was Professor Anderson-Rabern. The way she directed *One Man, Two Guvnors* gave him a model for how to help the actors empty themselves into their characters. At the beginning of the *Domestic Animals* rehearsals, his inclination had been, literally, to *direct*—to provide clear, authoritative instruction. After all, he'd written the play, so giving up control seemed a little perverse. "But then," Alec told me, "an actor would say, 'What about trying this?' and I'd think, 'Perfect idea! Makes sense,' just like Rachel would. And I'd give them more freedom."

Sometimes it felt like Anderson-Rabern was an invisible advocate by his side. When directing, he'd remember that she would never dictate how to play a character or scene; rather, she'd offer an idea for a line, or suggest the power of a glance or a stance or a freeze, in effect giving her actors the tools and freedom to create their own performances. One time he told me proudly how he'd adopted his mentor's method: "Yes, I had a vision, and I acted on it. How? By *letting go*—by letting others have a say in what went on. And, after tech week, by accepting that the production isn't even mine; it's the actors'. You give it to them and say, *'Take it and run.'*"

Take it and run.

As it turned out, that emancipatory idea, which Alec had gleaned from his professor, was the same one that his impressionable actors gleaned from him. And that sums up the just-do-it culture of a breathing campus. It's your moment, now. This one. Take it, make from it.

Alec Hersh is, as the saying goes, one of one—game, generous, imaginative, and organized. That said, *Domestic Animals* was the work of a pack and not a lone wolf. He drew upon a community of peers who would push and join and enthuse one another on the journey to invent. And he tapped into receptive professors who gave the kind of usable feedback that enables young people to improve their product, which helps creativity become a calling. It's a big deal that Brian Silberman took the time to read a lengthy manuscript of a novice writer he didn't even know—and to suggest a path forward that would ask a lot of Alec if he truly wanted to better his script. That's the pedagogy of involvement and the power of a creative ecosystem.

Developmentally, there's so much for undergraduates like Alec to gain with a mindset for creativity. They can sense that it's possible to imagine, to enact, to involve themselves in making with others. They can feel the rush of fashioning one's own product or raising one's own flag. They can realize that they aren't too young or green to do something now. They can absorb the benefits of practice and training, of being coached up to get better, which undermines the limiting fixed mindset myth that creativity comes from natural genius alone.[3] They can see what it means to walk back a false start or just simplify or turn a text from pretty good to very good with others' help.

It's especially powerful when one creates in the context of, or as a reaction against, some wound, pain, or prejudice—thus rewriting negative narratives and becoming through one's deeds the maker of a healing, evolving self. Which brings us back to *Domestic Animals*. You see, part of Alec's drive to create drama came from being exposed to an act of evil. On December 14, 2012, when he was fourteen years old, twenty children and six teachers were murdered in his hometown elementary school. While he did not lose a family member in the Sandy Hook massacre, he was floored by this appalling theft of life and innocence.

"Everybody in Newtown was traumatized," he told me. "None of us will ever be the same again."

In his early teens, he had to try to make sense of not only these shocking murders in a supposed sanctuary but also the absurd fact that many national political and media figures chose to explain away the dangers of on-demand assault weapons. If the adults couldn't even hold a conversation about gun violence, what conclusions could he draw? Was there any humane meaning to be found?

One time I asked Alec if this catastrophe somehow led him to his play.

"Absolutely," he told me. "Partly because *Domestic Animals* says that we should care about each other. But more directly, two years after the killings, a theater company came to Newtown with staff and actors. People were still broken. They created a show with children who were siblings of the dead or were in the school at the time. It was incredible to see. They had forgotten how to be kids, and this company allowed them to express themselves and be each other's friends again. I saw the positive change theater can make. I saw it as something much more than just fun."

In high school, he witnessed art for life's safe, absorbing the hope that drama might renew, repair, and reconnect. College then gave him the people and culture to act on that hope himself, rather than waiting or watching others. Franklin & Marshall activated his mindset to create—through which he wrote and produced a tremendous play, yes, and found that he liked invention and the relationships and teamwork it enabled. In other words, for undergraduates making is about more than the product; it's about creating connections and community, and from that, the fulfillment that feeds a mindset.

Point Two: Creators Develop Their Voice in the Service of Their Commitments

For Alec, F&M's culture was a benevolent force with many helping hands. But our campuses aren't always so affirming. Sometimes, when things go wrong or a crisis comes up, students move to create an innovative response—and, with that, progress.

Witness #BLACKYAK.

In the fall of 2015, just when Alec was falling in love with F&M, another first-year student, Jael Lewis, was finding the campus less than hospitable. An immigrant from Guyana who attended high school in Bushwick and earned a Posse Scholarship, Jael was an honors student with a passion for dance and law who was also a spark plug for community. Friendly, fashionable, enterprising, and raucously candid, she has a knack for pithy social commentary and hilarious impromptu impressions.

Although she made friends fast with many students of color that first semester, Jael found it slower going with members of the white, suburban majority. She sensed an ice-hard coating that blocked these peers from in-depth conversations with students like her. This was the semester when University of Missouri students were protesting the racial climate at their institution. In November, after the U of M football team vowed to boycott its games until the university president stepped down, F&M's Black Student Union (BSU) held a rally of solidarity.

Even though the demonstration had nothing to do with them, some students didn't like seeing their Black classmates chanting, and so they posted racist comments on the then-popular smartphone app Yik Yak, which caused headaches on many campuses for a couple years before going dark in 2017 and returning like a zombie in 2021. The app functions by displaying anonymous posts from users in the same geographic area, such as a college campus or a neighborhood. Its trust-crushing premise is that users will know that every post—no matter how targeted, vulgar, or vile—comes from a cloaked figure in their midst.

The cyberspace equivalent of bathroom graffiti, but with viral reach, Yik Yak provides a forum for harassers to disrupt others' sense of belonging. The gist of these 2015 attacks was that the rallying Black students should shut up and study, since they were only admitted to F&M because of their race.

Angry but activated, and refusing to be silenced, Jael pressed the leadership of the Black Student Union to call an emergency meeting. The year before, to avoid recognizing idiots, the BSU leaders had opted not to respond to a flurry of Yik Yak posts that disparaged African American men. With odiousness on repeat, many students felt that now they needed to act—even though doing so would be draining and time-consuming. Of course, they would call on the administration to condemn the attacks and uncover the harassers, but what else could they do? One thought was to "down-vote" the posts to make them vanish. Another was to fight back in the Yik Yak discussion threads or try to block the app on campus servers. So, what to do?

Already seeing herself as an artist and an activist, Jael spoke up even though she was just in her first semester of college. People shouldn't be paralyzed around hate and harassment—why not create a public art display that would challenge everyone to take a stand? The concept she proposed was a wall-sized, interactive display that she named, perfectly, #BLACKYAK, which would be installed in the student center atrium, a primary campus thoroughfare. The respected seniors Brianna Robinson and Sandra Welbeck quickly endorsed the first-year's confident proposal.

To create the #BLACKYAK, Jael printed enlarged smartphone screenshots that she had taken of about fifteen abusive posts before they had been down-voted. She mounted them on a towering eight-foot by six-foot sheet of paper with a large-lettered message: "You can no longer deny OUR EXPERIENCES." Her goal was to make this racism visible to all. She placed a second sheet next to that one, twice as big and blank, on which people could write their own messages with Sharpie pens.

For the next few days, hundreds of students and educators gathered at the display, somberly absorbing the anonymous posts and pondering how to respond. Some wrote, "No racism at F&M" or "Thank you to white allies." Others described micro-aggressions like how some students would posture as allies or change their intonations when speaking with African Americans. Thoughtful messages filled the canvas, far outnumbering the hateful posts.

#BLACKYAK conveyed Jael's authentic voice—for her, one that demanded audience engagement and refused to hide behind anonymity—which is what all educators want our students to develop. In fact, the year before, in his convocation speech, government professor Dean Hammer challenged the new students to create their voices in these unique college years of freedom and learning. Intellectually and socially, he said, "Voice is the communication of the commitments of what informs, and is informed by, your experiences."[4] And that communication happens, he said, not just with words but also with deeds, with choices that count. Like with #BLACKYAK.

Jael's protest piece did breathtaking cultural work at several depths. First, it was a *pro-speech protest*—the very opposite of silencing—that exposed the anonymous posters' cowardice as no one dared step forward to justify himself. #BLACKYAK also made visible the BSU's outrage and unity, demonstrating that the students would not acquiesce to cyber harassment. She showed bravery doing this, opening herself to personal attacks. As Spelman College president emerita Beverly Tatum likes to say, she opted not for a "safe space" but a "brave space," calling out racism. I call this leadership.[5]

In addition, with its call for counter-comments, the #BLACKYAK challenged the quiet majority. Have you experienced bigotry? Share it. You're *not* racist? Say so. And dozens of people picked up pens and did so in a unified chorus. #BLACKYAK even motivated a group of professors to create a companion display called the "Fac/Staff Yak" that embraced Black students and denounced prejudice of all types. That's impact. And, through the name #BLACKYAK, Jael called out Yik Yak for enabling intolerance with its cynical design. Complaints of this sort probably led it to go dormant.

No college is always communal, but conflict or even nastiness can incite creation too. Campuses rev up as people speak up. Hard topics rise to the surface. Class discussions get real. People let down their veils. Minds open. There's something at stake, so it's time to speak and stand. As Dean Hammer explained, "Voice comes from somewhere. . . . Voice is a critical awareness of what matters to you, of what expresses who you are, what you value. It is not something you are born with. It is cultivated in your interactions with *the world around you*."[6] And the campus around you.

Jael made a work of "critical awareness" that elicited anger and empathy, disappointment and resolve. The accruing voices became #BLACKYAK's voice, calling on the full campus to focus on Black students' lives. Her creation helped awaken moral imagination, and it contributed to a community reckoning that led to new steps to prevent harassment, promote inclusion, and increase faculty diversity, all actions Dr. Martin Luther King might call "the practical art of living in harmony."[7]

Because campuses convene people with divergent backgrounds and opposing views, there will be moments of disagreement, confusion, and offense. This is inevitable. How people respond to conflict can either nurture or negate a creative culture. Some, like Jael, create so as to catalyze a needed dialogue, inviting others to speak or create as well. That's the cycle we want—on campus and in society. As Dweck writes, "the growth mindset lets people—even those who are targets of negative labels—use and develop their minds fully. Their heads are not filled with limiting thoughts, a fragile sense of belonging, and a belief that other people can define them."[8]

Stories like this one complicate the current narrative of cancel culture on campus. Jael and the Black Student Union did not shout anyone down. They weren't snowflakes or cry-bullies—indeed, they were responding to snowflakes and cry-bullies who were afraid to own up to their racist insults. Jael invented a new venue to juxtapose the obnoxious speech acts of the few with the affirming speech acts of the many. In this case, sunlight was, indeed, a highly effective disinfectant. #BLACKYAK reminds us how creators can stir communities to confront difficult issues and bring people together more closely around values like civility, respect for others, and common educational purpose.

We saw with Alec that creating brings students together. As Jael's experience shows, it also brings out their voices.

Point Three: Creators Boost Their Critical Thinking and Problem-Solving Abilities

There's another kind of making that lights up college communities—the creation of new business ventures through which young people, often oblivious to failure, try to create a product or a service while learning core principles of entrepreneurship.

During my last few years at F&M, innovation took off as student innovators inspired one another. Ani Akpan launched a venture providing students with professional-quality head shots or photo collections from their campus events. Will Kiefer founded Bench Mark Program to help low-income Lancaster youth to build self-confidence and bodily agency through weight training. And, besides making #BLACKYAK, Jael Lewis created a makeup artistry business, Give More Face, serving students in Lancaster and friends at home in Brooklyn.

Each of these inventions was necessarily a business, as students tried to meet needs, create value, and bring in revenue. Whether it's commercial or social entrepreneurship, it's all the same makers' mindset. Not that every student wants to be an innovator, of course. One recent longitudinal study found that about 13 percent of undergraduates demonstrated "notable and significant growth" as innovators across four years. Students "who had many opportunities for cocurricular learning were nine times more likely to fall into the innovation trajectory group."[9] Supporting students who are inclined toward innovation can and should be central to the aims of educators—both for inherently valuable learning and personal development and for the practical fact that, more and more, our tech-fired economies will reward those with the mindset to create.

One undergraduate who embraced entrepreneurship was 2018 graduate Paraj Mathur. Curious about business and economics as a New Delhi high school student, he chose an American liberal arts college on the theory that interdisciplinary studies, rather than a single-field focus, would better prepare him for the reality of rapid disruption in business, health care, transportation, and communications. He saw opportunity in the likely erosion of settled knowledge and conventional business practice, but beyond that, he was open to many directions—one of which he found in his brain-bending, first-year Connections seminar, International Security Dilemmas.

The course was designed by business professor Bryan Stinchfield, who'd previously served five years as an Army helicopter pilot. In one of the first meetings, Stinchfield asked his students why hundreds of thousands of people would join the terrorist group ISIS. Paraj recalled that everyone agreed that the recruits must hate the West.

"Why?" Stinchfield asked.

"Perhaps because they are crazy," someone surmised.

"Hundreds of thousands of people are all crazy?"

"Because they were being manipulated," someone else conjectured.

"Why?" he asked again.

"Because they were afraid," someone guessed.

"OK, why?"

This went on, assertion after assertion, and class after class: Stinchfield never stopped asking *why*. What do you know, and why do you believe it? It was relentlessness . . . and stimulating. "Nobody likes such hard questions," Paraj once told me. "We often avoid them. But Stinchfield taught me that you can't solve a real problem if you're complacent with your questions."

The professor liked Paraj's lively mind and sensed he'd shine in the Business, Organizations & Society (BOS) major, which prizes curiosity and critical thinking. So, he emailed him a few times, offering him a seat in his upcoming Introduction to BOS seminar. Yet again, the pedagogy of involvement.

"I kept turning him down," Paraj said, "thinking I would major in economics, and then he'd email me back two weeks later telling me things like, 'Hey Paraj, a spot just opened up—Do you want it?' Finally, I said 'yes,' and that influenced *my whole education*. Because I was interested in innovation, in creating things, BOS was perfect because the major truly taught me how to ask unconventional questions with no fear."

At F&M, his first innovation was Strutzy, a concept he'd devised during a tech company internship the previous summer. The venture involved paying students to walk around Lancaster wearing ads for local businesses on their T-shirts or jackets. To assess the market reach of the ads, he came up with an algorithm combining data on neighborhood population density with variables such as time of day and weather.

The idea was clever, but few local business owners bought the pitch that Paraj's startup would increase revenue. "Honestly," he told me with a laugh, "I wasn't successful at building a customer base, partly because my data came from estimates, and partly because I wasn't great at sales." But he loved the thrill of brainstorming with friends and professors and getting some traction, plus the learning that came from innovating; the fact that his first venture fizzled only motivated him more.

His next one was SimplyStow.com, which began not as a new business idea but as a problem that needed a solution: Where could he store his stuff during the summer before senior year? This is a perennial headache, when students go back home or travel abroad or hold an internship in a new city. Who can afford to ship hundreds of pounds of junk back to Mom and Dad, just so they can ship it all back to campus in a few months?

With a friend, he created an app to match students who needed storage with Lancastrians who had space in their garages. After the local newspaper posted a story on this sparkly new business, about three hundred and fifty potential customers followed up. The prototype and the coding were easy, but how to handle the sudden geyser of patrons perplexed him. Busy with exams and summer preparations, he couldn't find any investors to help him hire the staff needed to pair up a rush of renters and storage spaces. Stinchfield talked through the concept with him while asking lots of questions, like if he had time to do this right and whether investors might have doubts about his experience and his staying power.

"At the time I was frustrated, especially with the college," he told me later, "because I thought this idea would be good for students. Why couldn't F&M just pay for it?"

Then he chuckled. "In fact, I was only thinking about my desire for a business and not thinking about the perspectives an investor—the college—might have." Like, for example, why should F&M allocate funds for this untested concept when it already had a storage contract with a local company?

SimplyStow.com helped him and about fifteen students solve a problem, even though it never took flight beyond that summer. Looking back after it bottomed out, Paraj realized that he'd viewed the project only from its end point—his definition of success—rather than embracing the need to research the problem to be solved, the likely value of various solutions, and the views of would-be funders. In other words, he needed more critical thinking, all the way through. More asking "Why?" as Stinchfield would preach.

Senior year, he took two purposeful steps to grow as an entre-preneur. First, the failure of SimplyStow.com spurred him to want to learn how investors think, so he obtained seed funding from the BOS program to start a pop-up club, Dip Ventures, which would host a one-day student pitch competition, with the winners receiving funding to make a go of their concept. Working to round up more than a dozen teams placed him in the funders' role. To differentiate among them given his limited investment resources, he asked them to present their business plans, targeted markets, and leadership teams. It filled him with pride to see all these teams competing. The winners proposed an app making it easier to advertise or attend campus events—an idea that the college helped the group test the following year.

Second, he signed up for an experimental seminar called The Ideas Class, developed by six faculty who visited Stanford University's Hasso Plattner Institute of Design, also known as the d.school. The professors' goal was to see how a multidisciplinary, project-based course might help students learn principles of innovation applicable to all sorts of endeavors. One of the leaders was Etienne Gagnon, who taught physics and astronomy. Others included Stinchfield, Kerry Sherin-Wright in creative writing, Dirk Eitzen in film studies, and Dan Ardia in biology. As Gagnon stated, their obsession with invention emerged out of an awareness that first jobs now increasingly require the combination of hard skills like predictive analytics or coding with soft skills such as collaboration and questioning.[10]

In students like Paraj, they saw energetic creators who yearned for impact. Campus culture was fueling their makers' motors, spurring them to innovate, and Gagnon believed the tools and methods of liberal arts education could be ideal preparation for the burgeoning creative economy. They didn't see any dissonance with the college's academic values since liberal arts education was all about intellectual agility and faculty mentoring. With some retooling to emphasize the effective framing and solving of problems, their version of liberal arts 2.0 could be more relevant than ever—and these faculty were early enough in their careers to give it a try.

Ardia, a challenging and approachable teacher, liked that "the faculty began to ask if we were willing to take the risk to leave the silos of our fields and collaborate on a new way of teaching." Could they help students learn the difference between a workable venture and a false start? Could they identify the precise skills and attitudes that would be most valuable? Could they give students the freedom to try out projects of their own invention that might not succeed? And how would they grade this kind of work?

Scheduled on Fridays and held in a funky caged-in corner of the library, the pilot section of The Ideas Class drew sixty applicants but had to be limited to eighteen. On the first day the professors brought in wood, nails, and tools and told the students to build their workstations. "This was incredibly difficult," Paraj said later. "It *had* to work, and the students had to rely on each other to create desks that didn't fall over."

After that, they met some successful innovators who talked with them about "solutions culture." A key discipline that they stressed was to listen carefully to those experiencing a problem before deciding what fix to propose. To practice this skill, they fanned out across campus to interview students, faculty, and staff about where change was needed at F&M, from course registration to counseling to campus social life. The faculty pushed them to probe more and not just to fall back on their own preconceived notions of the college's flaws or structures for change making.

Next, the class ventured into Lancaster to interview nonprofit leaders about hindrances to achieving their missions. Then it became time to turn questions into solutions. One team wrote a business plan for converting a vacant bar into an after-school tutoring center. Another helped an artist drive more foot traffic into her gallery. A third helped a local science museum attract more schoolchildren.

Paraj's team consulted with Penn Medicine Lancaster General Health, a large regional health system, to confront the problem of attracting new patients from the millennial generation. His group began with the assumption that the local urgent care centers that twenty-somethings frequented involved too much curing and not enough prevention. As a result, Paraj's first task was to research new prevention strategies for the chronic health problems of millennials, like stress, nutrition, infrequent exercise, and risky behavior. How might they make a new business model addressing these needs? Unfortunately, the more he researched preventive health care, the more the team churned over what exactly to offer.

Finally, after a month of getting nowhere, one of the team members challenged them to step back and reexamine their assumptions. Was their new health program for millennials in fact merely a solution looking for a problem? Why not tweak the existing urgent care model to make it more responsive to this age cohort rather than design a whole new model that seemed to have no engageable market? So, they pivoted to propose a plan to retool urgent care for millennials, and the hospital system readily seized upon their report. The major takeaway was to constantly assess each turn of the wheel of a new project, requiring intellectual agility rather than just drive and dogged labor.

"This was the best class I ever took," Paraj told me a few months after graduation. "It was collaborative, not competitive. The faculty were partners, not experts. We wanted to achieve as a collective. And we had different strengths—that made 'load sharing' both easier and rational. Why should I do something you can do better?"

Taken as a whole, Paraj's education amounted to a four-year process of creating with mentors and peers. As with Alec, involved faculty took seriously his inclination to invent outside the classroom and challenged him. Where else can eighteen-to-twenty-three-year-olds get four years of sustained mentoring from knowledgeable professionals, *whenever they ask for it*?

For educators looking to promote creative mindsets, three takeaways for Paraj's education stand out. First, great learning can happen in classes that help students ideate, explore, create, and evaluate in real time, and in the real world, rather than in simulated situations.[11] Second, as he told me, faculty can mentor students "to ask more questions—better ones" and constantly rethink their assumptions. Third, students will not be finished or polished creators just because of one class or one major or one degree; rather, creativity is a lifelong endeavor that demands sustained commitment, which is precisely why it's so valuable to galvanize the mindset for it during college.

In *Creating Innovators*, Tony Wagner summarizes research showing that scholars and business executives alike believe that fostering greater creativity and innovation is essential for America to create new jobs and sustain a competitive and adaptive national economy.[12] He argues that innovation is not a natural skill but rather is a process that can be inculcated through educational methods that reinforce the value of three things: play, passion, and purpose.[13] Paraj Mathur came all the way from New Delhi to Franklin & Marshall and left with all three, because he absorbed the value of curiosity and critical thinking in the creative process.

Point Four: Creators Claim Their Agency

On every campus there are undergraduates demonstrating how college fosters creative exploration and the mindset to make. It's valuable to notice them and not take them for granted, even though they often don't ask for help because the ecosystems that support them are doing extraordinarily valuable work for society. At F&M, for example, I saw how Anna Folz created a program on her own to bring hundreds of solar stoves to villagers in Guatemala, reducing dangerous wood foraging and smoke inhalation, and preventing kitchen fires.[14] I saw how Matt Rohn and Emily Ray assigned themselves the job of giving an inactive debate club the purpose, structure, and accountability needed to compete for national championships.[15] And I saw how young staff member Shawn Jenkins cofounded F&M College Prep, informed by his earlier creative experiences helping found the school's Sustainability House and its new form of student government, the Diplomatic Congress. Here's one more detailed story that shows how an imaginative student can pull together many campus resources to make a dazzling invention—and a mindset.

In 2015–16, while Alec and Jael were starting their incandescent college careers, the senior Alejandra (Alex) Zavala was finishing hers. That year she created—from the fusion of her life history, her Mexican American identity, her commitments, her education, and the campus's creative culture—a mixed-media photo exhibition so distinctive that, after displaying it, the campus museum purchased it for its permanent collection.

A double major in art and psychology with a minor in French, Alex entered the 2015–16 year with both personal pride and a troubled mood. Having come to America after first grade, she knew she was lucky. With secure legal status, her loving parents worked blue-collar jobs and prioritized education for Alex and her brother. She excelled at Octorara High School, winning a prestigious Lenfest Scholarship and dating a young man named Bradley, to whom she is now married. An excellent Upward Bound program helped her find F&M, where she loved her classes, picked up photography, studied in Paris, and forged true friendships with students like Andrea Smith from Las Vegas. Through it all, she felt an abiding love for her parents and their heroic sacrifices to give her the freedom to learn and build her life.

Hence, her sadness too. She knew Mexico as home, hope, family, faith, culture, life—a gorgeous land of godly people. But she also knew her country as a place of pain, where power reigns while the poor work, wait, hide, or leave. A first-year course with Professor Laura Sheldon helped her to understand Mexico's inequities through the lens of political history. She started to see how the corruption and cartels, the impunity and the violence, grew from the country's past and the power of its northern neighbor. And then a 2014 atrocity shook her soul.

On September 26 of that year, forty-three male students from Ayotzinapa, a rural teacher college, were traveling by buses they had commandeered (an annual event) to Mexico City for a protest observing the notorious massacre of college students in 1968. Tragically, their vehicle disappeared in the city of Iguala, Guerrero, and none of them have been seen or heard from since. Despite a national outcry, each investigation has failed to reveal who abducted them or why they were murdered. Many suspect a local crime syndicate, perhaps in league with local government or with tacit approval from higher-ups, but as months and then years passed the case went cold with no accountability for the families.[16]

About twelve months later, in the fall of her senior year, Alex and her mother had a conversation about the growing violence in Mexico. From the reports of friends, her mom felt that bloodshed was increasing everywhere, even in their home province of Guanajuato. It was outrageous, but what could people do? As they spoke, Alex formed an idea. She would soon be crafting a proposal for her capstone project in studio art, which she loved. Maybe she could create a work that would draw attention to the forty-three murders, at least on campus.

It occurred to her that if her parents hadn't come north, she'd surely be attending college in Mexico. Perhaps she would have been on that ill-fated bus, leaving her parents with clenched, crying hearts. And not just *her* parents. She imagined all the students at F&M whose family journeys started in her country. In her first three years, as the Next Generation talent strategy took off, the Latino community had more than doubled. There was Andy from Los Angeles, Ivanna from Santa Fe, Andrea from Austin, and Ruth from Chicago. In a different life, she thought, any of her classmates could have been killed.

Instead, all were cutting their own paths in America, and at Franklin & Marshall. Alex saw so much integrity in the way they pursued their studies. All tried their best and trusted the process. All held part-time jobs and helped their families back home. All supported the campus first-gen community—whether they hung out primarily with other Latinos or, like Alex, had a wider array of friends and roommates. And, with their number growing each year, they were all energizing each other and helping Franklin & Marshall become an even finer college.

She considered how the students at both F&M and Ayotzinapa were swept up in a vortex of history. In the face of brutal generational injustice, the ancestors of one group left while those of the others stayed. But they were all related—by culture, by aspiration, by humanity. She saw and felt these mystic bonds—and through her art project, others might too. The living could honor the dead and the Mexico that made them.

The art major imagined a set of portraits of her Mexican American classmates—forty-three to be precise. Then she began picturing the kinds of details that make the individual portraits cohere as a collection, such as background images of Mexico and America. "Creation is applied thought," Sir Ken Robinson writes, referring to how creators must generate sets of options and then make judgments about what to winnow.[17] That's exactly what Alex would need to do. For this tribute, she wondered, what expressions should her subjects take? What clothing should they wear? How would she show her country and the diversity of regions from which Mexican Americans hail?

As for so many undergraduate creators, deadlines made a virtue of necessity, and she made evocative choices. The exhibition portrays the students from the waist up, dressed in plain white, or shirtless for some of the men, with serious countenances, as if they're looking both back and ahead. Using an advanced image-layering technique that she refined with Professor John Holmgren and drawing upon principles of visual perception she learned from Professor Fred Owens, Alex struck for the depths of heritage. Behind each headshot she placed a map of the Mexican province from which the student's family hails, and in most, she added a faint image suggesting their US home. Hildalgo and Houston. Chiapas and Denver. Oaxaca and Chicago.

In about half the portraits she grafted in traditional Mexican headdresses or flowered hair clips to invoke the culture of home, while in others she superimposed images of the heart, lungs, or bones that all humans have. Each piece is exquisite—a striking subject poised in thought, embedded in cultures. Collectively, they blend and fuse and honor: Mexico *and* America. Universal *and* particular. Men *and* women. Life *and* death.

Alex called it *Hasta la Raíz*, or Down to the Root. Mounted in three rows, the forty-three seventeen-inch by twenty-two-inch portraits created a fifty-foot wall . . . of humanity. And there was a forty-fourth panel, to bring it back to Ayotzinapa: This panel displayed photos of the forty-three Mexican martyrs, from their student ID cards, arranged just like the F&M portraits. All murdered.

Hasta la Raíz asks its viewers to juxtapose the living and the disappeared, and then to learn and care about a heinous crime in this culturally and humanly beautiful country: Who were these murdered students? Why are there no answers?

It also speaks differently to differently placed viewers. For example, it invites the larger campus to look again at Latino students they'll surely recognize from class, clubs, or campus jobs saying, in Alex's words, "We are here, and we have a lot to offer—our culture is alive here." What do you really know of the love and labor and loss and towns and tenderness that brought so many of these young souls to North America and then to Franklin & Marshall?

To students in the portraits and Mexican Americans who might come to F&M in the years ahead, it says proudly, "We are one, and we are many. We are Mexican, and we are American. We are we." As a first-gen American and first-gen college goer, Alex paid homage both to the culture of her forebears and the country of her future.

In a 2002 essay, the Mexican American writer and theorist Gloria Anzaldua described creative expression as "an archetypal journey home to the self, *un proceso de crear puentes* (bridges) to the next phase, next place, next culture, next reality. . . . You realize that 'home' is that bridge, the in-between place of constant transition."[18] This is what Alex's art does, giving her a place to stand, a beam connecting the cultures that formed her, from which she can see and show and start to shape America's ever-renewing society.

Creating this bridge was an act of Olympian aspiration that brought myriad trials. Technically, her mentor Holmgren helped with countless quandaries in photographing the subjects, layering the images, and experimenting with types of print paper. Artistically, her hardest task involved constantly adjusting each portrait in relation to the others so that all would "stand out, but not stick out." Intellectually, the biggest hurdle was to integrate ideas from history, science, and language to give the work greater reach and resonance. Logistically, most onerous was finding, interviewing, photographing, and coordinating with forty-three busy students, all under the press of deadlines, which her boyfriend Bradley helped with immensely.

Hardest of all were the moral challenges, which she couldn't plan for. "The students shared their family stories," Alex told me, "and some of the feelings were raw." Many described the loss and hardship of loved ones. A visiting student from Mexico became very emotional. She found it unhelpful to try to suppress these roiling waves of sadness to just get the work done. Instead, the solution was to feel creatively.

This meant allowing herself to feel love and hope along with the cross-generational trauma as she made each portrait—because, in fact, it was love for their children and hope for their futures that powered the families to leave the only homes they knew for a perilous North American dream. Being together in the project made these disparate F&M students "more united" and reassured her "how strong the culture is, despite all the obstacles we have faced and the horrible things we have gone through."

In this way, *Hasta la Raíz* "moved from being a project to being real." It became uncomfortably personal with sharp feelings, searching questions, and self-imposed pressure to get it right. These were real people, real lives. Alex's sympathies expanded, and she touched deeper layers of love for the people of the Mexican diaspora, her people. She also felt a searing burn over the killings and the coverup as those injustices became more real too. Creating *Hasta la Raíz* changed her, affecting her down to her root.

When the moment of completion approached and the portraits began to align in a moving coherence, she realized that the exhibition was not just about the murdered forty-three students, her forty-three classmates, or the landscapes of migrant culture; it was also about herself and her brave parents. "My vision," she told me, also became to enable others to understand "where I come from and what my background is . . . and at the same time to have others understand me as the individual I am."

And that leads to three takeaways from Alex's experience. First, as with Morgan Kincade's senior thesis, capstone projects push students both to synthesize earlier learning and to devote time to producing an original work. Whether one makes a thesis or a case study or a scholarly finding or a symphony at the end of college, the act and fact of doing so gives students evidence of their creativity and their growth.

Second, colleges need to make sure students have stimulating places for invention. For Alex, a studio in the Herman Arts Building was her lab, her retreat center, and her home for a semester, as she bent time fusing her mind with the spirits of the many she hoped to honor with her creation. The same could be said of the Steinman College Center, where Jael mounted #BLACKYAK, and the Green Room Theatre, where Alec brought *Domestic Animals* to life. These are spaces for soul making. Let students spill paint there and write on white walls and lose themselves as the night lightens into dawn. It was with this reverence for the creativity of the young that, supported by philanthropists Ben and Susan Winter, we commissioned architect Steven Holl to create for F&M a glowing glass and steel visual arts building, its unique shape defined by the trees it sits within, for the making and teaching of art, photography, and film.[19]

Third, as we saw with Andrea Smith's senior thesis on housing insecurity, it's valuable to encourage students to create from consequential personal experiences. *Hasta la Raíz* emerged from Alejandra Zavala's soul *and* social context, growing in moral import as it progressed. This bravura work of art matters as a product and a process and a community-creating experience for the students, the viewers, and the artist herself. It *only* could have been made by Alejandra during her time at Franklin & Marshall College. As if channeling the poet Audre Lorde, because she used her strength in the service of her vision, she gained agency as one who can see and speak against wrongs done to her people. The same could be said of Jael Lewis with #BLACKYAK. Both women will know for the rest of their lives that they can interpret the world, disrupt silences, and enrich the lives of those they love with their maker's minds and eyes.

The mindset to make creates connections, voice, and curiosity. It also builds agency.

*

Create once, create again. That's the multiplier effect of maker cultures. We've seen that throughout this chapter. For novice creators, each venture sets the stage for its successor, as the young hone their mindsets for invention and make discoveries that will shorten the learning curve next time up. Being a lifelong creator requires continuous learning and improvement, of course; for the rest of their lives, these young people will have to keep innovating and improving and bouncing back up when they fall on their faces. For that commitment, a growth mindset matters profoundly, and it must start somewhere.

As entrepreneur Joan Fallon likes to say, when it comes to innovation, a great college "makes it possible, and makes it happen." People talk often about "creative destruction" in the mythologies of famous business disrupters, but college campuses are oriented differently, toward building up makers and community in what we might call "creative construction." We've seen some of those catalysts here—involved faculty, engaged peers, build-it curricula, capstone projects, makers' spaces, creative cultures. It's all doable, and it's all being done. All we have to do is increase what's working, while resisting one temptation: If we value undergraduate innovation, if we prize the rise of the maker's mindset in the young, we must resist the adult impulse to control student creativity, to de-risk the process of invention, to turn creation into a permission sport. The bottom line is that students need the pedagogy of involvement, but that's different than a pedagogy of control. When it comes to creativity, self-generated work that fails also provides invaluable growth as the young learn to pick themselves up, as did Paraj, and go find the next vista opening before them.

When it comes to creativity, as with riding a bike, once done no one forgets. Making becomes a mindset—for creating from ourselves and thereby re-creating ourselves. When we create, we change from being one who is acted upon—the condition of our birth—into being one who acts. This awakening to agency changes a person's understanding of how to be herself, of what to want and do with our "one wild and precious life."[20] The canvas is always ours, but many fail to claim it. One act of invention can change a person forever—and change the ecosystem, too, prompting more people to want to make.

And, whether expressed through poetry or performance, business or education, the creativity of the young is a gift to all. It's a form of energy. It moves light and makes change. It renews others. It feeds the human hunger to build and speak and stand upon one's own hand-plowed ground. To the musician Nick Cave, creativity comes from and expresses each person's unique spirit—a force we know and feel more strongly when we tap into it to create. He writes in his online journal, *Red Hand Files*:

Your spirit is the part of you that is essential. . . . Worry less about what you make . . . and devote yourself to nourishing this animating spirit. Bring all your enthusiasm to bear on the development of that good and essential force. This is done by a commitment to the creative act itself. . . . The more dedication you show to the process, the better the work, and the greater your gift to the world. Apply yourself fully to the task, let go of the outcome, and your true voice will appear. You'll see. It can be no other way.[21]

Alec, Paraj, Jael, and Alejandra did just that in college, aided by the culture of the campus and generous mentors who valued their impulse to create. In these four and so many more, I see the vital making center of our society. Their inventions provide an original insight, a start, a voice, or a lens. Their hearts beat to give and grow, to ask and experiment and add—and making from that centering spirit is now part of their identities. Whether on campus or in later life, such work is rarely solitary, for innovation emerges out of our involvements—with viewers and buyers and partners, with mentors here or gone, and with older ideas and a new world dawning.

In fact, innovation is one space where we meet and make that new world. The core truth that creativity makes clear is that with mind, soul, skills, and help, we can act upon our surroundings. Innovation is hope in motion. College provides the ideal place, space, people, and provocations for the creative mindset to take hold— and as we'll see in the next two chapters, creativity often flourishes and hope often moves when students get and give mentoring and learn to collaborate.

Chapter 2: Questions for Discussion

1. How do you understand the mindset to create? Why does the author believe that this mindset is a powerful resource for individuals and society?

2. The author describes the creative processes employed by Alec, Jael, Paraj, and Alejandra. What attitudes did they bring to their projects? What hard challenges did each have to overcome?

3. How did the campus ecosystem inspire and enable the four students to create? And how did their faculty and staff mentors assist them?

4. Often students take on creative projects outside of class, but doing so could divide their energies and detract from their formal academic work. What are the possible benefits of creative endeavors for their overall learning and growth?

5. The author claims that colleges need to take care not to "de-risk" the process of creating so that the students have the freedom to follow their inspiration. Do you agree with that?

6. How do student creators and their creations enhance the overall campus culture and community? What more can be done to encourage and support creativity and innovation among students?

3

THE MINDSET FOR
MENTORSHIP

Anybody can be a mentor, because being a mentor encompasses recognizing that you have something to share. We all have the opportunity to step up and take on a mentorship role, even if for a couple seconds. These moments helped me figure out, I'm doing this a lot. This makes me part of who I am.

—KEIRAN MILLER

WHEN WE FLY OVER A COLLEGE at night and see its electromagnetic energy levitating as light waves, our eyes turn naturally to the places burning brightest, like the library and the athletics complex, revealing them as major sources and centers of power.

What if we could also see the bio-fields of collective human energy generated by all the people who make up a college? If the glow were most bright where student learning is most intense, what might we see happening there? Perhaps first-year student Morgan

Kincade discovering new ways to think. Or sophomore Paraj Mathur hiring classmates for Strutzy's human billboards. Or junior Darrius Moore, who we met in the introduction, steering the agenda at an I.M.P.A.C.T. meeting.

That said, viewed by an engineer's standard, the people-powered energy system of a college might seem a bit inefficient. Why?

Academically, every semester all students must quickly orient themselves to a set of new courses independently designed by educators who may hold divergent beliefs about learning, knowledge, and standards of success in their classes.

Socially, all students must navigate campus cultures that have innumerable unstated rules and norms and a constant churn of new and graduating peers.

Organizationally, all students must learn the roles and procedures of a set of departments (i.e., academics, student life, health, financial aid, career advising, conduct, housing, and more) that can seem like an opaque maze of mazes.

Given such "inefficiencies," why is it that, year after year, many colleges do quite well at moving thousands of undergraduates into coherent patterns of learning? In part, it is because of stabilizing processes and structures honed over time, from the curricula to school policies to shared governance.

But there's also a practical force, a soft power if you will, which is the culture of mentoring, the getting and the giving. Think Morgan with Professor Misty Bastian, Paraj with Professor Bryan Stinchfield, Darrius with the senior Lorenzo Daughtry-Chambers. All three were supremely well mentored as first-years, propelling them forward, and—no surprise—all went on to pay it forward.

In stories of formation, going back to ancient Greek literature, the mentor is an archetypal figure. In *The Odyssey*, as the eponymic hero leaves home for the Trojan War, he places his son Telemachus in the care of his old friend Mentor and the swineherd Eumaeus. Recognizing the boy's trust in this sage advisor, the goddess Athena impersonates Mentor when warning him to stand up to the "suitors" threatening the palace with his father gone. From that story comes the noun and verb we use to today to invoke the person-to-person sharing of usable knowledge and experience—whose power has now been documented by reams of learning research and incorporated into virtually every theory of human development.

In college, mentoring happens, and needs to happen, all the time and in many arenas—academic, social, organizational, professional, spiritual, and personal. It's provided by faculty, counselors, staff, chaplains, coaches, and widely, fellow students, whose common perspective gives them unique knowledge and credibility.[1] A culture of mentoring is like a flywheel that smooths and channels the expenditure of energy by students so that they can more effectively pursue their goals and later help others pursue theirs.

For example, I saw the mentoring flywheel turn when Sydney Fass walked on to the tennis program in search of community and subsequently grew into a respected advisor for recruited teammates (and others), when the well-mentored Charisma Lambert later showed confidence guiding her mentees in three clubs, and in the intellectual development of chemistry major Trexler Hirn, who first learned the lab techniques of protein expression, purification, and crystallization from upper-class students Daniyal Tariq and Nicole Savidge. Trexler's peer mentors gave him the tools to secure a summer research grant with his classmate Caroline Kearney to explore new techniques for conducting gas binding experiments in an oxygen-free glove bag. While feeding his growth as a discoverer, these experiences also prepared Trexler to assist Brianna Papoutsis and Mike Lee when they picked up the project. The flywheel of mentoring shapes how individual students: (1) learn, (2) learn to learn, and (3) learn to help others learn—thus, (4) making the campus a more productive learning ecosystem for all.

In recent years, many educators have begun thinking about the "hidden curriculum of college," defined as "a set of unwritten norms, values, and expectations that unofficially governs how individuals interact with and evaluate one another."[2] In order to know and navigate these tacit norms, which influence success in the formal curriculum, good mentoring can help any and every student. It is especially valuable for students from first-generation, underrepresented, or international backgrounds, who, according to 2018 graduate Brandon Stevens, "are always told by their families, you need to go to college, but they can't tell you how to handle the stress and expectations when you're there." Checklists and guidebooks only go so far. Young people need timely, mind-to-mind assistance in many forms: academic coaching; advice about how to talk to professors or construct a class schedule or contend with assignment overload; guidance on campus resources, such as where to bring a problem or who to ask about a part-time job; and validation in the form of a timely text message or a helpful introduction.[3] It's especially impactful when mentors help mentees to see and then seek appealing opportunities—activating themselves—like James Ngo did with budding playwright Alec Hersh. As super-mentor Darrius Moore said to me, mentoring is about "speaking *positivity*" in support of mentees and their aims, meaning that the moral of a mentoring moment—*you* matter—can outlast the particular lesson being imparted and fuse with other can-do messages in an affirming chorus we carry with us for life.

Some undergraduates, like Darrius, mentor out of immense gratitude to those who showed them the way. Some, like Caitlin Brust, who founded an intellectual salon for students that met weekly, embrace education so passionately that they want all to enjoy it. Some mentor as a hallmark of identity. Some mentor as stewards of a club culture or to meet a crying need or as part of a formal role like math tutor or resident assistant. Of course, many of these motivations overlap. As we'll see, almost invariably, those who give continue to grow, often from the very individuals they've aided. One of my favorite stories is how a few fraternity brothers taught Sheldon Ruby, a first-generation student from a rural town, the basics of interview attire. Then he proceeded to win three national fellowships in two years, showing them how to strive.

It's clear that after graduation, the mindset for giving and receiving mentoring provides many advantages and matters in many contexts. As learners, it keeps us fresh. As citizens, it keeps us contributing. As workers, it keeps us productive. If being mentored helps us succeed in an organization, mentoring others helps us leverage that success for more impact, learning, and joy. Over the past four decades, the benefits, modes, best practices, cultural considerations, and ethical dimensions of mentorship have become a burgeoning area of research and thought leadership.[4] It's now a priority for many organizations that seek to optimize performance, strengthen workplace culture, promote inclusion and belonging, develop millennial and Gen Z colleagues, and in these times, adapt to the rise of remote and hybrid work.[5] In higher education, it's being emphasized as a must-build skill among faculty in every field.[6] As Lois J. Zachary writes, "Because mentoring combines the impact of learning with the compelling human need for connection, it leaves individuals better able to deepen their personal capacity and maintain organizational vitality in the face of continuous challenge and change."[7]

Over two decades, I've seen the campus culture of mentoring ignite the mindset for it in many undergraduates. Four points stand out. In college, mentorship is *constant and culturally valued*, as students regularly give and receive it, in cycles and at every stage of learning, encouraged by educators. It *opens and strengthens relationships*, enhancing meaning and belonging. It *resonates ethically* for both parties, promoting care and action for others, sometimes enabling students to use pains of their past for someone else's well-being. And, tying it all together, college allows emerging adults to experience mentorship as *desirable, growthful activity* that speaks to their values and the kind of person they aspire to be.

As a result of these dynamics, as they advance in college, many students start to give and receive mentoring more often and more comfortably. Why? Because they like it, because they do it well, because they yearn for it, because value it, and because, as good experiences build, mentorship becomes true to who they are. That progression is what activates a mindset. For young people eager for strong relationships, growth, and impact, the mindset for mentorship offers a good way to live—and college is a fertile place and time for it to flourish. Let's explore the four factors that make mentoring stick.

Point One: In College, Mentoring Is Constant and Culturally Valued

Years ago, the exceptional Georgetown University professor of theology, Otto Hentz, SJ, told me that he enjoyed thinking back on upon his initial encounters with students he knew well. Invariably, he would recall something telling from those first interactions.

That's how I feel about Keiran Miller, whose extended mentorship journey during and after college will provide the anchor case study in this chapter. I met him at a spring 2011 leadership workshop for ten New York City high schoolers we enrolled via the Posse program (which I'll describe in chapter 4). With warm eyes and an all-in demeanor, this seventeen-year-old son of Brooklyn immediately showed his ease and skill with group dialogue. I also have an early memory of Keiran bowling over an Open Mic Night audience with a lovely poem addressed to his ten-year-old brother that carried motivating messages for all:

> . . . work hard, young sir, aim to be great,
> With determination and struggle you will achieve your desired
>   fate.
> I know it may seem like a waste of time and spirit,
> But your destiny lies in your own hands; embrace it, don't fear it.
> Cause when you give crap you get crap,
> And trust me I ain't havin' that,
> I want you to realize your highest potential,
> And never settle for less; cause that's whack.

I share these recollections to make the point that F&M did not transform Keiran Miller into a mentor; rather, he was raised to respect and connect with others, to help and be helped, to make friends across any supposed divide, all of which he demonstrated long before his high-tops ever touched earth in Lancaster. What Franklin & Marshall did do was offer countless invitations from both sides of the mentorship equation, which he then claimed, grew from, and leaned into further after college when launching his career.

Those invitations started arriving on day one of college, thanks to several high-touch faculty mentors. Through Posse, English professor Patricia O'Hara sat with him biweekly for two years. She began their relationship by opening up about how her own under-graduate experience (she enrolled in her late twenties) moved her to support students who might feel out of place. Understanding these motivations led him to trust her, and over many talks, her wisdom sunk in: Prioritize your studies. Learn to turn down some invitations. Be there for everyone in your posse. In various situations he'd return to these maxims—sometimes echoing her wisdom when advising others.

Another early mentor was the historian Doug Anthony, who commanded his attention on, of all things, email etiquette—the diction, the font, the formatting, the professionalism. "Sometimes mentoring can be subtle," Keiran once told me with a chuckle. "Professor Anthony was blunt. 'You need to learn how to do this to make a good impression, to participate in the workforce.' He hammered it home—setting the tone for how I communicated with others." And then there was the charming and gracious Sands Hall, who saw the promise in everyone. One class, Keiran sat back as others delved into the assignment. Hall put him on the spot, getting him to admit that he hadn't written a word or read the prompt. "She took a quick two minutes to say I hadn't valued the work of peers enough to come to class prepared," he explained. "Besides the general embarrassment, it helped me see that I had let down my classmates, and it made me see the importance of the workshop process for writing." When he improved, Hall noticed the change and invited him to join the board of a publication she edited.

Not everyone can absorb and act on tough love, but Keiran could, whether the sources were faculty or student elders such as Walter Stewart, whose shrewd insights could slice fog. Walter always seemed a little more grown up, a little more in command of his views. One time a group of first-year men were bantering about nothing when the senior broke in with a message that landed. "He told us," Keiran said, that "it was fine and good that we all had different opinions on every issue, and that we could have a lot of fun together, but one thing we needed to understand is that no man of color was to take advantage of a woman or look away if one were vulnerable. Never. Period. We were all expected to step in or get help." Inside, of course, they already knew this. What mattered was that Walter said it out loud, for all to hear, so that no one would have to think twice when duty called. That's mentoring. Then there was the kind and driven Alia Allen, a high-altitude go-getter who'd always pause to check on him even if he was just a scruffy, argyle-attired freshman. Once, when he felt overwhelmed, she opened up the Black Cultural Center townhouse and sat studying with him for a few hours—for Keiran, an indelible example of "just in time" mentoring.[8] Yes, Walter and Alia were watching his back as he came up at F&M; more deeply, they were modeling the quality of mentoring they expected him to provide to the next waves of newcomers.

It felt validating to be aided and invested in by such esteemed faculty and students—and Keiran found that he liked synthesizing other people's insights as a part of framing his options. From that base, it seemed natural to try out mentoring himself, and so, at the end of freshman year, he applied to work as a peer mentor in the summer F&M College Prep program, which was run by the perceptive young staff member, Shawn Jenkins. This was July 2012, when the rising junior Darrius Moore also worked in the program.

The experience was an absolute blast. It enthralled him to observe the gifts of dozens of diverse high schoolers just two years behind him. They sure could think and try and team up and care. He loved whetting their appetites for college life, which Darrius would refer to as "pouring into people," and when they returned to their homes he cried because it touched him to see them bond and thrive in three short weeks. His presence, his guidance, and his care helped them flower. He felt a fullness that he wanted to feel again, leading him, as sophomore year started, to sign on to be a peer mentor for a cohort of incoming students being advised by Africana studies professor Carla Willard.

They were a powerhouse group who had been educated in KIPP public charter schools in Houston, Austin, and New York City. Keiran tasked himself with being their everything, believing "I was supposed to have the answer to any questions, solve every problem, dump all the knowledge I had on whatever subject came up." But that went nowhere, since he couldn't cure their first-year maladies, like one's paralyzing anxiety about academics or another's sharp longing for home. (Both went on to do very well at F&M.) He would touch base with Jenkins, himself a mentor par excellence, who'd remind him that his role was not to find remedies but to forge relationships. A second staff member, the new senior dean for student success, Donnell Butler, sounded the same note with his mantra, *seek to understand, rather than to be understood.* "You don't have all the answers," he came to realize, and it was *their* education, not his. "You are there to draw out their ideas," he heard from Jenkins and Butler. "Students come talk for different reasons. Sometimes they don't even know why. You don't have the responsibility to always give."

With this coaching, he relaxed and located the balance between "when to listen more and when to share more." It made him happy to see that by demystifying the hidden curriculum of college, he could help them claim their opportunities. This led him to mentor new student cohorts again in his junior and senior years, with more self-assurance. Of course, it was a dance, the steps and pace varying with each mentee—many of whom later credited him with enabling them to find resources within and without, at the right time. For the hard-charging Raven Charleston, it was helping her grasp how to advocate for herself with professors or financial aid deans with an awareness of what she could expect from their particular roles. Amanda Lopez-Fasanella needed something else; he helped her work through homesickness, or rather, *home culture-sickness*. And then there was the sensational Bendjhi Villiers, who exuded joy in learning; Keiran showed him that he could step up in myriad activities, from club leadership to spoken word, without adopting an inauthentic alpha-dog posture. In each case it felt rewarding to know that his mentorship could empower others "to catapult themselves to heights I could not imagine," like when Raven graduated with honors in three years or when Bendjhi joined the Writers House community with its many confident creators.

As Keiran gave to others, he gave to himself as well—that's the key point. Mentoring brought him "joy, excitement, and energy." It enabled him to learn from others and heed his own advice. I think the process helped him savor his non-mentoring experiences, whether it was maintaining diverse friend groups or listening open-mouthed when lecturers like Michael Eric Dyson laid out truth like a banquet. It brought him a five-star reputation among faculty such as the classicist Alexis Castor, who described guiding a first-year cohort with Keiran as an education in itself. Most of all, mentoring brought possibility to each day, for, across dozens of interactions from morning to midnight (or later), he'd have the chance "to step up and take on a mentorship role, even if for a few seconds." Over his last three years, mentoring provided an edifying cycle—give and grow, then give again and grow more, over and over, like a runner striding faster and farther with the realization of his powers and their purpose.

Junior year, after a semester in England, Keiran angled his mentoring flywheel in two new directions. First, having benefited from I.M.P.A.C.T.'s all-mentor-all culture, he sensed it was his turn to fan the club's enduring flame, so he volunteered to succeed Darrius as president. The role was less about one-to-one mentoring than about fostering helpful mentorship among the beloved community of brothers. He understood going in that "it wasn't my job to have every answer to any question or issue that might come up in our discussions. It was my role to make sure everyone had a voice and that we worked well together."

Second, coming back from England in January, he was enthralled by all the new students who were fiery poets. It made him think about how, two years earlier, his brain was raging but not his pen, causing him to "question my conviction" to write. As a result, he and his friend Natasha Kirnes began to brainstorm about founding a club devoted to spoken word poetry. For her, what resonated was to provide "a sense of belonging—and to help others control their freedom of expression." Intuiting others' needs, a hallmark of mentoring, they codesigned "a weekly space to give people an excuse to spend time with their craft" (Keiran's words) and a community of peers to help with anything, from themes and lines to tone and flow. The club would be about raising each other up, not rap battles—and so they called it L.I.F.T., for Levitate, Inspire, Foresight, Teach.

The group wasn't all that large—maybe ten regulars to start. They conducted it workshop-style. "We always made sure that everyone was included in an activity and felt comfortable within that inclusion," said Natasha. Keiran tried to channel the professionalism of writing teachers like Erik Anderson, from whom he borrowed an icebreaker in which they all described their morning routines replacing body parts with colors, like "I opened my browns and brushed my whites." Of course, he knew that for many, speaking their word and coming out emotionally would be an ordeal. "At first it was delicate bringing in the element of critique," Keiran told me, "so we needed to know what each writer wanted to accomplish. Was this a piece you wanted to get out of your system and be done with? Or was it something you wanted feedback on so you could hear how I heard your words?" The ethos was welcoming and appreciative, honoring effort, while also being serious about feedback. Keiran described their ground rules this way: "First, people were expected to give complete silence when you read, and then you were expected to be completely silent when they responded. Second, all commentary should be as specific as possible"—fine guidelines for mentoring of any type.

With this structure and culture, the L.I.F.T. community clicked and progressed. A first-year named David showed his "jubilant personality" in poems that juxtaposed natural imagery with the passion in his heart. Anjé McLish worked on performance. Bendjhi focused on helpful listening while Raheem Charles honed his understanding of how to direct his honest poetry toward an audience. Keiran opened himself to mentoring, too, trying out sections of an ambitious five-minute piece, "Everyday It Could Be." The poem called on listeners to breathe in the miracle of existence and feel they could give back "a fresh perspective on the life we all live," which might lead to small pleasures, like "peach cobbler on a Wednesday," and big changes, "Like no massacred children in schools,/Like human trafficking hitting gridlock." Not cynical, but not naïve either. I loved the poem's sure-footed opening:

> From sun-up to moon's rest
> The best of life's fruit hang ripe on the tip of your tongue and all
>   you have to do is
> Be brave enough to swallow.
> Let the nutrition kick-start your ambition like a super-charged
>   lawnmower

Decapitating a cornfield of the mundane.

I think, each day is magical.

Everyday that giant gas ball in the sky makes it its business to let
you know there

Is still hope in the world;

Some call it divinity, others say science,

I call it mystifying.

A multivalent art form, spoken word is meant to be heard, felt, joined, witnessed, and even acted upon. Any time I watched Keiran claim the mic, typically clad in his black I.M.P.A.C.T. hoodie, I felt that he was operating in three dimensions. First, there was the performance, in which he gave fully, animating the moods he sought to invoke, arms and hands moving fluidly like a dancer. Then there was the dialogue, as he would skillfully call upon the audience to give back with a word or a laugh, snapping or silence. And third, there were the messages imparted *as a mentor*, calling upon any listener to drink from the cup of possibility, as "The glass isn't half empty or full because it's always filled with something./And it's up to you to turn that something,/Into anything." Keiran used the medium of spoken word and the platform of campus leadership to "speak positivity" in Sensurround.

During the first three semesters of L.I.F.T., the members mentored each other in a few ways. One had to do with emotions, as the students found the nerve to share bruises of the heart with each other. Keiran would soak up "the silence backstage before one of our shows—so still that I could hear the performers drawing short breaths of feeling." By being allies in the effort to distill experience to its poetic essence and shadow box with the internal censor, the members coaxed and coached each other into a word-speaking community.

Second, they helped each other improve. For example, the first year, some participants suggested to Anjé that she move away from obscure language and avoid the safety of "list" poems. Taking that in, she practiced often between meetings. Keiran helped her memorize her lines so that she could experiment with the beats and stresses. When L.I.F.T. held a Valentine's Day showcase on the theme of love, it was Anjé's first time at the mic, ever. After taking a deep breath, she pushed out the line, "When the guy you like starts dating your friend . . . ," and won over the audience. Focusing on delivery was catalyzing for her and the others. It gave them mastery of the words, and something else, Keiran told me: By saying aloud—to listeners—what they'd drafted in the privacy of their minds, the poets started to grasp "which ideas they truly wanted to stand behind with conviction and which, once verbalized, made them flinch."

And, third, there was the force multiplier known as inspiration. Natasha loved the group's "camaraderie" and how one person's poem would move "others to be outspoken in moments when they had thought their only choice was to be quiet." Being present to each other's efforts, even when the syllables stuck to their tongues like peanut butter, became an invitation to all to stretch out, to push a little further, to explore what more they could say and feel and do with a poem. As Bendjhi remarked after a showcase event, "The talent spilling out of everyone is so incredible that it . . . makes me want to write outside the comforts of my margins to see what I discover once I get there."[9] That's the power of peer mentoring.

Keiran co-created L.I.F.T. knowing from his education that all can give and gain as mentors. His attraction to this way of relating to others blossomed organically—at first because he liked feeling the respect of wise people he respected, and then because he liked using his resources to help others. As he mentored more, he actively thought about the practice and took pleasure in the relationships.

His identity gelled around being an active friend and resource—someone with whom you could be yourself and who was generous—reinforced by being a citizen on a campus where mentorship was cultural, not counter-cultural. At F&M it was pervasive, expected, admired . . . and needed. Carol Dweck could have been picturing him when she wrote:

> People with a growth mindset are also constantly monitoring what's going on, but their internal monologue is not about judging themselves and others this way. Certainly they're sensitive to positive and negative information, but they're attuned to its implications for learning and constructive action: What can I learn from this? How can I improve? How can I help my partner do this better?[10]

What practical lessons can we glean from Keiran's growing skill and self-awareness through mentorship?

- First, faculty and staff mentoring is a booster rocket to help students propel themselves forward, feel known, and embrace high standards. We should make it feasible for undergraduates to have many mentors, from day one—especially those who may feel underrepresented, underprepared, out of place, or culturally marginalized. There's undoubtedly a need: In one 2021 survey of 2,000 undergraduates, nearly half reported being unable to identify a single mentor, defined "as someone who was not already a friend or a family member who was available to give advice on navigating college and planning for after college."[11]

- As we saw with L.I.F.T., when students become mentors, they often utilize the wisdom and adopt the examples of their teachers. That's one more reason why the professional development of faculty should emphasize mentoring along with teaching and scholarship.[12]

- Given the promise and prominence of peer mentoring, colleges should help students improve their mentoring through reflection, supervision, coaching, group dialogues, classes, and research.[13] This is low-hanging fruit for high-impact learning.

- As Peter Felten and Leo M. Lambert argue, colleges are relationship-rich communities that facilitate connection and helping as spontaneous day-to-day norms; this quality of culture needs to be celebrated, nurtured, and protected.[14] Interactive virtual platforms have their uses and their value, of course, bridging distances and facilitating exchange, but as we saw at the start of the pandemic, young learners crave connection and social contact. No one craves social distancing.

- Finally, as Keiran learned from roles he's held after college, faculty and other advisors should help undergraduates learn to articulate the skills and mindsets they have gained through mentoring, which will help them secure and succeed in first jobs.

Early in his senior year, Keiran began pondering what kind of work he might do after graduation. What was he good at? How would he grow? Was there anything he loved so much he'd do it for free? Whatever the question, his answer was always mentoring, for it had powered his days and ways in college and perhaps could shape his life after college as well. At the end of the chapter, we'll find out how he acted on that intuition.

Point Two: Because College Mentoring Is Interpersonal and Reciprocal, It Builds and Deepens Meaningful Relationships

Keiran's story shows how being mentored smooths transitions, builds competencies, preempts false starts, and hastens growth. In mentoring cultures, students learn through experience that it's usually more *effective* to seek out coaching than to plow on alone.

On campus, mentorship works—which is one reason why it becomes a mindset. It's productive.

A second reason is because it's gratifying. Mentoring creates warm feelings and relationships. Students like sharing experiences, being cared for, and having someone to look after—all of which can lead to friendship. Take Keiran. Freshman year, one of his mentors was Darrius. Junior year, one of his mentees was Bendjhi. Now, as adults, they're the best of friends, socializing together, regularly puzzling over the state of the world. It was mentorship that brought them into love. Hence the mindset.

Here's a story that demonstrates the point: During my first weeks at F&M, I toured one of our feeder schools—McDonogh School, outside of Baltimore—to hear how its students and counselors viewed the college. That day I met a luminous senior named Katie Machen, who'd just said yes to F&M. Thoughtful and sincere, with a listener's presence, she was avid about writing, languages, and service—an ideal fit for the college. Given how much she revered McDonogh, I remember hoping that she'd quickly find her people in college.

It turned out that was no problem; Mona Lotfipour found her.

They met in the pre-orientation program, Putting It Together in the Community (P.I.T.), through which forty new students arrive early to do service in the city. Focused on pre-med and public health going into her senior year, Mona greeted the Machen family at Ware College House and helped them unpack. How fitting, Katie later told me, because "from day one, she was *leading me into college*" in ways that unfurled like a destiny.

In P.I.T., Mona's crew of eight was assigned to patch up drywall in housing units and help paint a community center. In between jobs, she'd probe her team about their interests and march them around campus to meet professors. Her main message was that

F&M was totally accessible. Anything they might need could be found, like cookies on a platter. It caught Katie's eye that the senior was so genuine, so invested in her education, and so knowledgeable about Lancaster, especially the refugee community. Later she found out that Mona was a new American herself, arriving from Iran at age seven, and that she was already a social entrepreneur, having created one program to help local families get tax rebates and a second—in Cape Town!—that used sport to teach health and safety to youth.

After classes began, Mona invited Katie to meet the leaders of a club she might like, The Human Rights Initiative, or THRI. The group promoted awareness and action on human needs, global or local, wherever students wanted to focus. The year before, they'd hosted talks by human rights advocates John Prendergast on genocide and Layli Miller-Muro on gender injustice. "I'll introduce you to everybody," Mona told her, "and you can decide if it's for you."

It sure was. Dynamos like Becca Green and Emi Florez had much to say about their summer internships and concerns about injustices around the world. Mona's friends were overjoyed to be back together and brainstorming about that year's Human Rights Week. "It felt so exciting to be in a room with these people who had such big ideas and wanted to make the world a better place," Katie told me, "and to be treated like an equal by them." This was exactly the kind of college community she'd hoped for, and now, thanks to Mona, it had found her.

Katie jumped at her mentor's next invite, which was to help plan a national conference on refugee resettlement that the college was cosponsoring with Church World Service. Their goal was to convene health care, education, and social work professionals, along with policy experts and refugees, to improve the coordination and cultural sensitivity of services. In fact, Lancaster was becoming quite the hub for this work.[15] Somehow, despite being a full-time student, Mona had picked up a ton of responsibility. Katie joined a small team of students who spent several months building out the conference, with to-do items multiplying like guppies. "We put in so many hours of work on the conference together in our little home in the College Center," Katie recalled with fondness. "It was thrilling to build that space together." The "It Takes a Community" summit was a coup.

Mona also "led" Katie into college academics, as the senior strongly believed that new students should not put off the most engaging classes and professors just to fulfill requirements. She pressed her to register for an advanced community-based learning seminar on refugee issues being offered in the spring. It would bring her right into the lives of heroic newcomers while exposing her to the swirl of political, policy, and social issues affecting their lives. So what if she was only a freshman? Could there a better course for her?

The seminar introduced Katie and two classmates to a Bhutanese family that had lived in a camp in Nepal for twenty years. The students welcomed them at the airport and helped them get situated in an apartment secured by a resettlement agency. They aided the family with everything from where to get groceries to how to enroll their teenage son in school. It was so much more than a class; it was an experience of solidarity. They weren't just helping people; they were accompanying them. They weren't just bridging cultures; they were bringing them into relationship. And they weren't just learning new concepts as theories; they were applying them in Lancaster and becoming part of the fabric of the city. Mona had given Katie entrée into an expansive philosophy of education— premised on the idea that we can lower the boundaries of both campus and classroom to make space for experiential learning and wondrous feelings of connection. "She had the butterfly effect," Katie told me, "influencing so much of what I did and loved over the next three years," which included mentoring F&M peers and teaching adult refugees and schoolchildren in Lancaster.

If Mona *found* her mentee, the reverse is also true in that Katie *chose* her mentor. Some of the attraction, yes, was that the senior was supernaturally high functioning, linking so many nodes in the campus network. But really their synapse was far more personal than practical. Mona was kind and selfless "with this huge personality," said Katie. "She would make me laugh, and I loved being around her." It was a fit that made the mentoring easy and organic. "College students are on more level ground than a mentorship between a professor and a student," she reflected. "Even when one is a freshman and the other is a senior, there's more room for a relationship to develop naturally and more room for vulnerability," which can lead to friendship.

One time I asked Katie what she thought Mona had gained from her that year. "I guess the mentorship and friendship blurred together. I was a freshman trying to find my way and I soaked up being with her. But she had all these senior year concerns like applying for the Mitchell Scholarship and medical school, which I was barely aware of and couldn't help her with at all. I'm curious how she would answer your question."

I found out in a Zoom meeting with Mona, who was finishing her ophthalmology residency at the University of Rochester, where each day's work included mentoring and being mentored. She chuckled when I asked if she regarded herself as Katie's mentor.

"Maybe for about a week . . . just during P.I.T."

"That's not what she said," I replied, sharing Katie's comment about the butterfly effect.

Mona paused to recollect those first weeks and months—from move-in day to watching her jump in at the THRI meeting. With all this "positive energy," Katie was simply a welcome and winning new friend. "I learned so much from her," Mona said. "Maybe she was *my* mentor, not the other way around."

How so, I asked. "Well, I saw how she gathers insights before making a judgment and brings others into that process," which she did often in that year of exploration. "And Katie is extremely creative. That's a different lens than I had. So, with things like the conference, my approach was more like, 'Learn what needs to be done, apply it, and then go on to the next thing.'"

Then Mona alighted upon an even more subtle notion. With her sparkling mind and care for people and their values, the new student had helped the senior by allowing her to "re-experience F&M fresh, so I could show her this place *where I wasn't going to be for much longer.*" Yes, Mona led her into college, but it was Katie who led her into leading her.

This is a harmony I've seen in similar pairings. On any campus, there are always a few seniors, like Mona, who just seem to glow. They're influential, read-in, and all-in. They can speak to the essence of the community—and are often invited to do so. As a result, as fall turns into winter and then to spring in their final year, this type tends to anticipate graduation with a tinge of sadness, knowing how much they'll miss the place and the people and the life they've made there. Keiran was one of this fully rooted kind, as was Darrius . . . and as was Mona, a child of two lands and two worlds who created in college an education and a future for good.

Thus, as she first conversed with Katie, she must have sensed that this awesome new student was right and ripe for all that F&M could offer. Mona was ready to pass the torch and Katie valued the warmth of the flame. It's more meaningful for seniors to leave a school they love when they've shared its best with someone who'll still be there to live that love, their way.

In Mona's final hours in college, on a hot May day thick with feeling, these now dear friends came full circle. Right after commencement, I remember looking for Mona and her parents in the grateful crowd of graduates, families, and educators. Finally, I called her. Back in her room strewn with unpacked possessions, she answered with a sob.

"What's wrong?"

"Dr. P, I don't know how I'm going to leave."

"I know. I understand, Mona."

"I can't believe that it's over. My room is a wreck, and I have to pack the car and get home for a party . . ."

I knew, of course, that this emotion was probably coming from an excellent place.

"Do you need any help?"

"No, I'll be fine," she said through her sniffles. "*Katie's* helping me move out."

A complete role reversal from move-in day. How fitting. They'd met at the crossroads of their aspirations, one starting college and striving, the other striving and starting her exit. I don't think there's a word in English to capture such a relationship—a circle of mentorship, fun, friendship, belonging, and love as one steps into an experience that the other is preparing to complete. Whatever we may call this first stage of their friendship, it's what Katie and Mona made through the medium of mentorship.

There's another compelling way that mentorship and friendship coalesce in college, which is the reverse of how Katie and Mona came together. It occurs when students start out as friends and later become allies and partners in each other's growth. Doing so may mean reinforcing each other's pursuits, influencing each other's worldview, deciphering experience together, or completing each other's sentences to push the next daring reach or charge or change. Such relationships normalize the giving and getting of help as a desirable dimension of platonic intimacy.

I saw this with Andrew Foley and Brian Rivera, earnest young men who came to college from different universes. Raised in a ranching family in Chihuahua, Mexico, Brian attended Bell High School in Los Angeles and ventured east to Franklin & Marshall thanks to the divine access program College Match and our perceptive admission dean, Julie Kerich. Meanwhile, Andy, whose parents were educators and brothers were college graduates, attended nearby Hershey High School and applied to F&M in part because of its test-optional admission policy.

Early in freshman year, they fell into a spontaneous conversation in the Brooks College House laundry room. What started as small talk became a two-hour deep dive into the concept of free will, a topic in one of Brian's courses. Both had come to college to live and breathe ideas, science, and learning—and were energized to find a new friend who wanted the same. Coincidentally, both also planned to run competitively, Brian as a sprinter and Andy in cross country. At the outset, what connected them was their desire to go beyond themselves on what Brian called "the discovery journey," to claim and live the full promise of the mind. They shared high-minded ideals about education. "We knew we were so lucky to have this chance," Andy told me, and so "we reinforced in each other the mindset to absolutely gobble it up and consume as much as we possibly could."

Their relationship turned into a coursing dialogue . . . about everything. Classes, historical texts, poetry, philosophy, liberal education. No matter who spoke first, or what the topic, the other would pick it up. It was "*Yes, and . . .*" every single day. They talked in their rooms, they talked in the dining hall, they talked in the common room, and they even talked during late-night runs circling the track or the sleepy neighborhood streets. They'd swap readings from their classes with professors Jim Strick on scientific revolutions and Anthony Chemero on cognitive psychology. A recurring theme was the Catholicism of their upbringings, with its symbolism and its blind spots and its variances by culture. The first Thanksgiving, and many breaks or weekends thereafter, Brian was welcomed like a prince into the Foleys' loving home, where intellectual debate and impromptu kitchen dance parties were equally prized.

Some on their hallway viewed them as "nerds" or "geeks," but neither cared. They had no interest in fraternities or partying or guy talk. Nor did they wish to complain about the volume of academic work. They were possessed by the opportunity to soak up knowledge and loved the "daily discipline" (Andy's term) of discovering what more their brains could do. Most evenings back in their rooms, they "would report back from our independent voyages in academic life," Brian told me. "Andrew drew a lot from learning about my own discoveries, and I drew a lot from what he was learning." Not that they were closed off to others, either; that year they widened their circle to include fascinating classmates like Jess Dunbar, Dora Chi Xu, and Akbar Hossain, all of whom took in the liberal arts as food for thought and play and life.

Going back to antiquity, thinkers have sought to define the many modes of friendship. How should we think about Andy's and Brian's? The philosophers Dean Cocking and Jeanette Kennett argue that in some close relationships, friends don't merely enjoy or mirror one another but rather "play a more active role in transforming each other's evaluative outlook." F&M professor of philosophy Bennett Helm explains this idea further:

> [In] friendship . . . we are "receptive" to having our friends "direct" and "interpret" us and thereby change our interests. To be *directed* by

your friend is to allow her interests, values, etc. to shape your own. . . . To be *interpreted* by your friend is to allow your understanding of yourself, in particular your strengths and weaknesses, to be shaped by your friend's interpretations of you. . . . Hence, Cocking & Kennett claim, "the self my friend sees is, at least in part, a product of the friendship" (505).[16]

How did these two undergraduates become the "product" of *their* friendship? By influencing each other markedly, irrevocably, in ways that no one else on the planet would have done quite the same way. College gave them that.

To Andy, Brian was "profoundly original . . . with no interest in any external motivation like grades." With college inviting them to "rethink all that you've been taught," he exuded curiosity and would "enter any conversation bringing in other pieces of what he was excited about or interested in and wanted me to run with him on that." This electrified Andy, especially because Brian was a first-generation college goer who had to count every dollar and sacrificed for every opportunity. In Cocking and Kennett's terms, Andy was "directed" by his friend: "I was better at following patterns and jumping through the hoops . . . and his whole mindset was about originality. I just loved that . . . and it kept me from getting siloed, which was really important given the science and medical school tracks I ended up going toward."

In turn, Brian's outlook was influenced by Andy: "I was too excited early on trying to do everything," he told me, and "I drew energy from his commitment to take the long view and see the big picture" about how to focus himself. For example, while Brian wanted to "learn for the sake of learning," and earned high grades doing so, Andy helped him understand that "performance during a bachelor's degree (as judged from transcripts) contributes toward future education." He also showed Brian how to access college resources just by sending emails to professors or applying to join a research team. With his passion for health care equity, Andy helped him "apply the ethical concepts that I was learning abstractly in philosophy classes to a practical view through the lens of medicine . . . with an incredible awareness of real health care problems." All in all, most influential was that Andy became a witness to his family's journey and his "high achievement" of even being in college, which allowed Brian to feel seen and known, as he was and wanted to be:

> At one level college is also a place for sacrifice. It definitely was for me. Sacrificing being close to family, sacrificing working during that time to contribute to the family, even sacrificing free time for doing homework. I knew I was willing to sacrifice anything and everything to be the best in college. It made the world of difference to have had an admired peer have faith in my sacrifices.

First year, they learned about the Brooks College House Congress, where residents practiced what Andy called "the procedures of self-governance," similar to how a science class might inculcate the procedures for replicating research findings. This living/learning model reinforced the idea that education is a communal endeavor—and thus it was their role to foster the best learning environment for all. To do so, sometimes they teamed up, like when they lived in the Sustainability House or when, senior year, they cofounded the club Trace Elements to give students a place to discuss curriculum-crossing concepts like AI. But they also contributed to campus culture separately; Andy and his friend Nora Theodore created a hiking and camping program for new students, while Brian became a mentor in F&M College Prep, and after graduation, worked as an admission recruiter for two years.

In college, Andy and Brian were the kind of friends who would wake up at seven o'clock in the morning to discuss each other's assigned readings or who would spend a Friday night figuring out which Richard Feynman video to watch even though neither was taking physics. They came to college fired up to map the very landscape of knowledge—to know all things knowable and to transform themselves in the process—and as they neared the completion of their undergraduate studies, with their typical integrity, they also began to accept the limits of this quest. As Andy stated:

> I think by the end . . . that we helped each other get rid of the illusion that we were going to find solid ground on knowledge alone, and that that wasn't what leads to a fulfilling life. . . . This pursuit of something better might be supported by knowledge, but it was probably much deeper that had to do values and aiming for something that actually unlocked *someone else's* power or unlocked *someone else's* opportunity since you have already gotten that. . . . I think that was something that I wouldn't have gotten to on my own, but we sort of co-created. . . . We figured that out together.

True friends help one another grow into their most authentic selves, which is exactly what Brian and Andy did at F&M. They gave each other belonging. They prompted each other's thoughts. They helped each other to act. They influenced each other's choices. They shared enthusiasms, friends, and even families. After college, Andy went to Harvard Medical School and now practices family medicine in Lancaster. Brian has just finished his PhD in educational psychology at the University of Alabama, with a focus on math cognition. They remain in regular conversation as they move ahead in their careers. Andy told me that he carries in his wallet this passage from the poet David Whyte that captures the essence of their friendship:

> But no matter the medicinal virtues of being a true friend or sustaining a long close relationship with another, the ultimate touch-

stone of friendship is not improvement, neither of the other nor of the self, the ultimate touchstone is witness, the privilege of having been seen by someone and the equal privilege of being granted the sight of the essence of another, to have walked with them and to have believed in them, and sometimes just to have accompanied them for however brief a span, on a journey impossible to accomplish alone.[17]

Today, there's much angst about the male gender gap on campus and its negative effects among both those who attend college and those who opt out.[18] Less talked about are the mutually enhancing friendships that male students can co-create as undergraduates. One place to look for inspiration is relationships inflected, if you will, with mutual mentorship, which Brian and Andy continue living, and looking for, to this day. Such friendships lead to learning that's "impossible to accomplish alone."

Point Three: For Some Students, Mentorship Is Ethically or Morally Resonant

Mentorship becomes a mindset for a third reason, which is that doing it can feed and further one's ethical or moral life. How? Mentoring helps young people get outside of themselves to imagine other people's needs. It fosters positive feelings that come from being kind or helpful. It allows students to learn that, even acting alone, they can make an impact. When many people mentor, the character of a community strengthens: Students feel more connected and invested; the seeds of trust and loyalty spread more widely. Mentoring is a virtuous way to be a citizen—and a person.

Consider Mike D'Antonio, who mentored his fraternity brothers to think ahead and mitigate risk when hosting parties. Or Sarah

Haddon, a championship-level basketball player forced by a slew of team injuries to play as an undersized center on overmatched squads; despite this competitive disadvantage—or perhaps because of it—she became an essential mentor to her younger teammates, practice after practice, loss after loss, helping them hold a winning attitude and be sisters off the court. Or consider Keiran, Bendjhi, and Cameron Rutledge, who'd been outstanding mentors in F&M College Prep. In 2017, even though they'd graduated, they gave up one summer month to do it again because they were needed. In each situation, stepping up to mentor was the right thing. It's powerful when young people take pride in aligning their actions with their altruistic values. That is what I mean when I say that mentoring can be morally or ethically resonant—and, when students again yearn for that resonance, given the perpetual need for mentors on campus, they won't have to wait in line.

Mentoring can contribute to undergraduates' moral identity in a different way—when it allows them to use the lessons of their own wounds or sorrows to assist someone else, which is a privilege to observe when you know what you're watching. I saw this with Brandon Stevens, who came to F&M in 2014, and whose story I share with care for his anonymity. Growing up with his grandmother in rural El Salvador, Brandon enjoyed *campo* pleasures like playing outside and hunting for chicken eggs, but he came to miss close family members who had moved to the United States. In 2009, at age thirteen, and by himself, he made a two-thousand-mile sojourn to the US border, sometimes packed into pickup trucks or buses, walking long hours and sleeping beneath the cold sky, unaware of who was with him and if they might hurt him. The thirteen-day trauma ended with two harrowing nighttime crossings of the Rio Grande on a makeshift raft (he couldn't swim)—resulting in his being taken into custody by immigration officials near McAllen, Texas.

Brandon believes he was fortunate in that his odyssey to the north could have been tragic. When detained, he could have forgotten his grandmother's phone number, which would have kept him from accessing the legal process for unaccompanied minors. His forty-five days in a youth detention facility could have been inhumane. And the first magistrate who handled his case could have sent him back to El Salvador, but instead he released him to his aunt, a legal resident of California who then adopted him.

Adjusting to US life in his teenage years, Brandon was a self-described "good kid"—hardworking, considerate, and careful about whom to trust. A crucial early mentor named Mr. De La Torre helped him believe that he could learn English, despite starting at zero. Eighth-grade English brought a decisive choice: It was his turn to read aloud from *The Odyssey*—and the epic poem was a minefield of words he didn't know and couldn't say. He felt the eyes of the forty-person class trained upon the back of his neck. "Here comes Brandon," he told me, feeling again the churn and burn of that crossroads moment. "What's he going to do? Is he going to stay quiet or mumble? Or is he going to read and have people make fun of him?" He told me this story with quiet resolve to fight the fear of looking foolish or being bullied: "One of the biggest turning points was when I decided not to be shut down *by myself.*" He powered through the best he could without shame—understanding that he and only he could and must take responsibility for his life.

Throughout high school, his family lived hand to mouth, and he couldn't work, meaning his main job was to earn excellent grades—"not with any expectation of rewards, but because that was what I was supposed to do." He studied consistently and played a ton of soccer, at which he excelled, and on weekends he helped out with photography at his church. Still, at various immigration hearings, the government attorneys would petition the court to deport him, even though he was a model teenager. As a result, even with all his self-sufficiency, he had to accept that "there was no way to gain citizenship *through my own achievements*." This was the truth of his situation, but all the same, he resolved that he must not allow his lack of agency in the legal realm to deter him in other arenas. He hadn't walked through hell, faced down drowning, and nearly froze to death dripping wet in the detention center so that he could now live a stunted life. Thus, he crystallized a set of beliefs to inform his choices:

One: "There will be some limits, and you have to know them."

Two: "You have to do your best with what you have."

Three: "You have to prioritize what is most important—understanding that some compromises will be necessary."

Four: "You have to make your own choices, and keep setting high goals, no matter what others think."

With this prodigious combination of realism and self-reliance, he shined through high school, knowing "I had to be an excellent citizen *because* I was a second-class citizen." He was proud that he improved his English every year, from poor to basic to intermediate to finally proficient as a senior. Academically, he took supplemental courses at a community college, graduated sixteenth in a class of five hundred, and won the Principal's Award for all-around excellence. His final year, he put aside varsity soccer to focus on academics, which were "more important to my future," a choice that gave him the chance to help coach the freshman soccer team. "It taught me responsibility and time commitment," he told me, and he loved mentoring the players:

They respected me, and I respected them. That's the foundation of a mentorship—true respect, mutual growth. I was not there to tell them what to do, to tell them how to grow. . . . I was there to *influence their desire* to grow in a positive direction, because at the end of the day, if I tell you to make a decision it's not going to be as impactful as you making that decision.

Even with these accomplishments, Brandon probably wouldn't have made it to college but for an advisor named Gerry Oxx who understood the gravity of his circumstances. Without legal status, he couldn't take out a federal loan or hold a work-study job, despite wanting to help pay his way—so he'd need a full scholarship for tuition, housing, food, travel, and expenses. After a thoughtful recruiter from Franklin & Marshall visited the school, Gerry challenged Brandon to imagine himself out east. While F&M couldn't accept every applicant who had no financial resources, Brandon was supremely well-qualified, with talents tested by the vicissitudes of life and the soul of a survivor, and so the match was made. I would add that the admission staffer who saw his fortitude and advocated for him was Brian Rivera.

In college, right from the start, Brandon encountered so many "good people . . . who impacted my life positively." One was his future girlfriend Vanessa, who carried herself with an upbeat energy that meshed perfectly with his quieter demeanor. Another was the philosophy professor Lee Franklin, who led his cohort group with a calm and kind heart. His student mentors, including Cameron Rutledge and Prescott Owusu, shared experiences but never told him what to do, just like how he'd mentored his ninth-grade soccer players. He actually formulated an approach to being a mentee, hewn from his independence: "I needed to listen to what they have to say. But I'm not going to just do what they want me to do; I need to analyze their experience . . . and use it as it applies to my life."

One of his favorite classes was Geology, taught by the person-able Andy DeWet. Before the first test, he sweated pellets memo-rizing the names of all the rocks and minerals. After he earned a 98, the professor invited him to explore the field. Soon it was aca-demic love. "It excited me to be hiking or walking in the park," he told me, "and to come upon a rock sticking up and know how that rock came to be." The more he dug in, the deeper he wanted to go. When considering earth science as his major he circled the depart-ment to ask the professors about their research, which is how he got to know Tim Bechtel, who became, with his wife Felicia, a great mentor and friend. For sure, he faced challenges and needed re-silience. One semester he showed up with eight dollars in his pocket. Another time he had to decline Bechtel's invitation to be his research assistant in Switzerland because, of course, he could not leave the country. It was disappointing because he'd earned the offer but had no power to take it; even so, he knew how to accept reality and still move forward.

In his sophomore year, Dean Donnell Butler brought him an in-vitation that he *could* accept. F&M had secured a grant to enroll five students in the Deferred Action for Childhood Arrivals (DACA) program, which covers unauthorized immigrants brought to the United States as children. The program allows these young people, also called "Dreamers," to go to school or work with less risk of deportation, allowing them to raise their hands for opportunity. When Butler asked Brandon about mentoring these five students, he promptly said yes, excited to draw upon the reservoir of expe-riences with which he'd made his life and made life his. We knew they would be terrific, for recruiting strong DACA students was like finding stars in a planetarium. Every year we received applica-tions from dozens of teenagers who had earned top grades while dealing with the worry that they or a loved one might be shipped away, or that money might run out, or that a predator might turn their family into prey. That takes *talent*—and we believed that having more DACA students would enhance every student's education, especially if the Dreamers got off to quick, confident starts.

Let me skip ahead four years when all of Brandon's mentees graduated on time. Each had been a rock star. They earned superior grades, joined or founded clubs, and held part-time jobs, since with DACA they could do that. Each dealt bravely with the uncertainties brought on by the 2016 election of Donald Trump and the swift announcement that DACA would be terminated, which the courts later stayed. Today, these recent alums are working or in graduate school, still excelling, developing themselves in anticipation of the liberating legal moment when they'll finally be able to fully live and give with free and safe futures.

Brandon contributed to their success, as he welcomed them into F&M and built relationships on their terms. Along with his co-mentor Kristen, he would study with them in the library or listen to their first-year problems, like not being able to concentrate in their room or struggling to connect with a professor. Sometimes it would get deeper, when they would fret that they might be growing away from their families. His priority "was to offer them emotional support . . . and an outlet for the distress and expectations" in this immersive, expansive college experience, buoying them "to find their own solutions and ideals." Overall, the primary idea he hoped to instill, largely by example, was this: They must not get stuck in a mentality of being passive, or feeling out of place, or worrying about how they look to others, or being undocumented— for if he had done so, he "would have remained stagnant." He wanted to *influence their desire* by modeling for them his do-your-best-with-what-you-have philosophy:

> I'm going to be the one who asks the stupid question in class because, to you it may seem stupid, but for me it's new knowledge.

It's something I want to learn, and I don't care about what you think. I care about what I want to learn.

So, you have to step away from the mentality of "What are others going to say? What are others going to think?" and really focus on what you want to do with your life. . . . You have to live in the present. . . .

What I can do right now is live the best life that I can, whatever that means to me, so if it's going out of my comfort zone, it's what I want to do. And if it's a bad experience then I'll learn, and I won't do it again, and that's OK.

I want to learn, I want to fail, I want to fall back and get up, I want to do those things. I told them, "If you want to do it, go for it, and have no regrets because you made this decision. . . . If something makes sense to you right now, do it because you may not have that opportunity again."

For this group, he brought the right life-knowledge and approach at the right time. Once I asked how *he'd* benefitted from mentoring a group of students who, like him, came of age in the shadows. I'd thought he might say that aiding others gave him some solace, converting his losses of the heart into a force for helping younger Dreamers.

In fact, that wasn't his understanding at all.

By the time he started mentoring, Brandon told me, he had already figured out his philosophy of striving despite strictures. Mentoring five fellow Dreamers did not redeem his scars and losses, he told me; rather, it expressed and reinforced that the understanding he had long held. Which is to say, at an early age, Brandon "took ownership" of the trauma he'd survived and the restrictions he'd lived with. These realities led him to define himself by what he *could* control, and what he *did* value, and the actions he *could* take with no expectation of reward. Mentoring the similarly situated peers was one more in a long pattern of self-willed choices since he was thirteen years old by which he asserted his value, values, and bounded autonomy. Mentoring expressed the moral and ethical meaning of his life and furthered his hard-won sense of purpose, which was "to do what was expected" regardless of recognition and "to do the best you can with what you have" despite constraints.

Factor Four: Mentoring Fulfills Mentors

For Brandon, mentoring five Dreamers continued his long march to interior freedom. It gave him, again, the gift of moral agency.

For Katie and Mona, mentoring was different—both were easing into change, one entering a promising new world and the other completing her best years so far. Their relationship gave each other the gift of growth.

For Brian and Andy, fast friends first, strivers in their souls, mutual mentoring emerged over time as one aspect of what true friends do, helping each other chart and walk the ways of growth. It gave them the gift of accompaniment.

For each young person, mentoring took life to a deeper level, a desired and growthful way of being, stemming from their values and their identities. F&M facilitated this in ways that other institutions might emulate. Every new student begins F&M with myriad faculty and student mentors at their disposal, both to help them and to show that passing down experience "is what we do here." The college then provides early mentoring opportunities not just as part-time jobs but as conduits for growth in residential communities, in some classrooms, in new student cohort groups. New mentors get mentored on how to mentor, and faculty and staff sometimes partner with students as co-mentors. Today, some institutions are even having early success utilizing trained peer counselors in their counseling centers, expanding access to care and for some students destigmatizing it.[19] All this builds a culture of mentorship.

Having fulfilled themselves through giving relationships, Brian, Andy, Mona, Katie, and Brandon entered post-college life looking for more of the same. As did Keiran Miller, who entered his last weeks of senior year with several job offers to help lower-income students pursue and prepare for college. Most intriguing was the Pennsylvania College Advising Corps (PCAC), which places recent graduates in two-year college advising roles, mostly in rural schools. Keiran had mentored a few PCAC students in College Prep, three of whom went on to light up the board at F&M. It moved him to imagine helping teenagers cut from their cloth. Yes, he'd need to overcome the skepticism among families that saw college as a doorway through which their children would disappear—and that was a job worth doing.

The dedicated PCAC director Bob Freund recruited Keiran doggedly, like Stanford going after an Olympic swimmer, but two programs in New York City also made good offers. The positions were similar, but not the contexts: A mostly white school or all mentees of color. Small town or big city. Pickup trucks or subways. A foreign culture or a familiar one.

At the decision point, Keiran framed it this way: He'd lived and loved city life and would eventually come back to it. But, as with college, the unknown beckoned. When else would he have the chance to offer himself to farm kids and find out what they could teach him? Sure, he might be Shawn Carter playing to a Carrie Underwood crowd, but he'd figure it out. After all, he believed, sixteen-year-olds anywhere have so much in common with sixteen-year-olds everywhere once you get beneath the skin.

So, Keiran said yes to PCAC and was charged by Freund to bring his mentor's mindset to Columbia High School in the green hills of Lancaster County. A flat red-brick building perched on a bluff amidst cornfields, dairy farms, a highway, and a river, it was one of the smallest public schools in the Commonwealth, serving just four hundred students, at least 70 percent of whom qualified for the federal free or reduced-price lunch program. On day one, as he organized his desk and straightened out his bow tie, this Black Brooklynite with an elite education became the community's one and only college advisor.

Job one was to figure out the seventy-five seniors, using techniques he'd honed at F&M. Be approachable. Listen. Don't make assumptions. One of his first meetings was with a firecracker named Anita who wanted to meet "the college guy." Like most of her classmates, she divided her days between school and the Lancaster County Career and Technology Center (CTC), a respected community hub where students could work and learn hands-on in fields like dentistry, welding, automotive repair, website design, and much more. At the time, her interest was nursing, but she also liked school culture and activities such as volleyball and National Honor Society. She was a go-getter, so positive, but for her college was by no means a shining promised land of learning like it had been for Keiran in high school.

It was the same with the next few appointments. There was Mike, with a GPA in the middle of the pack, who really hadn't been thinking about college. And there was Julia, who had the highest grades in the school and was ready to apply to some competitive universities, and yet, seemed to lack conviction. None of these seniors were lasering toward an elite school like so many in F&M College Prep. Was that bad? No, of course not. "I realized fast," he later told me, "that many of these kids were different than I was at their age, in that they weren't focused on college. Maybe it was the military, or a trade, or nothing yet."

He thought of Donnell Butler's maxim: *Look to understand, not to be understood.* So relevant. Asserting that the Columbia students should value what he'd valued at their age would be a waste of breath and make him seem like a know-it-all. Far better would be to learn how *they* saw their futures and why—"to develop an understanding of the values and experiences of this community where they had lived their whole lives." To mentor well, he would need to hold some of his own views in abeyance in order to look and listen intensively, like the way a writer trains himself to see the world through eyes other than his own.

To do that, the twenty-minute commute to work became a godsend. That was when, with the music of Migos or Beyoncé setting a mood, he'd empty himself of expectation so that he could reenter the school building with a roving mind. Then he could try to learn from, say, the celebratory vibe of the morning announcements webcast on YouTube, or the different postures teachers took toward their students, or the details that made the CTC internships so popular. He tried to decode school politics and map which seniors had siblings associated with the school. He made sure to show up and pitch in, working the concession stand at football games and the ticket table at plays. Those community events brought in waves of families. Many of the parents worked on the land or in stores or drove trucks. Some ran their own businesses as electricians, welders, or carpenters. Some served in the military. They really cared about the school, and the school cared about the community. Pride was the current crackling through it all.

A natural synthesizer, Keiran adroitly eased himself and his role into the mainstream of the school. For example, within the first weeks he shifted his focus and title from "college advising" to "college *and career* advising." He gathered information on every kind of institution, never favoring the F&M model above community college, technical training, for-profit schools, part-time programs, and big publics. He made it easy for students to come see him without signaling where they were going—and in these meetings, he avoided making college the default answer to every inquiry. After all, what was wrong with working as a machinist or serving in the military? Nothing, obviously. His task was to help his mentees to learn more about the fields that intrigued them. Tone was essential: inviting, polite, caring . . . and never preachy or pushy or self-regarding.

With that approach, his first mentoring efforts landed well. He built a fast relationship with a basketball player named Joey, who was practiced at looking cooperative as a cover for letting things slide. "I saw my high school self in him, and let him know that, so he knew that I knew that his follow-through wasn't always the best," he told me. This gave them a knowing bond Keiran could work with as he challenged him to do more than wait for the supposedly inevitable scholarship offers to come rolling in.

The epitome of humility, with off-the-charts EQ, he gained respect quickly. One canny move was to create a "college ambassadors" program for ten juniors (his "minions"), which provided him some helpers, gave them a credential, and offered the concept of higher education a boost within school culture. Aided by his team, he put together visits to universities like Kutztown and Millersville that could be reached within ninety minutes. In November he organized a College Opportunity Week, with presentations from about ten colleges. Some open-access institutions offered on-the-spot admission, which created a buzz around the school.

That year Keiran enjoyed a lot of validation that mentoring was for him, but two peak moments were defining. The first involved a likeable junior named Richard, who took on any task at school or home. As he was one of the minions, Keiran thought he'd benefit from a crash tutorial on how admissions officers evaluate transcripts. But as he spoke, the boy began to lament that his grades were going to hold him back. "He felt that no one had told him what was at stake," Keiran told me, "and now it seemed too late." The exchange shook them both. Suddenly he felt the presence of deep-water currents pushing these kids' rudders back to the dock just as they were discerning new horizons. "I was trying to show them this vast ocean that lays before them," he said, "but because of how the ship was built, it's like, 'I don't know if I can actually make that journey.'"

It was more than disquieting. It was a crisis. Given his lack of experience, and the differences of upbringing and identity, what did he have to offer these students, really? Rationalizations for staying put and bromides about branching out? Doubting himself, he leaned on what had worked at F&M and sought out a new mentor, a veteran teacher and dean named Jim who was the picture of patience.

"How do you keep working at this when you see student after student being dragged down? How do you keep going?"

Smiling kindly, Jim gave a first response that made sense:

"You need to keep your own bucket filled. You need to re-charge yourself."

Keiran got that, as self-care was no new concept. Then Jim gave the real answer:

"You being here is far better than you *not* being here—so you need to make yourself useful. That is what the students need. They need *you* to keep going. You need to keep trying, because if you stop, the students are the ones who will feel the consequences."

Keiran took to heart this advice. Melting down wouldn't help his kids one bit. They needed him to try, try, try, and give, give, give.

That was the job that needed doing. His very best efforts made with optimism would certainly create more value for his mentees than pessimism could ever yield. Applying himself in times of doubt would lead to results, and the results would lead to meaning. He just needed to extend the timeline for gratification— "almost like a farmer who doesn't know what the crops are going to yield" but must keep laboring all the same.

One way he recharged was by making allies of the most involved faculty, so they would value him as an extension of their teaching. A second was by replaying life lessons from college. "I would think back on F&M and all these mentors," he told me, "and remember how they would ask me question after question, leading me to rethink what I said to them." This helped him become more assertive in making queries to get his mentees to say what was on their minds with weighty choices on their dockets, like Patricia O'Hara and Shawn Jenkins had done with him.

This method played out well with Julia, the valedictorian who'd become more tentative about college with each passing month. By February, she looked like a prime candidate to "undermatch" by staying at home and piecing together work and school. With her permission, Keiran asked if this was because of family responsibilities.

> She shared a moment of vulnerability and said "Yeah, that's exactly how I feel. These are things that I have to do to be able to support my family. I'm the most responsible person there." We just had an open conversation, which gave me the chance to say, "You're seventeen years old, and that's a lot of pressure for a seventeen-year-old to hold."

This exchange deepened their relationship. It became normal for him to politely remind her to consider her educational dreams and needs, but he never tried to tell her what to want or choose. Mentoring Julia reminded him that he had "an overlap of intuition, passion and skill" with which he could connect, person to person, as a believer in the students and their advocate. He liked how supportive questioning could be a form of wisdom. All in all, picking himself up and just doing the job that was needed the best he could helped him regain the feeling of meaning and self-confidence that had led him to make the bold choice to come to Columbia in the first place.

The second defining moment came in April, when he put on Columbia's first College and Career Declaration Day. Keiran had spent months getting every student lined up with something to announce—work, military, technical college, two-year school, or four-year school. In the days before the pep rally, he and the minions poured over every detail—from speakers and T-shirts to food and fun games. The entire staff and school attended—even the middle schoolers. Keiran played emcee as the seniors came forward with their news: Joey would matriculate at Wilson College. Anita, now dealing with a new health issue, would work for a year before enrolling at Shippensburg University. Julia had found the right fit, West Chester University, which was not too close and not too far, with strong STEM programs and a fine aid package.

With each announcement, it grew more raucous—especially among the middle schoolers, who whooped it up like end zone crazies. It was a day when everyone could cheer and be cheered—because, deep down, they were celebrating more than college or career, per se. The Declaration Day was about the community itself, how they all could "have pride and hold it close." And Keiran felt a justified pride too. His students had excellent plans in place—and the event had been a big win. It had more than paid off to heed Jim's advice and keep planting and plowing in hopes of a strong harvest.

A few days later, however, it dawned on him that his two-year role was half over, a sobering thought. Yes, he had much to look forward to—like launching the current juniors and making inroads with the younger students—but still, he would be departing. That was a fact. He couldn't make a longer commitment, not with international travel or graduate school on the horizon.

Keiran's second year flew by as he "sharpened and stretched" his role. Whether he was moving among friend groups in the cafeteria or working with the techies who liked his offbeat humor, he was comfortable centering the conversations on the students' twin desires—how to be true to themselves and find a path forward they could like. He beefed up the college visits. He also connected some I.M.P.A.C.T. men with a colleague looking for mentors for ten middle schoolers. And, to learn more about system changes that could make college counseling more impactful, he joined a working group of advisors digging into data sets and research findings.

Year two was rewarding—and it ended with an exclamation point. For his farewell party in the teachers' lounge, almost the entire staff showed up. Everyone praised his energy and effectiveness. It felt so gratifying to be seen and valued by all these long-term educators, some of whom, like Jim, were paragons of integrity, while he was just a newbie straight out of college trying to do his best. The Brooklyn/Columbia differences hadn't hindered him at all—in fact, they helped, spurring him to mindful acculturation. Everyone said not just that they would miss him but also that they couldn't wait to work with his successor, a redoubtable rugby-playing F&M Texan named Andrea Martinez, whom he admired. The growing number of Latino families in Lancaster County was one more reason why he was enthusiastic about the match.

When his colleagues produced a cake, it felt like a lot and more of a tribute than he'd expected. And then a door burst open revealing a group of his mentees carrying a cashew-colored chest engraved with their esteemed school's name. It was magnificent. For a month they'd made it with their own hands in the woodshop. Among them was Richard, who'd worked all year on a plan that would take him triumphantly to Thaddeus Stevens College of Technology with a scholarship. It was one of the great days in Keiran's life.

Driving home that evening with his Columbia High School chest in the back seat, new memories flowing through his brain, already indelible, he felt enlarged. The community's pride was an example to treasure and to apply. Mentoring there had been so fulfilling and enlarging and spiritually right—as had his roles in F&M College Prep . . . and I.M.P.A.C.T. . . . and L.I.F.T. His next step would be a year working at a university in Greece with a team of Americans. Directionally, mentoring and writing called to him. He loved both and wanted them in his life. They gave him friendship, they gave him hope and growth, they gave him voice, and they gave him an agency consonant with his values. They were core to his heart and his mind and his stride, he was now sure of that.

*

We forge growth mindsets in the kiln of experience, in our moments of reach or choice or challenge, when we know like a faith that, having, say, created or discovered before, we can do so again, perhaps even better or more ambitiously because that's what we do and who we are. That's also true of mentorship, a practical art that touches people personally. Those who have the mindset, looking outward to learn from or serve others, often live exquisite lives.

Brandon and Keiran, Katie and Mona, and Andy and Brian are some of the finest individuals I know. In their everyday acts of living, they seek to connect and give to others, from their ideals, from their humanity. Their kindness has an aura. College was the ideal place to feed their fire for mentoring. The culture of mentorship gave them growth, gave them joy and love, and gave them ethical gratification. The college and our society are both better for it.

One time I heard the lifelong public servant Madeleine Albright say to an audience, "I find that the older I get, the younger my mentors are." Having watched this group come of age and enter their careers with the mindset to mentor—"to speak positivity" and "pour into people"—I feel the same way. It's one of teaching's loftiest rewards.

Chapter 3: Questions for Discussion

1. How do you understand the mindset for mentorship? Why does the author believe that this mindset is a powerful resource during and after college?

2. The author compares mentorship on campus to a flywheel because the person-to-person transmission of information and advice makes the whole system work more effectively. Do you agree with that? What more can be done to build a culture of mentorship on campus?

3. The chapter describes how mentorship motivated and fulfilled Keiran, Mona, Katie, Brian, Andy, and Brandon. In what ways does mentorship benefit both the mentee and the mentor? What are the traits of a good mentor—and mentee?

4. The author shows how, with experience, Keiran grew as a mentor, becoming more self-aware and intentional. What are ways that colleges can help mentors improve—students and educators?

5. The chapter describes how Keiran led two student organizations and thus became a mentor to groups of students as well as individuals. What do these two modes of mentoring have in common, and how are they different?

6. What is "the hidden curriculum" of college? How can colleges be more intentional and effective in providing mentoring to students for whom campus culture and practices are highly unfamiliar and perhaps unwelcoming?

4

THE MINDSET FOR
COLLABORATION

College wouldn't simply be about individual advancement,
like high school. It would be about the work of collectives.

—KATRINA WACHTER

ALTHOUGH STUDENTS APPLY TO COLLEGE as individuals, and earn
diplomas that bear their names alone, much of their growth transpires in teams, as we saw last chapter with the spoken word club
L.I.F.T. Students think and talk together in seminars, live together
in intentional communities, and perform together in clubs and
jobs. They create campaigns together. They run youth programs
together. They compete for titles together. They serve together on
committees to address tough topics such as peer conduct and academic integrity. Often this experience is highly positive, although
teams made of eighteen-to-twenty-three-year-olds will also floun-
der or fail, for many reasons. But flops can be productive too—
moments for learning and for change.

Like people, undergraduate teams have their distinctive hopes and traits and vibe. They also have varying models and structures. Some are led by educators, others by peers. Some chase a singular goal; others, a more fluid range of aims. Some teams are closed, even intimate; others can be joined by anyone. This chapter will explore five forms of team experience that are prominent on most campuses: (1) the all-student organization, (2) the shared governance committee, (3) the cohort group, (4) the staff-led cocurricular program, and (5) the seminar. Through these models, colleges inculcate the growth mindset for collaboration, which Sir Ken Robinson defines as involving "people working together in a shared process in which their interaction affects the nature of the work and its outcomes."[1]

Moreover, college enables undergraduates to take part in many of these "shared processes" at the same time, thereby diversifying students' experiences of teamwork. A senior might serve on the executive board of the Hillel chapter while also playing the viola in the school's orchestra. A junior might deliberate with faculty to create a lecture series while also staffing the weekly produce market. A sophomore might train for the emergency response medical team while also recruiting donors for the annual Locks of Love drive. And, while playing these assorted roles, students are also taking a set of classes that require collaboration in myriad ways.

By "teamwork," I mean collaborative endeavor that creates a collective work product, which means that it's more than simply sharing ideas or being trained together. As Jon R. Katzenbach and Douglas K. Smith observe, teams "require both individual and mutual accountability. Teams rely on more than group discussion, debate, and decision; on more than sharing information and best practice performance standards. Teams produce discrete work products through the joint contributions of their members. This is what makes possible performance levels greater than the sum of all the individual bests of team members."[2]

Through shared labor, purpose, and products, undergraduates bolster aptitudes they'll use in and out of college—for agreeing on goals, for teasing out ideas, for divvying up tasks, for exchanging feedback, for stepping up and holding back, for sharing power and pushing growth, for bridging backgrounds and tending to trust, for negotiating and adjusting and iterating and debriefing, and, of course, managing mishaps. Some of the problems that need to be acknowledged and dealt with include personality conflicts and cliquishness, which are as inevitable as a rainy day, and group-think and the closing of ranks, which can be quite destructive. However, when teams function well, which is often, students get to see and feel the benefits of collaboration, like enhanced ideating, productive practices, and the addition of needed talent.[3] Clearly, team play is critical in an era when change constantly disrupts the assumptions of work and life. One 2016 study found that "over the past two decades, the time spent by managers and employees in collaborative activities has ballooned by 50% or more."[4] From an historical perspective, Robert Putnam and Shaylyn Romney Garrett argue that when Americans become more "we" centered, the United States becomes more equal, less polarized, and less fragmented.[5] As colleagues and citizens, as neighbors and family members, we must be able to cooperate and collaborate with others. Life demands that.

College students derive something else from their teams: the indelible rush of being partners in a triumph. As with mentoring, collaboration changes the collaborators. Imagine rowers on the river or musicians in the concert hall—practicing together, sacrificing together, devoting together, becoming together. When we co-labor, and coproduce something bigger than we could have made alone, we become bigger too. We expand our empathy. We extend our reach. We increase our awareness. We yearn to be more, stronger, better for each other and our climb. Teamwork brings out new features to our identity—self as facilitator, self as partner, self as linchpin or protector or spirit leader. Teamwork gives us community and acceptance. It creates shared memories. It grows our trust in trust. And, when collective work wraps up, like when the professor recaps the seminar or the house lights rise as the last cheers wane, you can feel a bond of meaning, a pride, and sometimes a slight sadness like love, the grateful longing for just a little more, where mindsets build. Andrea Smith, who grew up alone, summed up the moral meaning of teamwork this way: "Having an on-campus job, lab partners, housemates, and leadership positions increased my sense of belonging. It made me feel included, challenged, and excited to be part of a community."

The opposite is true too. Isolation rarely brings out our best. Loneliness, depression, and alienation have been worsening among undergraduates for a decade and, as for people younger and older, intensifying with the pandemic.[6] Collaboration is not a cure-all, but it can help. With partners, we co-know and co-make and co-shape our surroundings; in doing so, we re-know and re-make and re-shape ourselves.

Overall, there's a logic here, on campus and beyond: When we tie ourselves to a team and achieve goals no one can reach alone, we enhance ourselves. This is *the power of we*. College helps young people to internalize this power—to feel it, want it, live it, love it—through the five team models we'll delve into here. Each has value on campus and beyond, feeding and fostering the mindset for collaboration that we need in the public squares of our democracy and the more private pursuits of work and life.

Model One: The All-Student Organization

These are purpose-driven teams that are 100 percent originated, owned, operated, and perpetuated by undergraduates. What are some examples? Club sports and improv troupes, radio stations and newspapers, advocacy campaigns, tutoring programs, and so much more. Such teams demonstrate one of the most galvanizing ideas in the history of higher education, which is that, acting together, young people can influence any community they're part of, and quickly.

Sounds like a stretch? Across fourteen years at Georgetown University, I regularly saw the power of we. For example, in 2004, Students Taking Action Now: Darfur (STAND) designed an anti-genocide campaign that awakened the campus and spawned eight hundred chapters in school and colleges.[7] A few years later, the Out for Change team worked with the administration to create the first LGBTQ resource center at an American Catholic university.[8] Other all-student organizations focused on school spirit, campus traditions, supporting startups, and more. The students who committed themselves were informed, organized, practical, and motived by high ideals. Their work enhanced the university and sometimes even drove change beyond its gates.

I saw the same at F&M. One of the best all-student teams I observed was the Fellowship of the Strings, a quartet of classical musicians whose crossover interpretations of songs by Coldplay and CeeLo Green were staples of campus events. Another we'll read about next chapter was the club ".08," through which students promoted safer drinking at parties. And another was a team that founded the Muslim Students Association, drawing together domestic and international students for learning, friendship, and prayer.

Worthy teams help students hit high marks in the present while accumulating life lessons for the future. To see this more clearly, let's look again at the club Intelligent Men Purposefully Accomplishing College Together (I.M.P.A.C.T.), mentioned in the profiles of Darrius Moore and Keiran Miller. Founded in 2004 after a racist incident on campus,[9] the club's goal is to build community and success among men of color. F&M also has a comparable women's organization, S.I.S.T.E.R.S., an acronym for Sophisticated, Intelligent Sisters Teaching Excellence, Responsibility & Success. Both welcome students of all identities, including white students who are valued as friends, allies, and partners. Each I.M.P.A.C.T. meeting begins with the pledge that all members make:

> I am only one, but still I am one. I cannot do everything, but still I can do something; and because I cannot do everything, I will not refuse to do what I can do. For there is no one quite like me, and I can make an IMPACT.

Why has the club endured and grown for eighteen years? Mainly, because the brothers understand that, despite the college's many valuable ideals and offerings, bias still occurs and inclusion is still uneven, so men of color need to work together to achieve their individual goals. Given *this* important purpose, what does collaboration look like?

Organizationally, it means showing up for each other at the weekly meetings, all semester long, and practicing consensual decision-making.

Educationally, it means mentoring each other for success, and collectively analyzing and addressing any barriers to learning and opportunity, for the one or the many.

Socially, it means giving each other community, friends to hang out with, and a place to belong, which enhances learning.

Symbolically, it means representing each other well on campus, which is why the brothers don ties on Tuesdays and support women-led events like Take Back the Night.

Morally, it means standing together in solidarity and encouraging all to be who they are, as they change.

Spiritually, it means taking pride in each other's feats and growth as all strive to *accomplish college together*.

In all these ways, collaboration sits at the core of I.M.P.A.C.T.'s purpose and identity. There's a reason for the "T" at the end of the acronym. All are stronger *together*. In particular, there are two things that would not happen but for the brothers' ability to team up.

First, I.M.P.A.C.T. enables them to co-create and sustain a forum for *collaborative dialogue* based on the free and full airing of ideas. Across seven years of periodically attending meetings, I observed that any issue can be surfaced. One evening I watched Bendjhi Villiers and Keyla Ynoa from S.I.S.T.E.R.S. lead a discussion on sexist and homophobic language. Their tone was inviting, not judgmental, prompting a first-year student to admit—trusting that he could—that at home he'd sometimes banter with friends using derogatory terms, a behavior he now wanted to dial back. Another time I saw Keiran run a workshop on interacting with the police, during which a brother spoke from his hurt about being handcuffed by campus security—what he did, what they did, how it felt, what he learned. It was always stirring to watch these college men talk through nuanced topics like the roles of fathers in their lives or what kind of neighborhood would be best for raising children. And I would marvel at seeing a respected upperclassman like Cameron Rutledge or Matt Thomas lean in while a younger brother was struggling to say what he meant. Only through a purposeful organization can individuals have such a forum.

Second, I.M.P.A.C.T. gives these college men a venue for *collaborative action* to achieve big goals. For example, one night Jabari Benjamin and Luke Groff were discussing F&M's reputation in town. Luke, who is white and grew up nearby, confessed that most lifelong Lancastrians had no clear perception of the college . . . except that the students were all wealthy outsiders. "As we talked about this," Jabari told me, "Luke and I decided, 'Why should we wait on the college administration to fix this? *We* can do something.'" Motivating each other, they organized the brothers to mentor local youth and pitch in at a food bank, extending the club's work beyond the campus. "Individually we knew we could do good," he said, "but, *together*, the brothers realized we could be great." The experience led Jabari and his close friend Ramon Williams to stay in Lancaster after graduation for two years to assist college-bound students.

Jabari says that "bringing together all this talent with a focus on collaboration helps individuals achieve their 'why' and makes everyone's individual *impact* that much greater." Sometimes that can even mean collaborating to cope with serious adversity. For instance, in 2021 one of their members, Vicente Brambila, died in an off-road vehicle crash back home in Los Angeles. He was a vibrant dance major and student of culture who seized life and lived out loud. As his friend Guadalupe Vargas Razo posted in tribute, the ways he presented himself as a proud gay Mexican man "taught us how to live our best lives." Because of the pandemic, his broken-souled F&M friends and brothers couldn't even grieve in person. Former president C. J. Cortorreal was among those frozen in pain—until he realized, through a talk with Jabari, that the brothers could help the community move through the stages of grief. After a few Zoom meetings, they partnered with S.I.S.T.E.R.S. and other groups to raise $10,000 to plant a new tree on campus in Vicente's honor—something that would live and give for decades on end, in strength and beauty—just like their dear friend, whom there was *"no one quite like."*

Addressing our human need for a spiritual home base, collaborative student-led organizations like I.M.P.A.C.T. and S.I.S.T.E.R.S. create distinctive value in any campus ecosystem. They enable undergraduates to give each other a sense of belonging that aids growth.[10] They can help the young to widen horizons and deepen friendships, together. And they can provide a sense of solidarity that allows students to feel they aren't losing their core identities in a place where the default culture may differ from home. It's a model of egalitarian service-centered collaboration that sets a course for more co-creation in and after college. As Jabari once told me, one of the life lessons from four years of brotherhood is that "life is a joint activity—the where, why, and how depend not just on what you do, but *who you do it with.*"

Model Two: The Shared Governance Committee

"Shared governance" is the system and processes by which stakeholders hold joint responsibility for the operations, decisions, and direction of an organization. In higher education, the term typically refers to the rights and roles of faculty, but it's also relevant for student citizenship. When undergraduates join teams charged with shaping the policies and standards within which they live and study—a form of procedural democracy—they learn that, with effective collaboration, they can design structures and policies whose benefits may increase across time for the greater good.

At F&M, Katrina Wachter learned this lesson as early as one can.

One May morning in 2011, she drove to Lancaster for the one-day spring orientation program, Beginnings. With the application process finally done, she was excited to walk the lovely grounds of her new home and imagine the possibilities.

Katrina had always been an arrow pointed toward college. Raised in the Pennsylvania town of Bath, she grew up curious and active, organized, and positive. She relished everything about learning—the insights, the means, and the ends. Her parents, Stew and Denise, who had chosen not to attend college, made sure she saw herself as strong and capable with an agile mind. Although the Wachters certainly valued high achievement, far more meaningful was being a good and honest person. When it became clear that college would be in her future, Katrina's parents gave her the freedom to choose her path, both academically and geographically.

That spring day, she strolled the F&M sidewalks expectantly, soaking up the quadrangles and the gleaming life sciences building and the music hall where she would finally achieve her life-long goal of taking voice lessons. With the spring semester finished, the stillness made it seem as if the college were holding its breadth until her class arrived. The cozy, walkable campus reminded her why she longed for an intimate liberal arts experience, even when friends opted for mega-universities like Penn State. She saw F&M as a place where she could blaze her own trail as an aspiring doctor. The small classes and personable faculty gave her the feeling that "I was gaining a new family to guide me to my future."

Katrina especially liked the new system of College Houses, rather than big dorms, which was all about community. During a welcome reception at Beginnings, she received her placement in New College House (now known as Roschel College House), whose stately building was still under construction. Rising juniors Rosa DiPiazza and Robert Diggs (known as "Diggs") were recruiting incoming students for the summer committee that would draft the founding governance model and house constitution that all New College House residents would be asked to consider and vote on in the fall. *Why not start F&M a little early?* she thought. *It would be a great way to meet people.*

That summer, the team worked via tele-meetings. Rosa spearheaded the drafting related to the creation of the house's customs and traditions, and Diggs focused on governance. Rising senior Mona Lotfipour, logging in from South Africa, argued that the constitution should focus on the structure of the student government and the core principles of house membership. This idea dovetailed nicely with Diggs's conviction that, since they were only an appointed committee, they should leave the nitty-gritty decisions about conduct policies to the students who would be elected in the fall.

To get started, the drafting team reviewed the governance frameworks of F&M's four existing houses, such as the Parliament of Ware College House and Weis College House's Assembly of Peers. Their goal, as Diggs described it, was to create a new model "that would engage first-years right away and was distinctive, to set New College House apart." Intuitively, the upper-class students tended to favor the structures of the existing houses they lived in as first-years. Mindful of not letting that group dominate, Diggs always asked the incoming students like Katrina and André Douglass to speak up, to get them used to contributing.

The team settled on the organizational model of an elected senate, an executive committee, a judicial body, and house committees on topics like social life and sustainability. This framework established plenty of open roles for new students, to make sure "all first-years had a chance to engage fully in the life of the house from day one on campus," as Diggs expounded. Although they knew they couldn't legislate an engaged culture by requiring students to take part, it was their job to create a governance model that would organically draw them in.

Talk about building a plane when it's already in the clouds. Katrina hadn't even started college, and now she was helping create the New College House framework that would guide how she and about two hundred peers would live. "I've always prided myself in being a creator, and this seemed like the perfect opportunity to create something completely new and unique that could begin a legacy for years to come," Katrina told me.

They drafted and edited the language of the constitution through a Google Docs text, which kept the commentary concise and eliminated the need to coordinate schedules. Having a living document, rather than multiple Microsoft Word versions, meant that everyone could see changes in real time in order to crowdsource and sign off efficiently. The incoming House Don, the government professor Dean Hammer, edited very lightly, trusting the students to drive the process. Mostly he just asked questions: Are the senate roles sufficiently differentiated? Is the government's structure likely to have legitimacy? Will the committees attract participants? With a nod to Hammer, a scholar of ancient political thought, the team gave Latin titles to the house's four executive committee roles: consul, consul suffectus, quaestor, and scribe.[11]

Katrina loved making suggestions in such a receptive team of peers. The mystic chords that bound them were trust, respect, and an earnest belief in community. But she sensed that collective editing worked better for making tweaks than for introducing wholly new concepts. Her lingering concern was facilitating student buy-in. "At the time," she told me, "I worried that we would have a great document but that students wouldn't live into it," even more of a concern due to the new building's admittedly palatial design.

Something was missing. How would they make sure that all these incoming new students would assume the values of citizenship and community that the constitution called for? What else could they do to create culture? Ruminating in her family room in Bath, she had a eureka moment: *New College House needed an honor code.*

This eighteen-year-old wasn't shy about calling the question. After all, Professor Hammer and House Dean Suzanna Richter had repeatedly said they *expected* the students to design a model that inspired them. So, she fired off an impassioned email to Diggs, laying out her case. Even though he was skeptical about the viability of an honor code, since no other house had one, he thought better of discouraging a new student from running with her idea.

Channeling both the values the drafting team wanted to emphasize and her quick web scans of honor codes at other schools, Katrina came up with the three foundational principles—honesty, respect for others, and commitment to the house rules. She worded it succinctly and dropped the text into the Google Doc:

> As a member of New College House, I pledge to respect the academic work, physical belongings, and integrity of myself and my fellow classmates. I understand that failure to adhere to these principles may result in judicial action taken against me by the house judiciary, the house Dean, or the Office of the Dean of the College.[12]

After an easy discussion, the members agreed that the idea had merit and left it in the final draft. Now inspired himself, Diggs used it to write the New College House motto—*Hic Vivimus Et Crescimus*, or Here We Live and Here We Grow.

A few weeks later, when the academic year began, New College House installed an interim government and asked the new residents, mostly first-years, to reflect on the constitution and honor code. Both were approved, establishing a foundation for student self-governance that has now worked well for a decade. Today, when incoming students are inducted into what is now Roschel College House, they pledge to adhere to the honor code that Katrina brought into being before her first year had officially kicked off.

"I was lucky to be a part of all that," she told me a couple years after her graduation, observing that it also was her suggestion to warm up the house's Great Room by adding a piano. "I was a first-generation college student attending F&M with a Pell Grant and Gray Scholarship, and the committee gave me a sense of belonging and an immediate understanding of how students can work together to create great things."

In *What Universities Owe Democracy*, Ronald J. Daniels rightly calls on higher education to promote "the multifaceted ideal of democratic citizenship . . . supported by four pillars—knowledge, skills, values, and aspirations." In fact, the undergraduate team that drafted the constitution learned about all four. They started by gaining *knowledge* of the governing documents of the F&M's established College Houses. They utilized the *skills* of "critical reasoning and bridging . . . to translate ideas into collective action." They practiced the *ideals* of respect, self-governance, inclusion, and integrity in both the process of their deliberations and the substance of the document. And they demonstrated the *aspiration* "toward cooperation and collective action" for which Daniels calls.[13] It was a collective achievement—and a reminder that ethical college learning can happen in teams and outside the classroom.

Katrina went on to excel in many ways, within many teams. One time she told me that the constitution committee might have been only her sixth most impactful activity, given that she also collaborated on neuroscience research, sang in musical productions, directed the Broadway Revue, and helped lead the Kappa Delta sorority. In music, she teamed up with others to learn to perform arias in Italian, a language she didn't even speak. Upon graduating, she commissioned as an officer into the US Army and began medical school at the University of South Florida.

However, serving on the committee was the *first* thing she did in college. The project required visioning, listening, philosophizing, proposing, revising, compromising, and learning together—trust-based collaboration, the sausage making of democracy. "College wouldn't simply be about individual advancement, like high school," she learned from a process that acculturated her to a radically new way of being a student. "It would be about the work of collectives." The power of we.

Model Three: The Cohort Group

The New College House constitution committee vowed to realize a time-defined goal, and they won the day, creating a durable product. By comparison, in 2012 a team of ten first-years with fine minds and communal values, including Eddie Alsina and Natasha Kirnes, vowed to help each other get after goals that would unfold across the months and movements of their full college careers, mentored with consummate skill by the professor Ken Hess. Four years later, hugging teary-eyed in graduation robes they didn't want to remove, they too had won the day. There's much to value in their model of collaboration—*the cohort group*, which is a team of peers built and coached to progress and succeed together through much or all of their college education.

Eddie's and Natasha's cohort group arose from F&M's partnership with the Posse Foundation, the college opportunity turbine founded by Deborah Bial in 1989 that now works with about sixty upper-tier institutions. Through Posse, underrepresented students from the same metropolitan area attend college together and, mentored by a faculty member, pledge to support each other. The schools fund full-tuition scholarships, while the program coaches both the scholars and the mentors on strategies for individual and group success. A growing corpus of research and case studies support the efficacy of the cohort model for supporting student well-being and achievement.[14]

Franklin & Marshall began working with Posse in 2005, drawing annual cohorts from New York City. By the time I arrived in 2011, the program was deeply valued by many faculty and deans who loved and admired striving scholars like Shawn Jenkins, Eloisa Almaraz, and Maribel Vásquez. Hearing of this confidence, I promptly visited Bial in the Posse Foundation's Wall Street headquarters with its contagiously youthful vibe.

Fifteen minutes into our meeting, Bial began pitching an irresistible concept: She wanted to find ten leading institutions willing to turn the dial a touch and inaugurate ten new Posse cohort streams for undergraduates who wanted to study science, technology, engineering, or math (STEM). In 2006, chemistry professor Irv Epstein had piloted this approach at Brandeis University and worked out the kinks. Citing the national need for greater diversity and inclusion in these influential fields of the future, Bial asked me to imagine one hundred more STEM Posse students per year graduating from schools like F&M.

"Posse is perfect for this," Bial said with conviction, "and so are liberal arts colleges."

Something clicked, and I knew right then that such cohorts would mesh well with F&M's strength in the sciences and confidence in the program.

"What's more," she added irrepressibly, "you can choose any city where we work for your cohort."

Another click. I'd always been drawn to Miami, a multicultural mecca where dreams and talent flow like crystal tides. Bringing in ten Posse superstars a year from South Florida could be fabulous for the entire college. After a couple weeks of thoughtful discussions, our science faculty and deans agreed to give it a try.

Eight fast months later, we were shaking hands with our first ten scholars at an induction ceremony held at a local hotel. "Miami Posse One," we called them. These high school seniors were sparkling in their Sunday bests. Observing their proud families—parents and grandparents, siblings and cousins—I sensed that these young people possessed even more than their stellar grades. They were the offspring of hope and hard work, like Nicole Maurici, whose working-class family emigrated from Italy; Cameron Rutledge, the son of a single mom who was a children's advocate; and Carolina Giraldo, as we'll see in chapter 5, whose parents left their home in Colombia to shield her and her brother from violence. This collective force was awesome to behold, as the Miami-Dade County Public Schools superintendent Alberto Carvalho told them in a rousing speech.

For the students, taking the Posse plunge must have required bravery. After all, very few of their classmates would even consider going to college outside the Sunshine State, never mind at a small school up north with an ampersand in its name. And what about tying a four-year knot with nine random people you'd just met in a scholarship competition? Kind of like a reality show— hopefully more *Real World* than *Survivor*.

The Posse program cultivates trust and collaboration right away, before the new scholars start college. For the Miami group, this required somewhat arduous weekly treks to Posse's downtown headquarters for team-building exercises led by staff members Ben Bingman-Tennant, Jasmine Cato, and Keely Hanson. In these first sessions they learned of each other's sundry interests and identities . . . and of values they shared, like the desire to grow close, go deep, and give back. Many of them leaned toward medical school—Cameron and Tomilya Simmons, for sure, and Carolina, Marvin Nicoleau, and Maria Patino, quite possibly. Eddie and Nicole were thinking life sciences research. Amy Reyes liked computer science and set a tone for all with her openness and empathy. With her attraction to poetry and ideas, Natasha speculated that she might not stay with STEM, which certainly didn't trouble the others. Cristina Diez looked forward to college math, but, having dealt with a debilitating condition with the help of excellent caregivers, most important to her was not her major but pursuing an individualized education. One thing was for sure: Each was genuine, altruistic, and going places.

During these meetings they also started to absorb the Posse ethos about growth, which challenged them to trade comfort for learning. In sum, it went like this: They had worlds to gain from college, and college had worlds to gain from them. To go the farthest, they'd need to enter unfamiliar territories, like studying earth history or rooming with an ideological opposite or introducing aspects of Miami's culture into F&M. Doing so day in and day out would bring bouts of doubt, fatigue, friction, and vertigo. It had to. Discomfort was part of the deal—and they had a great deal to offer each other and the college. Thus, their unifying purpose: To be there for each other, come what may, by actively attending to each other's needs. No one would be alone.

The Posse trainers had them practice useful skills of collaboration. For example, to promote inclusive discussions, they taught the students to monitor who hadn't spoken yet rather than allowing a few voices to dominate. To encourage trust, they role-played falling blindfolded into each other's arms. To reward courage, they gave each other written affirmations called "warm and fuzzies." Such intentionality was persuasive: With preparation, the scholars could create a strong team culture *before* they would need it on campus. The real value, Natasha later told me, was not simply the exercises per se but the depth and commitment with which these open-hearted new friends did them. *"Trust the process,"* a Posse credo they loved to joke about, quickly became their go-to mantra. Said Cristina, "I liked how much our Posse trainers emphasized that we had a great deal to offer the college and surrounding communities. This recognition of our strengths gave us the confidence that we could collaborate well with other students."

In June, Miami Posse One came to F&M to get a glimpse of college-level science facilitated by Ken Hess, a wise chemistry professor who'd graduated from Gettysburg College as a first-gen student in the 1980s. Hess is the kind of educator who enjoys young people's individuality and unfailingly conveys faith in them while respecting the boundaries of his role. "I'm not your dad," he intoned with his wry Pennsylvania Dutch country drawl, "I'm your mentor . . . so don't ask me for money or rides to the store." The visit was a spectacular appetizer to college life. They met with friendly students and faculty, toured the college's cool research facilities and nature conservancy, visited the Penn State College of Medicine at Hershey, and best of all, bantered late into the night in the famously decrepit Deitz Hall. Everyone who met them came away dazzled, including the rising senior Andy Foley, who said:

Meeting them, I felt, *this* is the type of student this college was supposed to have all along—because every one of them had a different story and had lived multiple lives, compared to so many other people, and were so excited about the next step. Their joint excitement of honoring their families with this opportunity—all of them having a service-minded mindset—and then also all having a genuine curiosity for learning. . . . Brian Rivera and I were like, "This is it! This is what we were craving to see among other people in the school."

In the fall, Miami Posse One hit Franklin & Marshall College like a sunburst. They dove into the icebreakers, spoke first in class, and nosed around the labs. As we saw in chapter 1, Eddie immediately joined a genetics research team. Natasha began sharing her soul-baring poems. Tomilya set the standard for studiousness. Cameron and Marvin bonded like brothers. Together, the students forged a collective persona, which was that they were bought in and dialed in, undaunted. As Natasha wrote,

> And although I can't see worth a damn both figuratively and literally
> I find myself going places
> Like accidental stumbles were actual destinations
> Like every stumble was actually planned and every trip was worth the fall.
> And everytime I get up I see things a little more clear. . . .

As stipulated by Posse, for the first two years they would hold weekly group meetings with Hess and see him one-to-one every other week. The routine made touching base helpfully ordinary. Over a cider or Wilbur chocolates, they'd talk over their recent roses, buds, and thorns. Maybe the news of the week was a thought-provoking lecture or missing a sib. Or maybe a hot take on a study aid or a schedule change. If one of them talked about how they'd prepped well for a quiz or made an extra effort, all the others would snap their fingers approvingly. If anyone voiced a concern, no one dismissed it. As the days became denser and more demanding, ninety minutes of Posse love became more renewing.

For the students, Hess saw, teaming up on what was really a slow-motion transition would "help them normalize their day-to-day experiences" and avoid doubting their fit or their fitness.

From Lancaster, Hess would regularly place a call to Miami to share notes with the Posse staffers Keely and Jasmine. They were mentors to the mentor, listening to his observations and suggesting ways that underrepresented students might perceive campus culture or siren calls from home. He merged their insights with his own convictions, especially the idea that "every student was an unfinished *individual* with distinctive talents," who needed to be seen and valued as such, by each other and by him: "Their choices need to define their education. It's hard enough to go to college in a place with all this privilege. They have to feel that they aren't suppressing themselves to be here. You have to feel valued. Finding some of your people before you start can really help."

Also helpful, he knew from his own education, was the "holistic emphasis" of the liberal arts tradition. Learning about history and philosophy and art would strengthen them in STEM by helping them connect the dots among multiple ways of knowing. It would "foster curiosity and creativity, so critical to discovery in STEM," he once told me. And it would "give them outlets for their personal passions"—still to be discovered!—making college about widening their minds and not winnowing their interests. One of his roles was to help them all hold fast to the belief that they could succeed—"*because they could.*" And, if any were to decide they wanted an "off-ramp" from STEM, that would be fine and certainly no failure. In the future they could always find a new on-ramp, with added experience and self-knowledge.

Moreover, he expected that, on top of all the common first-year stresses, eventually his posse would have to wrestle with the demons of expectation—to excel for their families, to lock down their career plans, to live up to their billing as pathbreakers. "Once they realized how new it was for F&M to have ten kids like them all coming in doing STEM," Hess told me, "they started feeling the pressure of being 'the first.' If they failed, there might not be a second or a third. They assigned a lot of value to that," a worry he respected but didn't want to overplay, for there had to be some limit to their duty to future students. It was *their* education, no one else's. He encouraged them to taste some of F&M's enticing new fruits of opportunity. It made him proud, for instance, that Eddie went on to make an experimental film. Why not? On what tablet was it proclaimed that experimental scientists could not also or instead make experimental art?

In mid-October, as midterms loomed, Hess could feel the rise in his mentees' blood pressure. All part of the game, he'd preach. Their universal challenge was calibrating how to use their study hours. You could work all night every night and still fall farther behind, I remember Maria Patino saying, while Natasha couldn't help thinking she was "the weakest link" of the posse. "College academics require constant adjustment," Hess counseled in reply. "Make consistent effort, but don't overdo it. Do your best, talk to your professors, and be there for each other." Eventually, he knew, they'd have to change some of the ways they studied, relying less on stamina and memorization, but that would come in time, and for all it did.

That fall, right after midterms, Hess saw that they all were fried, so he threw out the Posse playbook and turned the next meeting into a madcap game of Pictionary. Everyone got into it, like it was a party back home in Miami. For some uncanny reason, Eddie and Hess melded their minds like psychics. One would sketch a few swirly figures and the other would blurt out the correct answer while everyone else was left scratching their heads.

The laughter got more raucous, particularly between the mind readers. It was so normal, like a family. Now, Hess trusted the process, too—and everyone saw it. Said Cameron,

> He balanced being hands-on and hands-off, which allowed our posse to form the relationships we did with one another. He was like, "This is your journey, and I'm here to help you along, but you are the centerpiece of it, so you'll contribute best to one another's journey, and if you need me, you can ask me, but for the most part, this is about you."

It was my biannual ritual, two weeks after each term, to look for patterns in the grades of the student body. In both semesters of 2012–13, Miami Posse One's average STEM-heavy GPA exceeded that of their class. Not that they always shined, or that they were always upbeat, but they were cutting it academically . . . and making F&M their home. In fact, rather than hurrying back to their beloved Miami for the summer, most decided to stay in Lancaster doing research or mentoring in F&M College Prep.

That year, they grew together like a stand of aspen trees, which share a communal root structure beneath the earth that keeps each individual sapling upright and well-nourished. Three aspects of their collaboration seem most impactful. First, they committed to being *interdependent* toward the goal of graduating together.[15] This meant sharing new know-how on everything from preregistration to how to send a print job from their smartphones. It meant celebrating birthdays and taking the occasional Saturday to go ice skating. It meant keeping a positive attitude, especially if others were dragging, and surfacing issues like adults when necessary. Miami Posse One was a team that had agreed upon and kept to, in Cristina's formulation, "a structure for accountability." Occasionally someone's corny jokes or quips on a Facebook photo would be annoying, but that grew out of their intimacy. So was the joy—delirious screaming during their first snowfall, discovering riches of Lancaster like the Central Market, waxing nostalgic about the *croquetas* and the coastal humidity back home. They were pilgrims on a shared journey they believed in fully.

Second, they also committed to give each other the space and grace to pursue intriguing interests *outside* the Posse, without jeopardizing their standing within it. For example, Maria and Eddie made new friends quickly. Cristina became active in Ware College House. Carolina rowed crew, Natasha tried out the sustainability club, and Nicole played with photography. Some became close with members of the Posse cohorts from New York. Bottom line, no one held back anyone else. "It actually happened organically," Hess told me, and didn't require much negotiation, "because they supported each person's individuality." They formed and fashioned themselves as a team of strivers devoted to helping each other lift off. Go forward, go deeper, find yourself. The cohort was a well-stocked base camp they could come back to for nourishment, not a space colony they had to stay within.

Third, they vowed to be there whenever one of them was fed up or laid flat or brain weary. As Cristina said, "If you had a problem, you knew someone would step up—it didn't matter who, but someone always did." They were great at sharing resources—a friend, a contact in financial aid, or a new way to clear the head, like walking over to the dog park. Each gesture of support made it easier to seek out someone the next time.

I once asked Cristina, "What if someone slipped up? Would there be an intervention?"

"That wasn't how it happened," she replied. "More often we'd just remind each other, 'You are here for a purpose, and you're the only one who can know what it is.'"

For thorny issues, their Posse trainings came in handy. One time the student newspaper ran an insulting op-ed surmising that Posse scholars detracted from F&M's academic caliber. It was an arrogant claim by a guy none of them even knew, but still it hurt. Did others hold the same bias? And why would the student editors even publish such a hit piece?

During their summer sessions, Keely and Jasmine had forecasted that they would likely hear objectionable statements in college. *Attack the idea and not the person* became another program mantra. But what should "attack" or rather "counterattack" even look like with commentary that was aimed at them like a missile? One night they lingered in the dining hall to hash it out. As Natasha later recalled, Cameron, Nicole, and Eddie were the most vocal in saying that the article was "stupid and should be brushed off." Sadly, going forward they would all face such gross ignorance in their careers. After all, there was a reason that people who looked like them were largely left out of STEM. One way to strike back was to go talk head-on with those who harbored such prejudices. Another would be top-notch achievement. They would show anyone who cared to look that Miami Posse One was a badge of honor for F&M and at the same time prove the larger point that lower-income students will excel when given a fair chance. Hess liked where they came out, but he also worried about yet another degree of pressure.

Over the next three years, I witnessed some of the byways and beauties in each student's journey. They all defined themselves in research and in service. They all found faculty mentors and took on mentees. They all relished classes outside of STEM, many in the arts. Junior year, Cameron, Eddie, Marvin, and Amy even spoke at a White House conference on STEM education. And, they all inspired Ken Hess, who didn't do effusive, to tell his colleagues, particularly the skeptics, that Miami Posse One "will change how you think about teaching. They will remind you why you got into this."

As their careers advanced, most took on peer leadership roles with research teams, the College House system, or New Student Orientation. As mentioned earlier, Natasha cofounded the poetry group L.I.F.T. Marvin and his friend Gio Shepard saved a failing rugby fraternity. When the racist Yik Yak posts blew up the campus their junior year, Cameron led I.M.P.A.C.T.'s response, calling on the college to do more to undo discrimination. Whenever one of them stepped up, all of them stood up to chip in or cheer. They had come from the same city. They had begun and branched out, together. They had united in friendship and hope. Each person's efforts were every person's pride.

Consider Cristina. After first year, along with Cameron, she worked in F&M College Prep. She loved how mentoring enabled her to become productively "invested in someone else's life." When the summer ended, she immediately told all her friends that, after graduation, her goal was to direct the program. Sophomore year she became a peer mentor for a cohort of first-years that included Charisma Lambert. She showed adult judgment right away, powered by inbuilt empathy, her Posse-honed collaboration skills, and her conviction that most people can solve their problems with the right support. She loved connecting, listening, intuiting, helping. All good . . . until it was time to decide upon a major late in her second year.

One of F&M's best traditions was an all-class Declaration Dinner to celebrate the sophomores' choice of majors. As the event neared, her anxiety climbed. What was she doing in math and STEM, *really*? The classes were fine, but they lacked the relational ethic that moved her as a mentor. What she was coming to love was Spanish—the language, the literature, the opportunity to study abroad and become truly fluent. And then there was campus life, and all the ways she was growing through relationships, leadership roles, community—which all pointed to Spanish as well. But what would the cohort think if she dropped STEM? And how would she feel? She went to Dean Donnell Butler, who listened carefully before telling her, "You already know what the decision is." Ken Hess also waved off her worries, reiterating his thoughts about the STEM off-ramps and on-ramps. "You do you, Boo," said Amy, channeling the entire posse.

So, Cristina made her choice and then made it work. Taking Spanish courses she liked, and throwing herself into service, she shot up as a school leader. She took a leadership role in the women's group S.I.S.T.E.R.S., helped form a new chapter of the sorority Alpha Xi Delta, and again mentored over the summer in F&M College Prep. She found new faculty mentors, especially Barbara Nimershiem, a warm math professor known for treating all with respect. One of her best decisions was to join the Public Safety Committee. Sometimes she'd don a yellow vest and ride around in a squad car to view her student peers through the eyes of the officers sworn to protect them. In this way, she found her form as the kind of leader who stands in the middle of a foggy bridge and invites the parties on both sides to find each other. "It still took me a while to get over the idea that I had let the posse down because of my major," she told me appreciatively. "But that was my issue. The love and respect everyone consistently showed helped me get over it."

In sum, Miami Posse One teamed up across four rich years to serve each person's freedom and flourishing. Keeping this commitment was an act of integrity and love, and it fostered a mindset of collective care, building to graduation day on May 7, 2016.

Adorned in customized blue stoles reading "Miami STEM Posse 1," they cheered loudly for each other as they strode across the stage. Then they held one last meeting in the science lecture hall where they'd spent and bent so many long hours, this time with their families, friends, teachers, and mentees looking on.

I forget who spoke first—probably Hess—but what I remember was a quiet story or two, some sniffles, and then the tear ducts bursting like geysers as the scholars tried to give voice to feeling. Ten for ten. They had done it. They didn't just survive, they thrived. "We brought change, showed that we belonged, and paved the way for others," Cristina said. So much had transpired in these four cross-layered years, but now it was time to scatter with the winds. Six of them had secured research positions all around the country. Natasha and Tomilya were starting with Teach For America in a matter of days. Cameron would soon be leaving for a year working with youth in South Africa, and Cristina, indeed, had secured her dream job directing F&M College Prep. Four years of college ended that day—but not their posse and their hold on one another. They took that with them. Seven years later, having been part of many successful research and work teams, they still hold spirited check-in calls and have reunions over holidays in Miami. As Cameron told me, "It is a family. We are each other's life partners."

It's tempting to sum up the efficacy of the cohort model by reciting some of the scholars' latest achievements—graduate degrees and formidable jobs, teaching and healing, organizing and discovering. But I don't think that's how Miami Posse One would want it. Their F&M story speaks to their *collective* aspiration and support. Such collaboration sticks to the mind and soul, becoming a way of being, and we who work in higher education would be wise to find more ways to enable it.

"Home is where we start from," T. S. Eliot wrote. Some teams become a home too.

Model Four: The Staff-Led Cocurricular Program

Some of the most impactful learning experiences come through campus programs in which an educator, usually a staff member, directs and drives undergraduate teams in challenging activities like athletics or orchestra or emergency medicine. The rosters evolve year by year, as seniors graduate and new students join, but what endures and gives coherence is a program leader whose values, goals, and actions instill high-level teamwork.

One appealing example is the F&M men's soccer program, led by a practical philosopher of teamwork, head coach Dan Wagner. He's emblematic of an unsung cadre of coaches across intercollegiate athletics, and not only in Division III, who teach team and life through sport. I first sensed from one of his players that Wagner might be special. One day in 2011, when I was new to the college, I was standing in a coffee shop line holding Stephen Ambrose's *Band of Brothers*,[16] which tells the story of F&M's most acclaimed alumnus, World War II infantryman Dick Winters ('41), when a lean young man came up and pointed to the book:

"We're watching *Band of Brothers* right now!"

"Who's 'we?'" I asked, having loved the HBO miniseries.

"Men's soccer. We break it down on the bus after matches."

One of thousands of paratroopers airdropped behind the German defenses on D-Day, Dick Winters became the combat leader of the thirteen-soldier regiment Easy Company. A mystical blend of training, judgment, and character allowed this 1941 economics major to reassemble his unit in the fog of war and then wipe out a group of enemy howitzers that was raining fire on Allied troops coming inland from Utah Beach. That maneuver, called the Brécourt Manor Assault, has become a case study of how an agile unit can defeat a larger force defending a fixed position. Winters continued to show heroic battlefield leadership as the Allied forces fought their way into Germany to defeat the Nazis. In his later years, he praised F&M for giving him the philosophy of doing the best he could in everything he tried.[17]

I now know that it's typical of Coach Dan Wagner to use the Easy Company story as a text for teamwork, as he bases his program on values like selflessness, commitment, accountability, respect, and hard work. For players to stick to these values given the demands of college, and to play winning soccer while also changing and maturing over four years, one thing is paramount to Wagner: They must be reliable teammates. No one succeeds alone.

To Wagner, pledging to the power of *we* is an almost sacred commitment. "Teammates should love each other in that they should consider each other more important than themselves," he wrote in the program's statement of principles. They should speak truth to each other, be patient with each other, work hard for each other, feel joy for each other in times of success—choosing aspiration and optimism even in the face of a crushing defeat or the loss of playing time. "We all need teammates if we're to dare greatly and do good," he believes, drawing upon his Christian faith without saying so directly.

The program consistently makes deep runs into the NCAA tournament, now holding a Centennial Conference record for consecutive bids, but what the students talk about first is their brotherhood. Wagner allows no hierarchies, expecting the seniors to do the mundane tasks like collecting the balls and cones after practice. For Jim Connolly, the coach's genius is that he focuses the players on team goals that require "individuals to realize that it is bigger than themselves." With that, Janse Schermerhorn observed, they aren't defined solely through their sport, as Wagner expects them to share non-soccer experiences, "but still as a group," like learning about Dick Winters or touring the battle-fields at Gettysburg. Sometimes he asks students to lead a team talk on personal themes, like the afternoon I watched Wyatt Fabian and Zach Colton, both of whom had lost a parent before college, speak about resilience. "We invest in each other," Paul McWhirter said in his 2018 end-of-season banquet remarks.[18]

All these values carry over on the pitch. To Robert Maze, referring to the head coach, "Wags gives us the direction for success, knowing that it comes down to our commitment and chemistry," which is why trust among teammates is essential. All must be bought in to their roles, aware of in-game strategy, and ready to pass up a good shot when a teammate has the better one. Wagner prepares them to push the action relentlessly without getting red cards or having run-ins with the referees. He also expects constant communication, saying they should be able to play their positions with their eyes closed. In one of his favorite drills, he connects the members of the defensive unit to each other with eighty-foot-long ropes affixed to their waists—teaching them to know where each other is, sync their steps, and listen to each other. It's a method and a metaphor for what it means to be teammates. We're all connected. No wonder most players wear a rubber bracelet that reads, "I Am Second." Team first.

Robert, who graduated in 2020 and still wears his bracelet, says that dominant ideal he absorbed was servant leadership—the conviction that "teammates serve each other, no matter the circumstance," winning or losing in competition, confiding in each other over a meal, dealing with a problem like someone drinking the night before a match. One Sunday in Robert's last year, the coach asked the seniors to draft a statement of core principles. They spent a few hours writing concepts on a whiteboard, discussing why certain values defined them, and then voted on the ones they thought were best. "We came up with the acronym SCORED," Robert told me. "Selfless, Committed, Ownership, Relentless, Enthusiastic, and Disciplined. We were entrusted with that responsibility to define what we were doing and who we were. And more important than just defining the principles was trying to live them out and embody that as a collective whole, no matter what, adversity or success."

Not that there aren't complications. Some students, like Wyatt or Eric Elicker before him, were individualists needing a bit of space out of season, which Wagner respects. A bigger challenge is when a student doesn't uphold the program's values, on or off the field. While Wagner deals with these incidents directly, he prefers to work through team leadership. He tries to marry very high standards with a spirit of empathy, which means acknowledging that we all fall short sometimes. "Our staff's job is to set the North Star," he says, "but it's all for nothing if the players don't hold each other accountable. The coach-centric, Bobby Knight leadership style does not work with the modern student-athlete."

And then there's playing time. Wagner and the players have an understanding; because they aspire to win, the coach may need to make changes as the season unfolds. Sometimes veterans must accept reduced playing time as newer players improve, which was the case for Janse Schermerhorn. The conference Freshman of the Year in 2014, he dealt with injuries and ended up playing less as a senior. But he made his role crucial, working hardest and cheering loudest from the sidelines. Now he's a stand-out recent graduate of the Uniformed Services University, the nation's military medical school. "I learned from Wags," he told me, that "no matter what your role on the team, you can somehow provide *value*." Says Jim Connolly:

> Our team builds our culture on the theme that joy for one means joy for everyone. Therefore, if you are not playing as much, you can take

joy and excitement in the fact that someone else is getting to play a lot and contributing to the team a lot. It is hard to watch someone play over you, but it's also really cool to see your best friends crush it on the field, which is why building relationships within the team is so important.

Injuries are a constant X factor that, ironically, can strengthen team cohesion. One year, All-American goalie T. J. White suddenly was forced to retire from the sport because of dangerous concussions. When Wagner elevated third-stringer Trevor Britton, a feisty junior who'd played sparingly even in high school, the defense rallied behind him and, together, they set a school record for shutouts. Another year it was midfielder Matt Regueiro and Wyatt Fabian. After season-ending injuries to captains Ben Wild and Jeremy Levine, Wyatt was deputized to captain the team and Matt stepped into the challenging "libero" position that Ben and later Jeremy had played. Despite the adversity, or because of it, the team rallied and won their way to the NCAA Elite Eight. "Next man up" only works if everybody is mentally and physically ready for the call.

F&M soccer shows the value of the program model for instilling and activating the mindset to collaborate. The educator in charge offers a coherent approach to teamwork. The students get the chance to opt in and stay in. Relying upon each other, they forge their friendships and make their memories, passing on the program's values to the next students coming in behind them. This model shows up in many corners of a campus. For example, for more than thirty-seven years, F&M senior director of instrumental music and conducting studies Brian Norcross has joyfully built a "culture of we" among the students in the orchestra and wind ensemble. Anyone can be involved if they stick with it. Likewise, to help students improve as writers, Dan Frick nurtures an assets-oriented culture in the Writing Center, training student tutors to help their peers take pleasure in clarifying and expressing their ideas. Said former tutor Katie Machen:

> The center's tenets are very community-based. So much of the tutoring was about listening to students talk through what they already knew and believed and then repeating their ideas back to them. In this way, we equipped our peers to find structure, connections, and clarity in their writing. We were trained to offer a *reciprocal* presence that extends beyond tutoring sessions and ought to be the basis of any sort of community.

Which brings us back to F&M soccer. One more way that Dan Wagner instills a team culture is by enabling all his players to see the sport they've been playing since they were children through a wider lens, a global perspective. Every three years, he brings the whole program to South Africa to experience the culture of "football" eight thousand miles from home. In 2017, I had the honor of joining them.

The trip combines introductions to South African history and culture with lots of football. Each day offered unforgettable moments, like peering into Nelson Mandela's Robben Island cell or visiting a nature center that protects elephants from poachers. It was most memorable to spend five days in the township of Khayelitsha, near Cape Town, which the owners of apartheid constructed as a ghetto for disenfranchised Blacks in the mid-1980s. It's still impoverished today, and vastly more populated, with 40 percent of its million-plus residents under age nineteen.

Wagner began his efforts in South Africa in 2008 after the shocking death of one of his players, Chris Campbell, during a preseason training run. Chris's passing left his teammates bereft and led the Campbells and Wagner to discuss a living memorial. Ultimately, they decided to support a nongovernmental organization in Khayelitsha working to create a safe place for children to play the sport they and Chris loved. Wagner and the Campbells raised $1 million to construct a synthetic turf field that has become a safe hub in the township. They partnered with the organization AMANDLA, whose mission is to train local adults to teach "fair-play football" and life skills to children, benefiting the mentors and mentees alike.

During the trip, I loved seeing my student-athletes connecting with people in Khayelitsha. One afternoon our students were trained in the tenets of fair-play football by AMANDLA staff, called "PlayMakers." The next day, we competed against a local club in a match that ended with both teams laughing and panting in Wagner's spirited shooting drill, "Chicanery." Another night the students divided up and played for local teams in Khayelitsha's annual crime prevention tournament.

Clearly, this work is a calling for the coach—one that enhances the education of his student-athletes by inviting long thoughts about themselves, the program, and their sport. As Robert Maze (then a freshman) expressed in the team travel blog, the trip provided a "revelation of the meaning behind all the hard work" he'd put into many years of soccer.

One such revelation was that the sport through which they've shaped their identities is, in fact, a kind of global religion. Our students loved seeing South African ten-year-olds dribble through double-teams or happily pound the turf after a teammate's amazing pass. It moved them to witness children's passion for this "dance with the ball" despite all their deprivations. Soccer is a game that dwells in the dreams of the young and the memories of the old. It has so many meanings in so many cultures; Wagner built the program to make sure that every student can absorb and process this reality together. Says Connor Whitacre, who went after his freshman year: "I'll never forget the energy and excitement the kids had when arriving at the field just for the *opportunity* to play that day, as well as the respect with which they treated the game. I think it gave our group a new appreciation for soccer as a unifying tool that really has no barriers."

Another revelation concerned the privileges they'd enjoyed relative to most players around the world. This came out during a team meeting Wagner held near the end of the trip. Zach Colton noted how, at home, as kids start travel soccer, each season's cleats, gear, and uniforms must be paid for, as do league fees, tournaments, travel, meals, summer camps, and manicured fields. Connor offered that he could no longer take for granted "the magnitude of our own opportunities that others would give anything for." The Nigerian student Ugo Ukolie, an All-American, made everyone laugh when he vowed not to complain about aggravations like practicing in the cold. Jim Connolly said that, now seeing himself as a member of a global football culture, he hoped to give more to it in the future, like Coach Wagner. The next year he won a Fulbright scholarship to return to South Africa as a teacher.

The experience also deepened their collective appreciation for the respect and honor with which Africans regard the sport. When they played exhibitions, the matches were physical, with both sides straining, but the tenor was entirely one of good will. No one dropped their heads or barked at the refs. The fans cheered for both sides. After competing, the players would linger for handshakes and hugs, group pictures, and the exchange of jerseys.

To Wagner, the trip also invites the students to experience football as a form of global citizenship rooted in the history of athletes against apartheid. For decades, a totalitarian system of racial classification had made it illegal and taboo for Black and white athletes to do something as human as testing their mettle on a pitch. In this way, apartheid flouted the core values of sport—equality, integrity, teamwork, the best playing the best—values that eventually led most of the world's athletic communities to ban South Africa from the Olympic Games and other international competitions. Perhaps this history explains the warmth with which South Africans now welcome teams from around the world.

"Sport has the power to change the world," said Nelson Mandela. "It has the power to inspire. It has the power to unite people in a way that little else does."[19] Each generation has the chance to inherit and extend sport's noblest values. Leaders like Coach Wagner show us the way—and teach that team sports can open windows and build bridges, extending the concept of "team" well beyond the roster. Hence the motto of the program, which Wagner borrowed from Spanish football club Barcelona FC: *Mes que un club*. More than a club.

As the team boarded the plane in Johannesburg to come home, it was evident that they had gained both a wider aperture on the world and a tighter bond as teammates. What more could they do and be, together? For the first part of the flight, the chatter was about competing for a national championship in the fall. They had the talent, the team, and the fire.

That didn't happen—but something just as meaningful did.

Which was that, as a team, they grew their grit in the face of adversity. Before the 2017 season began, three starters suffered season-ending injuries, including star forward Ugo Ukolie, starting midfielder Alex Bilodeau, and Robert Maze, who'd been a first-year sensation. Then they started losing—three of their first six contests. It felt disorienting to come up short, but they hung together. With their expected sets and strategies disrupted, Wagner had to push players into new roles and ask even more of seniors Wyatt Fabian and Jason Tonelli. But teams don't reinvent themselves overnight. After ten matches, their record was 4-5-1, meaning they'd need to run the table in the last six matches just to make the conference tournament—very long odds.

"It wasn't the start we were used to," Connor Whitacre said later, "but I don't recall there being any shred of doubt" that the team could win out. Down so many key players, the team showed intense poise, especially on defense, and went unbeaten those last six matches to squeak into the tourney. Wyatt anchored the defense with athleticism and intelligence, allowing Wagner to focus on building a new offensive scheme around Stephen Sherbahn and Jason Tonelli, who could rifle the ball from toe to net like a marksman. Said Connor:

> We leaned on the camaraderie we had built up until that point, and trusted one another, knowing that any of our thirty guys could step on the field and play as good as, if not better, than the guy before him. Dealing with injuries and subsequent adjustments throughout the year was tough, but whenever the opportunity was presented to the next man up, we rallied around his success. The belief and dynamic carried huge momentum and only takes place with strong relationships on the team.

In the championship tourney, they won two 1-0 marathons to claim the crown, edging Gettysburg in the semis as Connor shut down one of the top scorers in the country. I was there for the title match and watched the team push mind, muscle, and heart in foul weather to hold off Dickinson after Colton blew a penalty kick past a goalie who'd unwisely dared him to put the ball in the net. That year, winning turned out to be testament to the mindset for teamwork.

In college sport, few teams end the season with championship hardware. This one did, although it wasn't the national title they'd hoped for. Their glory was found elsewhere, in honoring their values and holding close as teammates when their loftiest competitive dreams got derailed. I remember watching families snapping photos on the rain-soaked field right after the conference title match—about six months after the South Africa trip. Everybody was drenched. Some were filthy and bone tired. Others hadn't gotten off the sidelines that day. Still others like Ugo and Robert wore street clothes and leaned on crutches. Their arms were all draped around each other and their grateful and gratified head coach, Dan Wagner.

More than a club.

*

So far, we have examined the models of the all-student organization, the shared governance committee, the cohort group, and the staff-led, cocurricular program. When they are successful, such teams create layers and levels of value for one and all. The most potent takeaway of teamwork is that in collaboration we can do, make, want, share, be, and become so much more. Teams transform us. They elevate our imagination. They teach us to transcend ourselves.

However, in some situations, the collective can be stultifying, demoralizing, isolating, or simply a waste of time. Perhaps every unhappy team is unhappy in its own way—but still there are ways to make sure students have growth experiences and not bad ones. Here's two that stand out.

First, through training sessions and cross-group learning, colleges should try to instill the attitudes and practices of A+ teamwork. For example, student clubs should write mission and goals statements and have outside moderators. Cohort groups should formally evaluate their strengths and weakness. Faculty and staff should be able to learn more about methods to facilitate effective teamwork. Student portfolios, which are being utilized by more institutions, should include categories related to collaboration and teamwork.

Some of the more promising innovations I've seen have been in response to the risks of insularity among student groups. At F&M, we created the Harwood Seminar to bring together athletics captains and other club leaders to learn together about team building. We also held a Day of Dialogue that enabled diverse student leaders to converse in each other's spaces (think: the football team invited to the women's center, or S.I.S.T.E.R.S. visiting a fraternity) to learn firsthand what each other values and how they are perceived. At Georgetown, President Jack DeGioia came up with the masterstroke of hiring the clinical social worker Mary Dluhy to work with student/educator teams trying to develop new approaches to highly charged issues like inequity or sexual misconduct.

Second, there is always the danger that the power dynamics in a team will become unhealthy or that teams will close ranks if a member breaks a rule. To prevent or address both problems, a few things are essential. One is clear rules and expectations for conduct, so that students know that participation in a sport, Greek organization, club, or student government is a privilege and not a right, contingent on their adhering to community standards. A second is involving student leaders in the process of setting or implementing those standards, as we saw with the New College House constitution committee. A third is reassuring students that the systems for adjudicating misconduct will be consistent and fair. And a fourth is ensuring that the educators who lead programs commit to those standards and expect their teams uphold them, as, for example, coach Dan Wagner does as a matter of course and character.

Model Five: The Seminar

There's one more model for teamwork that is found on every campus—perhaps the most powerful of all for activating the mindset to collaborate—*the classes themselves*. At F&M, I liked watching professors like Rick Moog blend seminar participants into powerhouse teams, using myriad methodologies such as group projects, collective problem-solving, breakout discussions, role-playing, and more.[20] Here, students learn that intellectual practices like forming hypotheses, surfacing counterarguments, and making informed predictions can, in fact, be done collaboratively in the pursuit of a collective work product. Yes, some group projects will fall flat, when, for example, they fail to align with stated course objectives or include students equitably. But when team-based pedagogies succeed, they prepare students for professional life, where teams typically take on the most ambitious and rewarding tasks, and most promotions involve more collaboration, not less.

Take, for example, a course that dance professor Jennifer Conley created based on her reconstruction of the 1934 Martha Graham piece, *Celebration*. As a feat of collaboration, the twelve-person recital reminded me of a trapeze act, requiring focus, stamina, kinesthetic awareness, and communication. It began with the dancers standing silently in a tight, outward-facing circle. Then, they jumped up and down in unison for forty-five seconds, transforming the floor into a beating drum. Next came four minutes of choreographed urgency, bodies firing in every direction—leaping, spiraling, surging, crisscrossing—a fierce display of power and trust, for one misstep could sprawl the bodies like bowling pins. The closing section brought them back to the circle formation, but this time they faced inward to lock eyes and share the moment. The finale included two long phases of grueling jumps moving inward and outward from the circle. As the lights dimmed, the dancers' breathing became audibly and inevitably synced, twelve as one, fused through performance. Years later, I asked 2016 graduate Emily Hawk about Conley's class:

> Before *Celebration*, I thought of dancing as a primarily physical endeavor: You train, you rehearse the choreography, and you can trust that your muscle memory will take over onstage. And it is true that *Celebration* was one of the most physically demanding experiences of my life. But under Prof. Conley's supervision, the experience was a combination of physical endurance and intellectual discovery. She encouraged us to *think* about what we were doing, both in rehearsal and during the instance of performance itself.
>
> For me, it was an exercise in vulnerability, especially as a first-semester student who didn't know any of the others beforehand. I had to learn to trust my castmates socially as well as physically. This process happened quickly, since we rehearsed in four-hour intensives each week and saw each other *a lot*. Rehearsals were often followed by cast meals at the dining hall or hangouts in the college center. The upper-class students in the cast soon became some of my dearest friends and most cherished peer mentors. I felt a duty to pay this mentorship forward when I became a veteran in the company.

Learning and practicing *Celebration*, element by element, gave the students the chance to reenact a supremely challenging piece that no dance team had attempted in decades. To achieve their potential, Conley believed the students needed a communal understanding of Martha Graham's artistic significance and the context in which she choreographed it. The dance had to make sense to them and have meaning. So, using archival video footage, she enabled her class to see both the full cast and the dancers in their individual roles. She also brought in images of the 1930s Manhattan skyline, so they could link the geometry of the architecture to the sharp lines and angles in the choreography. Emily later told me,

> Our costumes came from the Graham studios, and even had the names of previous Graham company dancers pinned in the collars. In this way, the process of staging *Celebration* not only required us to collaborate as castmates, but to collaborate with the legacy of Graham herself and with the dancers who had performed this piece before. It was a profound experience for me to enter into the embodied memory of the piece, and an experience that sparked my interdisciplinary interest in becoming a dance historian.

In the fall dance recital, the team brought down the house—but the professor had one more goal for her class. After the semester, she kept them rehearsing for two months so they could perform together one final time—in a multi-university showcase hosted by the Martha Graham Dance Company in New York City's fabled Joyce Theater.

Before this class, none of the students had ever performed in a Graham reconstruction—and now their mastery of *Celebration* would be evaluated by professionals and critics. Entering the theater, wrote Bianca Santos in her class blog, "it felt intimidating" to see all the full-time dancers with their pricy leotards and immaculate hair buns. But the F&M students knew how hard they had practiced and so, Santos said, when the heavy red curtain rose, they put aside the butterflies and let loose. "We never jumped so high as we did that day, and we never felt stronger," she noted, describing a collective peak experience. "We executed the piece to perfection and with conviction. I'll never forget how proud I was of our growth when we took a bow—and I was so grateful that Professor Conley was there to guide us on our journey."[21]

In these exhilarating moments, when a team's efforts and outcomes merge into meaning, we create memories for a lifetime. This is the power of we—students following an educator who believes they can soar together and helps them to do so. It gives learning a double dose of meaning—personal and collective—enabling students to fuse feelings with identity to make a mindset that will last long after the project winds down.

Another example is Susan Dicklitch-Nelson's class Human Rights, Human Wrongs, through which students help detained immigrants apply for political asylum in the United States. Their collective job is to develop human rights country reports to be submitted in court. This requires them to learn quickly about, say, the persecution of Coptic Christians in Egypt or LGBTQ people in Uganda, and then to put together a report that will be credible to a judge.

I remember when my mentee Akbar Hossain was taking the class. Their client was a Sudanese man named Aadam, who had been tortured in Darfur and was awaiting a hearing in the York County Prison. As a central part of his claim, the students developed a 376-page report on human rights in Darfur. The need to do this job exceptionally well became very real. Being deported would likely mean more torture, more trauma, even death . . . of a man they now knew personally. The class was in court when the judge issued his ruling. "WE WON!" Akbar screamed into the phone right after the decision. From the din behind his breathless summary, I heard the F&M team cheering and chanting like they'd won the Super Bowl. Akbar later called this "the most empowering moment of my life."[22]

When a class collaborates and coheres, the students feel like they've embarked on a quest. It's a mission, a galvanizing idea—to construct an answer, to make a report, to apply an insight. The binding agent is their united pursuit of a brass ring no solo striver can grasp alone. It's as if the class is the hero of a story, banding together to take on an imposing adversary—a wrong that needs righting, a question that needs answering, a dance that needs doing. It's a battle of forces—the seminar against the problem, with thirteen weeks to get the win. As the professor steers them, and students help each other, and relationships form, the class takes on a personality.

In fact, this fusion can happen whenever students work together in pursuit of a noble goal. Think of the collaborations described here: Accomplishing college together. Drafting a constitution. Testing teamwork in sport. Becoming life partners as a posse. Reconstructing a fierce dance. Saving a refugee's life. Building the muscle and the mindset for such teamwork—also called citizenship—is needed not just for a pluralistic campus but also for a pluralistic democracy. Says the historian Carol Quillen, who led Davidson College for eleven years:

> What we're trying to do in higher ed is prepare students for a world that we cannot predict, and that really means helping them deploy multiple analytical frameworks on a single problem, reframe a question that's given to them when the question that's given to them doesn't lead anywhere, speak intelligently and persuasively across multiple audiences, and learn to live with people who are really different from them—which is really the best argument for the kind of residential education that we offer. We bring together people who are really different, and they live together and figure out how to manage their collective lives.
>
> You learn [in college] how to be a fully participating citizen in a free society whose institutions rely on citizen participation to exist

and to be sustained. . . . If we don't acknowledge that we can help people learn how to do that without indoctrinating them or telling them what to think, then I don't see how these fragile democratic institutions that structure our public life survive.[23]

Shared goals and effort lead to shared achievement, growth, and meaning, all reinforcing a mindset for collaboration. There is so much hope and aspiration among the young. When they direct themselves *together* toward common purpose, they can achieve even more and feel more connected. The teams, team cultures, and team models of college evoke that feeling repeatedly across a four-year education.

And then the dance is done, the semester ends, or the clock runs out on a season. There's always still more to learn or ask or do. If only there could be just one more week, one more meeting, one more discussion. . . . But, inevitably, in class, and in life, all teams will run their course.

When the seminars disband, or the teams wrap up—with more to do, more to say—our hope as teachers is that wherever life takes them, our students will seek out their next edifying collaborations as a matter of mindset, knowing they're good at it and hungry for it, because they have touched and been touched by the power of we.

Chapter 4: Questions for Discussion

1. How do you understand the mindset for collaboration? Why does the author believe that this mindset is a powerful resource during and after college?

2. The author asserts that campuses are collaborative cultures, with students working on myriad teams every day. Is this a valuable feature of college life? How does it help students to grow?

3. The chapter presents five different models of collaboration and teamwork: the all-student organization, the shared governance committee, the cohort group, the staff-led cocurricular program, and the seminar. Are there other important models?

4. One story concerns a team of students charged with drafting the constitution of the College House where they and about 200 students would live. It may not be the norm to give students such a large role in campus governance. What are the benefits of doing so, and are you familiar with other successful examples?

5. The chapter argues that seminars can become memorable experiences of team learning and achievement. Do you agree? What needs to go right for this to happen? What can go wrong?

6. This chapter provides a highly positive account of collaboration and holistic learning in a Division III soccer program. Is this example too exceptional for replication elsewhere? Why or why not?

7. What can be done to help undergraduates improve their collaboration skills and avoid dysfunctional behavior, particularly in student-led clubs and organizations?

5

THE MINDSET FOR
STRIVING

Sometimes we give up something we love because there is
more we are called to be.

—CAROLINA GIRALDO

SOME UNDERGRADUATES CLAIM THEIR EDUCATION with a passion
for possibility. They form and chase goals. They seek out resources.
They apply themselves fully. They savor their experiences while
looking ahead. Critically, the growth they go for stems from their
values, whether enduring or emerging. Their learning matters to
them, deep down, as a part of who they are . . . and may become.

"My goals are my life force," the marvelous Miami Posse One
student Carolina Giraldo once shared. "It's what I'm here for. Even
if I hadn't become so focused on medical school, I know I would
have felt this way about something. It's who I am."

These are the undergraduates who don't waste a day. They
reach for reaching's sake and value expeditions into the unknown.

Hungry for what they haven't tasted, they anticipate learning and then act on aspiration. When they get frustrated or fall short, or hit a brick wall, they can self-correct and recharge, drawing energy from their values and their willpower. Carol Dweck would love them. They don't simply acquire education; they chase after it, they create it, they live it. That's their mindset—they're strivers.

Because such students forge forward as acts of selfhood, some may regard striving as a natural trait, like eye color, that's made and not molded. But that can't be right. Upbringing and experience surely shape the mindset to strive. For Carolina, while it may feel to her like a "life force," in fact, striving grows from her *life experience* and values, and thus is not an inbuilt essence but rather an acquired and malleable element of her identity. It can be activated.

On every campus, it's important to look for, and draw others' eyes toward, the strivers who make self-challenge their choice. At F&M, one was Dominic Akena, a film major from Uganda who lived for life after having survived abduction by Joseph Kony and the Lord's Resistance Army as a child.[1] A second was the swimmer Becca Meyers, born with Usher syndrome (which causes deafness and the loss of vision), who persisted for seven years to earn her BA in history while also winning gold medals and setting records in two Paralympic Games—before standing up as a public advocate for all disabled athletes by withdrawing from the Tokyo 2020 Games because the US Olympic Committee assigned only one trained personal care assistant for a team of more than thirty competitors.[2] Another was Kelseyleigh Reber Hepler, who conducted increasingly complex turtle and dolphin research in Central America and Australia during summers while also publishing two teen reader novels and serving as head tutor in the Writing Center. One more was Jonny Teklit, a creative writing and psychology major who, mentored by Professor Meg Day, won the Academy of American Poets Most Promising Young Poet Prize for his "Black Mythology" sonnet that blended the flight from slavery with the story of Icarus.[3] Yes, these are impressive achievements, but more important is the force and fire with which these restless souls acted on opportunity and drove the kind of growth that they envisioned and valued for themselves. That talent for striving will be their engine across the decades and doings of adult life—and an example for other students during their college years.

To be sure, the journey into striving overlaps with the growth mindsets for discovery, creativity, mentoring, and collaboration. It can be powered by any value that a person holds dear, like community, family, self-reliance, wellness, spirituality, or social justice. Sometimes, however, undergraduates strive *not from formed values, but into more fluid ones.* Called by the unmarked road, many undergraduates do not strive from fully held values or toward highly defined goals—and yet they throw themselves headlong into everything they try. They may have only inklings of their future adult identities or commitments. In fact, that's the point; they're ready and able in college to act on those intimations without putting down a pin on precisely what they expect to find. All of which is to say, strivers challenge themselves for growth that stems from what they do value now or may value after their exertions. They're guided by an anticipatory inner voice as they push themselves into possibility.

Activating strivers is critical for higher education and for America. Why? First, an old and eminent answer: Because education should draw out and develop the talents of human beings so that we can flourish across our lifetimes. This notion of education entails, as the saying goes, not the filling of a pail but the lighting of a fire for lifelong growth.

But there's a newer answer, too, given our time's vertiginous developments in technology, information systems, the economy, research capabilities, demography, politics, climate, and more. Our quickening society requires leaders in every field and sphere who can learn fast and learn often, who can handle disruption and sometimes push it, who can draw throughlines from ethics to action, and who can embrace sharp swings in how, where, and with whom they work—not simply because they have to, but because they *like* doing so and they can, and they are motivated by their values. In other words, America needs strivers.

For this type, campuses provide good soil, given the array of stimulating people, prompts, ideas, and opportunities. While striving is inherently self-led, educators can feed and foster this mindset if we get what makes strivers tick. This chapter explores four points that are especially helpful:

1. The roots of striving can take hold before college begins;

2. The mindset for striving often emerges from a winding path of new pursuits;

3. When hardship hits, strivers often tap their values to get back on track; and

4. The mindset to strive integrates action and reflection.

Point One: The Roots of Striving Can Take Hold before College Begins

Witness Carolina Giraldo, who is now finishing her medical degree at the Philadelphia College of Osteopathic Medicine. To appreciate how college supported her striving, it helps to know something about the influences that seeded her mindset at an early age, back when she was a child in Colombia.

In the early 1990s, Carolina's parents were part of a rising class of university-educated professionals. They both overcame real obstacles to get there. Her mother, Patricia, had been born into comfort but, after her mother died, she was sent to relatives who raised her as a second-class person. Her father, Luis, came from a poor farming community with a father who toiled and saved so that his children could excel in school and create better lives. Also, Luis grew up suffering from a painful biliary tract condition that required many surgeries and taught him to savor every day of life.

Luis and Patricia met and fell in love as students at the Universidad EAFIT in Medellín. After graduation, both secured good jobs in the city—Patricia as an accountant and Luis as an executive in a company that made airplane parts. They brought Carolina into the world in 1994 and their son, Luis Felipe, four years later. Although they had love, little ones, and promising careers, the Giraldos began to accept, with dread and then panic, that their children's lives could be stunted or stolen due to Colombia's worsening civil conflict involving paramilitary forces, guerrillas, and drug cartels. The late 1990s brought increases in terrorist bombings and assassinations. Even today, Carolina recalls the staccato echoes of gunfire from a nearby park. Rebels and criminals started kidnapping the children of professionals for ransom. In response, her elementary school added armed soldiers, barricades, car inspections, and bomb sweeps.

No surprise, at the age of six, Carolina started suffering from anxiety attacks about being abducted. With such violations and violence, the impunity of terror, Luis and Patricia began to consider uprooting their family. They faced a cruel irony; the economic independence they'd worked so hard to secure was just an illusion, as they could not ensure safety for their children. Leaving Colombia would be wrenching, with no guarantees, but staying would be denial. If something happened to Carolina or Luis Felipe, how could they live with themselves?

Thus, they made the fateful, child-centered choice that has defined migrant families for millennia. The Giraldos walked away
from all they had known—their homes and pasts, their jobs and
relatives, their identities and the ladders to professional advancement they'd constructed. They set their eyes upon America, the
nation of immigrants, settling in Miami. Patricia gave up her oc-
cupation, and Luis secured a job with an aviation company, and
with that came citizenship, so that their precious children, the
core of their lives, could grow up safe and free.

Crossing worlds created daily aftershocks, beginning with the
good-byes to friends and loved ones, some of whom opposed this
move. They had to accept uncertainty and live torments of the
spirit while trying to navigate an unfamiliar land. They traded
fear for loss and home for hope—a quintessentially American
choice requiring them to start all over, four fused as one, aware
that initially they would not be seen or counted or cared for.

To carve out new lives, the Giraldos had to rely upon each other,
giving Carolina empathy and adult eyes at an early age. She grew
up absorbing her parents' strains and sacrifices. Her mom would
tear up in front of her, lamenting the evaporation of her career,
afraid of losing her soul if they stayed and of losing their lives if
they went back. Sometimes they were forced to choose between
food and health care. They knew they could not rely on a benevolent society or a larger guiding hand. What they had was their
one blessed gift: family. The parents' main job was to protect the
children's future . . . and the children's was to get an education.

Because learning was life, Patricia would tell Carolina that she
needed to take responsibility for her achievements—a scary message for an unsheltered child who knew they had no safety net.
"When it comes to my goals and dreams, my parents brought me
up to work hard. They taught me that you are the one who benefits

the most from your accomplishments," she explained. "That's a lot of responsibility for a child—but I knew that's what I had to think. Nothing would be given to me except the love, support, and examples of my family. The rest would be on me. That started the development of my *grit*."

That concept, grit, which Angela Duckworth defines as the combination of passion and persistence in the pursuit of goals, is typically a rich resource for strivers.[4] Some young people who have defied the odds see it as their superpower. That said, grit and striving are not synonymous, because specified goals are essential to Duckworth's notion of grit, but not necessarily for striving. Some strivers have formed defined goals, but many do not . . . yet. Indeed, as Agnes Callard argues in her philosophical study of aspiration, the hunger for experience may well precede and promote goal setting rather than resulting from it.[5]

Clearly, Carolina's upbringing (the disruptions and difficulties she faced, and the determination she learned in response) put her on a course to value giving her all to learning. She excelled at MAST Academy, a renowned science and technology magnet school, leading to her selection for F&M's Miami Posse One cohort. I first met her with the other Posse members at the welcome luncheon in January of her senior year. Familial pride ran through the room like sound waves. It was memorable. After the Posse cohort posed for a photo with their future mentor Ken Hess, Carolina walked her parents over to me and placed my hand in hers.

"President Porterfield, I want to tell you something. Franklin & Marshall is giving me an incredible opportunity, and I'm going to work very hard. I just want to tell you that I'm not going to let you down."

Her mother and father nodded approvingly, as did Luis Felipe (then an eighth grader who would earn his place with Posse and

F&M four years later). The Giraldos were all-in on Carolina's education. With respect, I tried to loosen the clamp of expectation:

"Carolina, you earned this scholarship. This education is yours to create. No one will judge you. Make it your own, and F&M will always support your choices."

"Oh, don't worry," she said with a blinding smile as Patricia and Luis looked on. *"I'm going to make every single day count."*

Carolina's story speaks to an important if sometimes overlooked fact, which is that many students start college cherishing deep beliefs, values, habits, life lessons, and role models that will fuel their striving in and after their undergraduate years. *This is a potent form of talent that colleges can draw out if we get to know the assets in our students' lives.* Aicha Camara came to college with it, as did Keiran Miller and Brandon Stevens and many others profiled here. Too often institutions fail to appreciate that many of their students, especially those from modest or distressed backgrounds, have cut through brambles and scaled steep cliffs on their journeys to make something of themselves, and so they bring to the college opportunity deep strengths of character inculcated by their climb. As we'll soon see, Carolina's lifelong commitment to striving was a flexible resource that she often tapped and her professors often fed. It was forged in the crucible of her early life, and she carried it proudly to Lancaster, for self-discovery and self-fashioning. F&M's role was to activate it.

Point Two: The Mindset for Striving Often Emerges from a Winding Path of New Pursuits

Allie Morey is a 2015 F&M graduate from suburban Boston who was recruited by field hockey coach Missy Mariano to play goalie.

Her story shows how striving can be a unifying theme across the twists and turns of one's college education; although her drive never wavered, she changed directions a few times precisely because of her abiding quest for meaning.

A "passionate serving kind,"[6] Allie constantly aspired to help others. Her first year, she was immediately drawn to Mariano's holistic approach of valuing cooperation, respect, and integrity in all aspects of college life. Like Dan Wagner in men's soccer, Mariano was a decorated college athlete who became a championship coach and an even better educator. During Allie's first two years, when she desperately wanted to contribute on the field but rarely got to play, Mariano's emphasis on character helped her appreciate being a dedicated teammate in practice and campus life.

Sophomore year, wondering if teaching might be her calling, Allie commuted to nearby Millersville University for education classes not offered by F&M. Yes, it was a chore to find the courses and manage the logistics, but her real problem was feeling like an outsider at that relatively larger university. She applied herself but knew that Millersville wasn't scratching her itch to grow as a leader who helps and serves others. How could she find what she desired? The answer was to get much more heavily involved on her own campus beyond athletics.

One avenue for that was the social scene, which she thought about often. Sometimes when friends reveled together, it felt almost timeless, as if the party were really about something loftier like love or youth or community. Of course, with alcohol in the mix, there was always some risk of harm too. Drinking didn't bother her, but its dangers did. And, having been exposed to alcoholism as a teenager, she knew that prevention aches a lot less than healing.

Allie understood that alcohol abuse was a problem on every campus, with the risks worsened by the fact that colleges either had to crack down on underage use or close their eyes, neither of which was helpful. Given these realities, Allie felt, there was only so much the administration could do by itself—but students could take more responsibility for everyone's well-being with common-sense actions like cutting down on pregaming or calling campus Public Safety for escorts at the end of a night.

A second-semester sophomore, she aspired to tie together her values and actions in the service of a worthy cause, so she joined the student club ".08," which promoted safer socializing with or without alcohol. The group had formed a few years before after a highly regarded recent alumnus died of alcohol poisoning. The club was proudly pragmatic—cooperative with the administration but also independent.

It felt right to devote herself to strengthening the wonderfully *protective* aspects of student culture, drawing upon values like friendship and teamwork that she also embraced in field hockey. Enjoying ".08" and the nuanced thinking needed to make a difference, she quickly earned an invitation to join the club's executive board, which brought her into more conversations about how to promote safety and de-risk parties. What more could she do, she asked herself late in sophomore year. One friend suggested she run for president of ".08," while another pushed her to try to lead a new sorority, Alpha Delta Pi. Why not both? She wanted more from college life. It was exhilarating to imagine how she might use these platforms for good and be the kind of leader that others can look to. As the school year came to an end, she won both elections.

Back home in Boston for the summer, however, the thrill of being chosen began to wear off as she tried to imagine meeting all these new responsibilities in the fall with field hockey in season. Something had to give—and it couldn't be ".08" or ADPi. It was time for a big change. The field hockey team didn't really need her, she reasoned, since their all-conference goalie would be back in the net as a senior. So, in August she went to Coach Mariano and her assistant, Kaitlyn Eager, both of whom she idolized, and tearfully shared her decision to leave the program.

It's not easy for a coach to lose a recruited athlete, because the gap can't be filled for at least a year, but Mariano gave Allie her blessing. Her teammates did too. If the ideal of the scholar-athlete is to mean anything, programs must allow the young to grow and change, perhaps applying lessons from a game they love in the new callings that an education brings to the fore.

Junior year, she sacrificed downtime, sleep, and studies to help make F&M's nightlife more safe and no less fun. She formed partnerships with clubs and Greek groups to de-center drinking at their gatherings. She worked with Public Safety to make the shuttle service more attractive to students leaving events or even bars. It was practical leadership toward a principled goal. One wintry night I rode along as she delivered free pizza and water to parties where students were being students. During the run, we came upon a group of her former teammates celebrating a win. It must have stung, but all she revealed was levelheaded poise.

Her sorority had an excellent year, too, growing its membership. She spoke about sexual assault at the annual Take Back the Night march and talked up bystander intervention as a workable practice. She also helped coach a local high school field hockey team because she could not entirely let go of her sport.

Within her friend group, her new visibility on campus required finesse. "There's always a danger of coming off preachy," she told me. "I often felt I was threading the needle between being a trusted friend and becoming an untrustworthy pseudo-administrator"—a liminal balancing act that is part of the luggage of leadership.

At the end of the year, she went home for the summer happily depleted, with a well-earned sense of accomplishment. She'd devoted hundreds of hours to the campus—from meetings to fundraisers to planning to presentations. She'd learned tons about getting things done through "backstage F&M." People throughout the campus knew her name. She couldn't possibly have given or grown more.

However, as she began with her planner's mind to formulate hopes and goals for senior year, a sublimated idea caught her by surprise, which was that she missed the intimacy and belonging of the field hockey program. True, her former teammates were still her best friends, but she yearned for the special ties of sweat and purpose. She longed for the culture Coach Mariano instilled, the discipline to do things the right way—and the intangible moments, the fun and love of it all. All these values she'd put aside were still alive. She realized that she still prized going after greatness with these friends and began to imagine being part of a memorable final season, together. That's striving.

Expecting to hear "no," Allie brought her hopes to Mariano. The coach knew it would be dicey to bring back a senior who'd left the program and thus had never played with half the roster. But she believed that Allie was sincere, and so she gave her the chance to regain her spot—if she could earn it in the team's sweltering late-summer practices.

Allie brought the same work ethic she'd shown in ".08" and her sorority, but, physically, getting back into playing shape was quite the test. She needed to reboot her reflexes for the challenge of thrusting a foot or a forearm in the path of stick-flicked projectiles. Spiritually, it was worth the misery "to put the field hockey program back in my life, to experience the team again, to *contribute*."

Which she more than did. Winning the starting position, she played full seventy-minute matches for the first time since high school. That season the team went 18–3 and recorded twelve shutouts, including five in a row in one supreme stretch. She loved those moments of transcendence—the shrewd pass, the painful save, the drama of sticks bashing desperately as the ball bats among them. It felt amazing to be counted on, to play well, to have fun, and to win.

Like most fine seasons, this one did not finish in storybook fashion, but F&M played to its promise, earning an at-large bid to the NCAA tournament. The only squad to defeat them was conference rival Ursinus College. While the gap narrowed with each match, the Bears earned their three victories over the Diplomats, and so, that year, they were better. After the season ended with a tight loss in the NCAA tournament, Allie lugged her gear to the bus and settled in for the seven-hour drive to Lancaster. She felt grateful and gratified, having reset the relationships she'd yearned for:

> I knew in my heart that I wanted to play for Coach Mariano and with these women. I had to push myself as a campus leader my junior year, and having done that, I most deeply wanted to come back to the team. I wanted to belong. Of course, I was disappointed that we lost, but most seasons end with a loss. Doing my personal best as a member of the team that achieved a great deal is something I'll never lose.

"There are no moral victories in sport," some fans say after a loss. In fact, that's incorrect. Any endeavor to which we devote ourselves gives us the chance to grow. In college sports, defeat is not death but the chance to take stock and make meaning. For Allie, the striver, it was a season in which she acted on what she "most deeply wanted," which was "to come back to the team [and] . . . belong"—after having also acted on what she most deeply valued the year before, which was to be a campus leader. Allie Morey was no dilettante; each pursuit arose from her heart, and she pursued them all with full force. Her experience shows that striving is an adaptive process, difficult to plan linearly because the passion with which strivers stretch themselves creates the lessons and longings that will guide their next values-oriented pursuits.

By understanding this, Coach Missy Mariano showed her excellence as an educator. She cared to, and was able to, adopt the lens through which Allie valued her one and only college education. Because of her empathy, Mariano could let a recruited athlete leave her program without giving her a guilt trip and later allow her to earn her way back into the fold. In college, strivers will be the ones who explore unfamiliar activities, who sample untried fields, who change majors, who join new friend groups, who undertake everything with elan. Their turns and pivots are always aspirational, and we should encourage them. As Gwendolyn Brooks once wrote about her rambunctious, striving little boy, "his lesions are legion. / But reaching is his rule."[7]

Point Three: When Hardship Hits, Strivers Often Tap Their Values to Get Back on Track

As educators, we may hope that every student can go for growth without heartache, but as we saw with Julia Ramsey, often life has other plans. Let's see how two high achievers, Nadia Johnson and Jeanette Berlanga, retuned their striver's mindsets midway through college as soul-serving responses to crises that could have derailed their educations but instead enhanced them.

Nadia grew up in a low-income community in New Haven, Connecticut. Even with a good college prep curriculum at Achievement First Amistad High School and a supportive first-year cohort group at F&M, her onboarding was brutal: crushing first classes, cultural isolation, and constant fretting about money and her mother's needs back home. Initially, she was turned down for club activities that had been strengths in high school, like mentoring and singing a cappella, which she couldn't help but take personally, because (as I knew) she was excellent at both.

Looking back, she ached to recall the top student she used to be—one of the stars, a person of promise, pursued by many colleges. In a few short months, her identity had been swept away like dust. How could that be? At Amistad, she'd beaten the odds by outrunning the pack. Back home she was loud and proud, a bit edgy, but at F&M she'd lost her swagger. Feeling adrift in some classes, and always alone, she first tried buckling down, withdrawing, studying longer hours, and clamping down on any hint of self-pity. That just led to depression.

She felt like a failure—always anxious, always behind—and she sensed it wasn't helping to carry herself as untouchable Nadia. She saw the need to be more flexible and strategic in the pursuit of her education, like the way some back home in New Haven's Black community achieved their goals. This meant she needed to humble herself just a little to ask for help. Instead of nursing her pride, she sought assistance with study skills. She began showing vulnerability with trusted friends, sharing childhood stories. The summer after sophomore year, she chose to stay in Lancaster, which was uncomfortable, and work for the belonging that she craved in a place that she didn't fully understand. This is what strivers do—as Callard might say, they aspire to gain a value by actively learning it.[8]

In time, that's exactly what happened. She saw anew some of the good things that college could offer. "I saw that this was my chance to tap into learning for learning's sake," she told me. "I started going to lectures that weren't required—and not just for the food! I would go to them and walk away with something else."

Belonging wouldn't just be about making friends, or feeling that F&M wanted her, but it also would come from actively aligning her emergent self-propelled purposes with the school's educational mission. Nadia was developing her "agency," which the scholar Anindya Kundu refers to as one's class consciousness, awareness of social constructs, and readiness to think critically about one's position in society.[9] She was embracing her agency as a means of growth.

From there, Nadia began delving into sociology and gender studies, which shed light on intriguing concepts like double consciousness, white privilege, and body shaming. Rigorous study with Katherine McClelland and Ashley Rondini showed her that an F&M education could provide a foundation of both knowledge and intellectual procedure upon which any student could build. "Learning here is all about the next step," she said. "I learned that through the literature review in Sociology: You have to know what came before so you can find out what you are going to add." Now she was studying real-world topics that mattered to her while creating the toolkit for more advanced work—*and she knew it.*

Junior year, Nadia took the risk of re-applying for a cappella and youth mentoring—and this time she was chosen for both. She also helped lead the campus conversation about racism and white self-segregation, building on the protests over Yik Yak. More than once in town hall meetings she invited peers of all identities to be brave and go beyond their social circles. Using her voice, she grew her voice. As a senior, she became a mainstay on the Dean's List, sang, mentored, helped lead all-school Day of Dialogue, and signed on through Teach For America to educate children in Baltimore's Black community.

I was in the room one time when she spoke with new first-years who had graduated from her school network, Achievement First.

One secret to her college success, she expounded: "I'm resilient! Things started very poorly here, at least in terms of the expectations for college success that our high school inculcates. But I have made this place work for me. And the reason why is that quality that I will bring with me to every opportunity I pursue the rest of my life, which is resilience. I am resilient. I know I have that."

For Nadia, resilience included discerning what she valued and building up her agency, and not just tripling down on effort. As she said, "Sometimes grit allows you to know you need *something else* to use grit." For Nadia, that plus factor was wise humility to accept that she could and should recraft her approach to F&M: "There is a set goal in high school: Get to college and go," she explained to me. "But in college, *you create your goal*. You have to fail in order to realize what you can do"—meaning that setbacks can be seen as an element of success. In her case, "failure" and humility allowed her to rethink her educational purposes, reclaim her core values, reawaken her striver's mindset, and reinvest in growing her agency.

Over the years, I've seen that many strivers take pride in having the passion and goal-focused persistence that Angela Duckworth calls grit; but sometimes too much persistence can lead to problems. Some research shows that, among people whose social groups must contend with enormous structural and systemic barriers to achievement, the relentless pursuit of certain goals can create high stress and low self-esteem.[10] Striving—which is aspiration fueled by one's *own* values—may provide some protection against such stress. People who face ongoing discrimination may benefit when their aspirations affirm what they *actually* value rather than what some elements of society imply they should value. Maybe those personal values are service or solidarity, empowerment or hope, resistance or racial pride, or love or something else. Such values are a wellspring for strivers. That's why agency matters so much—it connects people who have been marginalized to values and perspectives that support their strength and dignity. Kundu puts it this way:

> Grit is based on an individual's long-term goals and adherence to them; agency specifically revolves around a person's position in their social world, largely related to their socioeconomic status and ability to navigate constructs of power. . . . Agency and grit are mutually beneficial and especially so if someone is provided the right support systems and healthy environments they need to thrive. Agency, if supported by social and cultural resources, can allow someone to form specific goals as they start to see themselves in a new and improved light. Grit is the mechanism or tool used to help a person stay focused and on track.[11]

I see striving as a growth mindset that can draw upon and deepen both grit and agency. A striver's mindset may soften the stress of perpetually having to fight for achievement and recognition amidst intransigent social forces because, instead, it's about aspiration that grows from one's core beliefs and resources. This is exactly the turn that Nadia made, strengthening her agency by reclaiming cultural and community values, deep as a river, with which she could apply herself passionately and authentic to her intersectional identity. That's a striver's mindset.[12]

I also observed this process with Jeanette Berlanga, who graduated from a KIPP school in San Antonio. The child of Mexican immigrants, she and her three siblings grew up immersed in both the infinite love of family and the travails of low-status labor. Tragically, when she was in middle school, her father died of a mysterious ailment. He had been her rock, her lion. The family suffered a horrendous wrong—not just from fate, but also from dishonorable behavior from people they had trusted. While the story need not be told here, what happened caused Jeanette to get after her KIPP education with an intensity of a kick boxer—helping her mother, studying every night, and playing soccer so ferociously that she earned a spot on the boys' team and eventually became co-captain.

College was never easy, not for a day. From her first classes in fall 2013, she had to claw forward among advantaged peers. She had to adjust to a different brand of soccer—prep school style—and to rarely getting in the match. And she had to get used to the moneyed white majority of the team and the campus—which she did with an open mind, making real friends and no excuses.

Jeanette was all fire, all grit, all the time . . . until, abruptly, an unexpected gale blew out the blaze.

Junior year, she tore her ACL on the soccer field, ending her season. It was hard enough to scrape up the funds and go under the knife far from family, but much worse was being vanquished from the pitch. Losing soccer felt like her soul had been ripped away. She'd weep several times a day and couldn't focus on academics. How could a mere knee injury do this, given all the cliffs she'd scaled to get to college?

The answer, and how she recovered, shows why willpower alone isn't always enough. This opportunity warrior didn't lose touch with her drive because she couldn't play soccer. She lost it for a more fundamental reason. Years before, when she was little, her father had introduced her to soccer. He'd bring her to a neighborhood park to watch him compete, teaching her to dribble, pass, and tackle. He was a phenomenal player. After he died, Jeanette began to preserve their connection by devoting herself to the sport he loved.

She took his uniform number—7—as a living tribute. It was not her number but theirs. It was almost mystical. Soccer was freedom and joy. Soccer was Mexico. Soccer was family. Soccer was her father, Armando Berlanga. And while she loved all these associations, it's also true that for seven years playing soccer helped her fend off a daughter's grief and rage.

Being sidelined with a shredded ACL, sadly, resurfaced the anguish of her father's passing and left her thrashing about in a weltering sea of emotion trying to find a true self upon which to cling. She felt hollow and alone, desolate. She told me, "I went numb. After my father's passing, I had found a way to deal with my grief. It almost felt like I was going through it all again. Except this time, I felt more helpless and could not find how to move forward."

Her normal approach of willing herself to out-effort a problem wouldn't work against this more elusive foe. She needed a new perspective, a consolation, and it did not come overnight. Her soccer teammates showed empathy, helping her see that "they loved me and not just my feet." She talked with a nurse about her feelings. And, as soon as rehab began, she began to feel that she could exert control over her recovery instead of being defined by the injury.

But most important, she sensed that she had to find a new way to stay close to her late father. How to do that? Wasn't soccer their sacred bond?

Actually . . . no.

She realized that the truth of Armando's life was not soccer. *It was their family.* Her father's legacy was his love of his children—two of whom, her young brothers, needed Jeanette's presence and example so that they too could learn to act on the faith that through education they would brighten their lives.

She came to see that depression and mourning were enduring states she couldn't put to rest with soccer and doggedness alone. She could not undo her father's death through the sport, but she could change its meaning by recommitting to her values and purpose, drawn from her father, to make the most of her life while also helping her little brothers. "Being an example never fell off my agenda. I always strived to be a modeled and exceptional example for my siblings," she once said. "Now, it would have to be away from the sport, though. . . . I had to rethink my whole person and who I wanted to be in life." That would keep her father present within her being.

After she came to this understanding, soccer still had a place in her life; she just couldn't ask the game to provide more than it can deliver. She rehabbed hard to get back on the field. And, in an act of tribute and renewal, she designed the large tattoo that now adorns her left shoulder—a soccer ball encircled with names of her parents and siblings, with "Armando Berlanga" at the top.

Senior year, she came back to the team, to her classes, to her schoolwork. Her tears dried and her grades rose. The final game of her career delivered a lovely moment: As a surprise, Jeanette's teammates pitched in to pay for her mother to visit campus for the first time and watch her play. Her suburban friends might not have fully grasped her struggles and her world, but they knew of her character and wanted to show their love.

Her plan after graduation was to work in San Antonio for two or three years before starting law school, which is exactly what she has done. "I never thought I could get to college," she said on the eve of her F&M graduation. "Now, I want more. Once you achieve a goal that felt out of reach, you learn and understand that you can do anything."

For Jeanette, what is "anything?" After college, it was first going home, hanging out with her siblings, helping her mom, finding a local soccer team, and in time moving toward law. Her mindset to strive included reintegrating with her family and community after and because of her college learning. Striving brought her back to where she began to know and make herself anew. She wanted to breathe. She wanted to weave together disparate strands of experience—that was the next goal of her striving. Drawing upon her values as a response to searing pain helped her understand and act on that desire.

Allie, Nadia, and Jeanette all graduated proud of their development and eager for future chapters of growth. Each one powered their learning by leaning on and living their values. For Allie, the striver's challenge was to swallow her pride and ask her coach if she could come back to the team. For Nadia, it was to act on values from home that allowed her to feel authenticity as a learner at school. For Jeanette, it was to find the rope she needed to pull herself through the fog of grief. College was the environment in which all three young women could meet these challenges and launch themselves into more growth. It's not surprising to me that each has sustained a striver's mindset in their early careers in education and law. Because of their values, reaching is their rule.

If we who teach want to activate striving, we need to learn and care about the values that motivate our students. We need to honor growth that occurs in deeply personal, nonlinear ways. And we need to help young people rebound from setbacks by tapping the values, older or newer, that have led them to strive in the first place. This may sound like a tall order, but really all it requires is a community of educators projecting with words and deeds that we care what students value, that we want to get to know them, that we believe their abilities are not fixed, and that, in those inevitable times when inner confusion rages like a storm, we will try to guide them to resources both within and around them. To see another example of what this can look like, let's go back to where this chapter started, with Carolina Giraldo, who started college with hopes and goals for growth that were grounded in her family's values, and who learned that, with experimentation and discernment, she could choose the forms of self-development most meaningful to her.

Point Four: The Mindset to Strive Integrates Action and Reflection

Having seen firsthand Carolina's fervent drive as a high school senior, I wondered (and worried) about how she'd steer through the choppy waters of first-year Biology, Calculus, and Chemistry, a fitful voyage for most new students. In fact, she navigated quite well, earning A's and B's while contributing to her Miami Posse One's culture of mutual support. Even so, she went home in December a bit rattled, sensing that her herculean high school study habits "weren't going to cut it in college." The pace of math and science was too fast to survive just by memorizing facts until falling asleep. Given her honor roll grades, how was she able to see this?

"Because I saw that to get where I would need to go in science, I had to change," Carolina reflected.

Despite having only one semester under her belt, she had the perspective to reassess her learning style in light of her longer-term aspirations. This is a key dimension of striving—the inclination to reflect and then self-regulate in order to pursue something one values, or suspects they will value, which for Carolina was fulfillment in science. Mentored by Ken Hess, who tried to demystify the new skills needed for each academic progression, in the spring semester she shifted her approach from "hours laboring" to "learning achieved"—a risky move for one who to that point had primarily relied on blunt force effort to achieve virtuoso results. "Now, I had to be strategic," she told me. "I had to focus on grasping the core concepts rather than every detail. I had to go see my professors. I had to ask questions of my friends. I had to learn from observing others who knew what they were doing. It wasn't natural, but I had to change."

As an excellence-valuing striver, Carolina grasped the need to teach herself new methods of studying before she would need them. Would "worrying forward" counterproductively induce stress, I asked her one time. Her answer amounted to an intriguing defense of the growth mindset: "People handle stress two ways. One is that they think they can control it; the other, is that they feel that outside forces control you, and you're a victim of them. You feel less stress if you don't think the outside has control."

For Carolina, having control also meant exploration beyond science, because she valued being receptive to many types of experience and meaning. One of her early choices was to venture onto the Susquehanna River with the women's crew team. With the long limbs and strong shoulders of a classic oarswoman, combined with her tenacity, she made rapid gains. She got the strokes down while adopting a philosophy about the agony of burning lungs and tearing muscles. Mind over body, she'd repeat. It's just pain, it's not me, so plunge into it. The sport reinforced her belief that no true effort is futile, whatever the initial outcome, because it takes a grind to make the climb. Coach Rob Weber called her one of the most impressive novice rowers he'd ever seen.

Powering through first-year science and a freezing river had a lot in common. Both demanded a philosophy of performance. Both were taxing. Both had objective benchmarks of excellence. And both involved a community of young people supporting each other's striving. That year Carolina came to love the ethos of the boat when the rowers lift the pace and energy crackles off the oars.

But then, at the end of a stellar first year, she received crushing news. While in Boston for a regatta and on the eve of finals, she received a distraught call from her mother, Patricia, with the news that, at the age of forty-seven, her father, Luis, had died suddenly of a heart attack.

I remember talking on the phone that day with a bereft and confused nineteen-year-old. While she didn't know what to do or what it all meant, she knew to let her college community take her hand and walk with her. Her teammates chose not to race that day, and one flew with her to Miami. From campus, the Posse cohort rushed to her side, especially Maria Patino, who put on hold her final exam preparations to attend the funeral. Hess helped her reach out to her professors, who gave her the time she needed.

A week into this nightmare, when Carolina came back to take her exams, I suspected that love and duty would lead this star student to transfer to the University of Miami to be near her mother and brother. Who would blame her? She'd be following her father's example: Put family first, and then restart life. Our role as her college, I thought, would be to offer her every option to stay while accepting her larger need to leave.

Except, that's not what she chose.

A couple weeks after the funeral, Patricia Giraldo called to express gratitude for the good people in her daughter's life. Reading my mind, she cut to the chase:

"Carolina will be back, I want you to know that. She needs to come back. She needs to continue what she started."

And so, that summer after her first year, she remained in Lancaster, hurting and half-functioning, trying to distract herself productively. Her one certainty was that she had to persist. There was no choice. She couldn't change her father's death, but she couldn't alter her identity either. She had to stay. She had to plow on, wherever that might lead. It wasn't about joyful growth; this was about fighting forward, willing herself onward in the hope that someday she could focus on more than keeping the pain in check.

During that season of mourning, she joined Rob Jinks's genetics lab, where her Posse friend Eddie Alsina was also working, to help research a rare genetic mutation with Lancaster's Amish population, WDR73, which causes developmental disorders in children. She worked with a rising senior who would go on to Tufts Medical School, Abby Benkert, to learn how to identify protein function using co-immunoprecipitation assays to mark protein interactors. This first lab experience taught her about both the absolute need for precision and the relentless ethic of getting it right. It was rewarding, not discouraging, to see that research is typically arduous and slow. And she noticed how Abby knew how to operate independently to advance the research—a model to admire and perhaps live into later.

One day I visited the lab so the students could show me their work. Her affect was completely flat. Some of those long summer days of smothering grief must have been excruciating. When her sophomore year began in August, I asked how I could help. "Just be there," she said honestly, knowing she'd soon need to steer herself into a new semester, even though she wasn't yet whole. A few years later when I asked her to describe this horrible time, she spoke expressively, as if past and present were one:

> The grief was so powerful. I felt my world had stopped and everyone else's was going on. But I knew I had to go on. It was the same force that keeps me—when I'm crying and saying I want to quit

physics, but I get up the next day and go to class. That same force got me to keep going even though I was in a terrible state. That was the core of my grit. This was the biggest test I have ever had to go through. Months later, I truly realized I was strong. That's when you know. You have what it takes to keep on succeeding.

Fall of sophomore year remained a pounding slog through ashen waves of mourning. Crew helped, and so did a mentoring program with the anesthesiologist Bob Falk. Shadowing Dr. Falk in operating rooms helped her to see the wonders of how the body could "withstand being cut open, sawed away at, stapled shut and somehow find the dynamic equilibrium necessary for life." In December, a vicious bout of bronchitis sent her to the hospital for a few days. Taking some exams at half-capacity, her Organic Chemistry grade suffered, which she feared would limit later options. Not a chance, said Hess, who was discovering new ways to be a faculty member through his intensive trial by trial mentoring of his ten Posse scholars.

Over the holidays, while convalescing at home, she resolved to relaunch herself in January. Spiritually, she was like a bloodied boxer getting off the mat, knowing she could and would get her legs back. This was a pivotal insight, like when Jeanette recognized that her paralysis came not from a knee injury but from the unearthed pangs of loss. Carolina knew she had to reignite her light to explore and expand. The Jesuits have a spiritual concept that illuminates this process (even when pursued secularly). It's called being a "contemplative in action," the generative cycle in which reflection informs our behavior, and vice versa.[13] Whatever comes first, the blend of action and contemplation is manna for strivers, fueling constant adaption and growth.

Ready to try out other talents, she signed up for Introduction to Drawing. At first, her instinct was to draw precisely what she saw, but Professor Jun-Chen Liu got her to adjust, saying, "If you want to capture a scene exactly, take a photo. Here, let yourself interpret." He taught her core techniques, and she loved improving with his guidance. One day she decided to depict the head of Michelangelo's masterpiece, *David*. Professor Liu had a better idea. "Pick a small detail. Just something revealing that you want us to observe the next time we look at the statue. Art is in the eye." So, she drew a sharp portrait of just *David*'s eye, her best work yet.

If the first half of sophomore year was about hanging on, it set the stage for her return to striving second semester in art: "Grit helped me get through grief because it gave me purpose. This was almost innate. My soul was driving me. It got me out of bed. You have to keep on going." Keep doing what you need to do, keep doing your best, keep being positive. That striver's soul was in there, willing her on until she had healed enough to make choices again from her joy and wonder in growing. There's faith and hope in every step when we can move, even if we feel numb—and later glean meaning from the movement.

Rowing made things better too. As a sophomore on varsity in 2013-14, she earned all-conference honors. She was so dominant that the University of Pennsylvania invited her to live in Philadelphia that summer and train with its Division I program. She accepted that offer while also compiling a bucket list of novels, relishing a few months away from academics to rest up and reel in the lessons from that first lonely year without her dad.

Always thoughtful, Carolina used breaks as a chance to assess her experiences, setting the stage for new insights. Training at Penn, taking long city walks, reading at night, she looked ahead to her final two years: College was now half over. She never could have predicted all she'd done and dealt with. There was the pre-med curriculum, rowing, art, and perhaps a return to research.

What was her true heart's calling? Did she still really want to be a scientist or a doctor, more than anything else?

This is what strivers do. They choose, act, and evaluate, over and over, to inform their next plunge into experience. Coming back for the fall, Carolina made a difficult, values-based decision, growing out of contemplation, about where to apply herself. It came down to this: She loved crew; she was excellent and still improving; it felt sensational to pull the oar through the current, to fuse with teammates at the peak of good pain, to push for personal best on the indoor rowing machine and in the weight room.

And yet, she needed to leave that love behind.

Science and helping people heal were, in fact, the twin stars providing the gravitational pull of purpose. If medicine was to be her mission, her life's work, she knew that she would now need to dedicate herself to gaining mastery of its central concepts—right now, as junior year began. "Emotionally, it was heartbreaking," she told me later. "I came out of the summer ready to give it my all as a rower, but I had to put aside my dreams for the sport and joys and friendship because of my duty to myself. . . . Sometimes we give up something we love because there is more that we are called to be."

More that we are called to be. As a striver, Carolina again showed that she could excel in the moment while still lifting her gaze to envision other vistas of growth. Early in her education, she valued exploring broadly, but now, to honor her deepest longings, she now had set priorities. Our culture tells people that they can have it all, but that's not true. Strivers learn they must eventually say goodbye to some endeavors their large-hearted drive has led them into, painful as that break may be. This was the moment when Carolina truly claimed the direction and meaning of her F&M education by making a painful choice that grew from and further ignited her mindset to strive.

Propelled by the choice, in her final two years, she pushed herself to grow in two meaningful ways. Remembering how Abby Benkert led in Jinks's lab, she asked biochemistry professor Christine Piro if she could be a part of her research team in the burgeoning field of lab-created or "unnatural" amino acids. The project was to explore incorporating the new enzymes into the protein lysozyme to see how they affect the structure, which had never been done before.

As Piro's lab partner, she had to be able to direct aspects of the project, like purifying the protein and making crystal trays. Each week, she needed to stay on top of the status of the research and be able to set benchmarks for progress toward the ultimate goal. Given the unpredictability of timing, she learned how much her own persistence and agility can be strengths. "The research isn't cut and dried," she elucidated. "The outcome may be a failure. When you are purifying a protein or working on a project, you expect it to come out a certain way, you have to tweak the conditions of the experiment. You think it will take two days, but it can take months."

Why do it? In this case, the big hypothesis is that if one can incorporate an unnatural amino acid into lysozyme some diseases might become curable. Carolina saw in the research professor the kind of passion and self-reliance that was a part of her own mindset. She admired her expertise and her example. From a year working in her lab, she gained an intellectual mentor and role model. It was Piro's recommendation that helped secure a postgraduate research position at the University of Pennsylvania.

Her second breakthrough came through art, because, having loved drawing, she aspired to see how fast she could improve in painting. Professor Liu was offering an introductory class, but it conflicted with Carolina's biochemistry lab. True to form, this generous educator offered to give the novice artist an independent study around the openings of her schedule, which meant Saturdays.

With that, Carolina lit a new region of her brain. As with drawing, she made the rookie misstep of trying to be too precise. Endearingly, Liu would occasionally smear his wet brush across a languishing work and tell her to tap the heart. "You paint on top of mistakes," he taught her. "You paint wrong on wrong on wrong until you get it right. Art isn't about being precise. Art is about putting your emotion on the canvas and having the feeling. You want your viewers to feel what you were feeling."

For the independent study, she wanted to focus on campus scenes—not for their beauty, but rather because, at this point in her life, Franklin & Marshall was her home. Influenced by Liu, she developed a theory: Art is about translating in the mind; the byproduct of the translation is the created work. "I wanted to take a look at F&M and paint my definition of it. I wanted to show these very warm images. F&M is home and a place where I grew—my toughest and greatest moments. I wanted to express the amount of love I've received at school, and to express my fondness for this place."

With that, she started painting the residence halls, the bookstore, the campus clock. Often, she would text me a photo of a finished work. I could sense the mood of belonging. She told me Professor Liu was teaching her to break an object into its components and then get the relationship right among the parts. He also was teaching her how to bring the viewer's eyes into the flow of the painting.

Sometimes he would have her paint an image for a while and have her turn the canvas upside down and keep working. "He would tell me that it all needs to occur in the subconscious. You learn techniques and then have the mind think about them subconsciously, so that all of these considerations are happening as you work, in the flow." He truly was a master teacher, totally dedicated to each student's growth and agency as a budding artist.

"Does painting require persistence?" I once asked her.

"Sure, because you want to develop a technique and it takes time. You incorporate other approaches into your style, and it evolves. One day you look at something really good that you painted, and you don't know exactly how you did it. Science also requires persistence, but it's the opposite: You must be able to replicate the specific conditions. In art, it's not knowing exactly how to do it again but rather having the *confidence* that you can."

And this confidence comes not only from the doing and the mentoring by educators but also, essentially, from the active contemplation of our pursuits. Strivers create experience and then discern its meanings for the next ascent. That is their mindset. College provides endless opportunities and many mentors to help that mindset take flight.

*

Carolina, Jeanette, Nadia, and Allie are remarkable people. Their stories show that those who seek values-grounded growth often draw upon formative early experiences, pursue growth improvisationally, tap their values to make meaning from adversity, and integrate action and reflection. It was a privilege to witness their striving in wonderful, self-initiated ways.

Do I think that their growth *only* could have happened at Franklin & Marshall? Of course not, although each was seen and valued there. Clearly, these four students could have developed their striver's mindsets at Spelman or Smith or Reed. They could have done so in a community college or a job or the military because striving comes from and expresses who they are.

That being so, the qualities of our learning or work environments matter for the activation of growth mindsets. I believe that the structure and campus resources of a four-year undergraduate education, with mentors and motivated peers and stimulating courses and endless out-of-class growth opportunities, can provide an ideal ecosystem for strivers. If you're a parent who wants your child to move through life with a confident yearning for authentic experience and growth, college is a phenomenal place and system to activate that strivers' mindset. But there's still more that can be done:

- Colleges can invest in mentoring, from faculty, staff, and peers, to expose students to unfamiliar growth opportunities, coach them on success strategies when trying something new, and help them explore the values and beliefs that motivate their learning.

- They can provide resources and incentives for reflection—within classes and beyond, including through counseling, to help students process experience, clarify values, work through blocks, act mindfully, and share distilled self-knowledge with others.

- They can encourage and support students in forming peer groups and cohorts, like I.M.P.A.C.T. and Posse, that reinforce the virtue and value of striving and changing, and of recruiting more strivers into the school for the benefit of all.

- When strivers face blocks to their progress, colleges can help them to identify the actions and resources to help them achieve their goals—while also being open to the possibility, especially for students from underrepresented communities, that the school may need to develop new resources. Three things that don't work are to try to solve students' problems for them, minimize their worries, or tell them what their values should be.

- And, in their messaging, colleges can stress and celebrate the power of defining and pursuing one's own values and path, as Carolina, Allie, Nadia, and Jeanette all did, as a way of being in school and beyond.

These are some ways to see and support the mindset for striving. The benefits come in many forms—in meaningful moments, in thriving across the arc of a college education, and in longer-term flourishing, for individuals and for society. For two decades, the scholar Laurie Schreiner has studied undergraduate thriving, which she defines as being "fully engaged intellectually, socially, and emotionally in the college experience." Schreiner has identified four primary pathways that enhance students' levels of thriving: (1) Campus involvement, including with peers; (2) high-quality and frequent student-faculty involvement; (3) spirituality, which includes a sense of meaning and purpose; and (4) a psychological sense of community on campus.[14] From these stories of striving we can see that each of these pathways was available to Carolina, Nadia, Jeanette, and Allie—although perhaps not all at once or in equal measure. It was their initiative and resilience as strivers that prompted each to take willful steps to pursue new activities, to try again after setbacks, to seek out faculty and staff, to get help when it was needed, and to join others in community. Each woman truly valued her growth and truly worked for it—each one shaped it, made it, owned it—while the college and its educators met them all in their striving and provided the resources and relationships for which they yearned. That is what activating strivers looks like and the power college has to do so.

I'm moved to remember Carolina's graduation in 2016, cum laude with a major in biochemistry and molecular biology on her way to a research internship and then medical school. The night before commencement, the college honored her and other graduates at a dinner her mother and brother attended. She and I posed for a picture with Patricia and Luis Felipe, now a foot taller and headed to F&M himself. After the photo, I watched the edges of her smile drop just a touch. It took me back to that first Posse luncheon four years before, when she told me and her parents, *I'm going to make every single day count.*

That she did. As a result, in the decades ahead, when the trials and tests of adulthood rise before her, Carolina Giraldo will pull strength from her college education, when she lost her father and her hero, held on for dear life, and then got back to striving for him and the family, and for herself, by doing and thinking, thinking and doing—a contemplative in action. Raised in the crossways of Medellín and Miami, this emerging American original more than kept her high school pledge—only now I understand that she'd really made that commitment not to her parents and the president of her future college, as it had seemed that high school day, but to her future self.

When talented individuals like Carolina are supported in devoting themselves to growth, trusting values old and new as their divining rods, college is doing its most glorious work. This is what helps make free and flourishing adults, as we'll see next in the triumphs of Akbar Hossain, Sheldon Ruby, and Markera Jones.

Chapter 5: Questions for Discussion

1. How do you understand the mindset to strive? Why does the author believe that this mindset is an empowering resource in and after college?

2. The author defines striving as constantly going for new growth that, crucially, reflects and stems from one's *existing or emerging values*. Strivers aspire to challenge themselves and climb high heights for personal, intrinsically meaningful reasons. Is this an important concept for students today? And does college really enable this?

3. In presenting Carolina's mindset to strive, the author says it is valuable to understand her life history and the assets and beliefs that she brought to college. Is it helpful for faculty and staff to know more about their students' backgrounds? What guidelines or guardrails are needed?

4. Carolina, Allie, Nadia, and Jeanette all leaned into learning passionately and made each day count. In doing so they dealt well with defining difficulties. What more can and should colleges do to help students make meaning from hardship?

5. The chapter invokes Angela Duckworth's notion of grit and Anindya Kundu's definition of agency. How do you understand these two terms, and how do they relate to the author's notion of striving?

6

GROWTH MINDSETS, SOCIAL GOOD, AND
HUMAN FLOURISHING

O chestnut tree, great rooted blossomer,
Are you the leaf, the blossom or the bole?
O body swayed to music, O brightening glance,
How can we know the dancer from the dance?

—W. B. YEATS

FOR TWENTY YEARS, on the evening after graduation, I made a point of visiting the commencement site for one last look before the set would be broken down and taken away.

Each time it was the same. A space that just hours earlier had teemed with life and love and pride and grace, with hugs and tears and melancholy smiles, was now a ghostly scene.

Gazing upon the unruly sea of empty folding chairs, and the spare commencement platform cleaned of its banners, and the forlorn statues of the founders, I always felt a bit depleted. Commencements call up emotion in waves. We see each other's intensity, we feel and share meaning, we attempt our awkward goodbyes, and then it ends abruptly—everything—the event and the work of the year and the seniors being students.

Standing alone, I would replay parts of the day. Robing before the ceremony. The procession and the musical tribute for the departed. That glorious first moment at the podium looking into the expectant eyes of the graduates. Most of all I would think about all these young people who'd strode confidently across the stage, having created the education they came for. You've read about some of them, like Carolina and Katrina and Keiran and Wyatt, so perhaps you see why I have so much faith in them and the good and great deeds they'll do with their educations and growth mindsets.

Those evenings, in the quiet of twilight, with memories swirling, I would ask myself, *What was it that just happened here, this weekend, and this year? What is it that I believe in?*

Reflecting in this manner year after year, each time with a new group of graduates top of mind, I came to my answer: I believe in learners *and* learning, the people *and* the process, which are two beauties braided into one. Education is about human beings in formation—the thinkers and the thinking, the doers and the doing, the dancers and the dance—with benefits for the one and the many, when we kindle fire in the young so they may find and fuel their growth through life.

Yes, higher education faces many challenges. But we won't fix anything if no one speaks up for what matters and what works. I've watched young people I care about grow, and own their growth, and take on mindsets for more growth—and I've witnessed this process in stories and in patterns, allowing me to make this case for college today:

First: Our change-challenged world, wobbling like a top, needs young people with the growth mindsets to discover, create, mentor, collaborate, and strive.

Second: A holistic college education demonstrably activates these very mindsets in eighteen-to-twenty-three-year-olds, providing daily experiences and epiphanies for them to build with and upon throughout college and beyond.

Third: Growth mindsets form when young people *actively* create the education they seek. There's gold for all students who apply themselves and lead their learning.

Fourth: It is exciting to envision the myriad actions educators can take to enhance this core power of college. In sum, they fall into a few buckets. We need to ensure that all students have access to involved faculty, active learning pedagogies, impactful out-of-class growth experiences, and engaged peers from the full American mosaic.

Easier said than done, of course. Some of the bigger institutions have softened their emphasis on personalized undergraduate learning. Some of the smaller ones still do that well but are struggling to fund and finance their mission. As a society, we need to put much more money into student financial aid, which enhances the whole school, while also challenging our campuses to become much more innovative in how they activate growth mindsets. And we must win back public sentiment by decreasing the cost of college and student debt while increasing the value—a combination that will require our institutions to do something many don't believe they're good at, which is change.[1]

So why should society encourage colleges to ignite growth mindsets and give more resources to those that can? There's a social case, a business case, and a human-centered case, each of which is relevant both for individuals and for our democratic-capitalist society.

The social case is that providing equitable access to higher education promotes the greater good—building culture, bridging differences, burnishing upward mobility, and bringing more talent into our professions and problem-solving. Citizens who can discover, create, and collaborate in this era of accelerating change will hold the country together. And in today's world, those who lack a college education may have trouble holding even their own lives together, given, as the scholar Anne Case writes, that "Education divides everything, including connection to the labor market, marriage, connection to institutions (like organized religion), and physical and mental health, and mortality. It does so for whites, Blacks and Hispanics. . . . There are two Americas now: one with a B.A. and one without."[2]

The business case is that the benefits of education outweigh the costs, given that a population primed to learn and adapt constantly will advance America's prospects in today's tech- and science-powered global knowledge economy. Investing in higher education is key to sustaining any country's competitiveness as viral change sweeps through the world order.

The human-centered case for holistic education goes like this: All people are more than our cells and more than our circumstances. We have but one life, and it is each person's life project to inhabit her promise and create her most true self. "What I do is me: for that I came," Gerard Manley Hopkins wrote—to give and be and do our best, to live deeply and freely down to the root.[3] A central aim of college, therefore, is to help each student live for and live into the ancient Greek concept of *eudaimonia*, a flourishing that comes from doing and developing well. Michelle Obama celebrates such growth as "becoming," which she calls a "forward motion, a means of evolving, a way to reach continuously toward a better self"—authentic, active, open, and hopeful.[4] We should want such free and rich becoming for one another, humans for humans, because each person has equal dignity and thus equal worth.

This chapter closes my examination of how college activates growth mindsets with the stories of three superstar human beings who activated their growth mindsets at F&M. Given the challenges of their childhoods, it's likely that, in earlier eras, Akbar Hossain, Sheldon Ruby, and Markera Jones would not have gone to college at all. But they did and they soared. Now they're young professionals with advanced degrees who are living, giving, growing, and serving our world in ways that speak to the potential of all young people. Their education shows that the business, social, and human-centered arguments are, in fact, complementary strands of a single coherent case for college in these times.

Akbar Hossain

Akbar Hossain is a force of nature—and a gift to America. To make the social case for college, look no further. A 2013 graduate, he parlayed his F&M education into a scholarship to the University of Pennsylvania Law School and numerous public service roles, leading to his appointment, in 2023, to the executive team of the new governor of Pennsylvania, Josh Shapiro.

But to fully grasp the value of college in the journey that Akbar has made, we need to look closely at how he got there and what he did with his opportunities.

I first met him on March 1, 2011, my first day at F&M, after inviting students in a late-night town hall meeting to tell me what they loved about the college. Neatly dressed, wiry and bespectacled, the sophomore came right up and offered, "The best thing about F&M is the faculty."

Every professor so far had helped him, he said, especially Susan Dicklitch-Nelson, who'd taught him in a seminar on the working poor. Through that class, he was able to volunteer at the Lancaster labor center helping immigrants apply for the Earned Income Tax Credit (EITC), the federal tax refund for low-wage workers. Akbar advised a Burmese husband and wife with three young children whose combined income was about $27,000. It felt momentous to help them secure a $6,000 EITC refund to pay down some of their debts getting to America. I recall asking that night what he was learning, so far: "That we can use our education to make a difference, right now! We helped forty families claim more than $800,000 in refunds. We did that as *students*."

That semester, Akbar regularly came to my Friday office hours. I was struck by the way he relished classes and campus life, ideas, politics, and people. It was there that this thoughtful young man first shared details of his family's global journey.

The oldest child of Mir and Shahida Hossain, he was born in Comilla, Bangladesh. Akbar's parents met when Mir moved to Comilla for work and became Shahida's academic tutor. Both were the first in their families to earn high school degrees. The day of their wedding, with vows and prayers, their assembled loved ones couldn't possibly have known how much courage and resourcefulness would be required of them.

When Akbar was about four years old, his father left home for a better-paying job as a welder in Saudi Arabia. Mir would shuttle three thousand miles between the two countries, saving every penny for his family and a larger circle of parents and grandparents. He swelled with pride at being the provider, but it also cut deep to be an absent father and husband. Talk about being a striver.

Wanting more from life and for his children, Mir made the fateful call to bring Shahida, Akbar, and his youngest son Kabir to Saudi Arabia, where they had their third child, Ayesha. For six years the family lived in a community of migrant laborers in Jed-dah. The children studied and played with kids from Pakistan, In-dia, and Nigeria. Their mothers schooled them at home while their fathers held factory jobs. The community was alive with strong but poor Muslim exiles trying to eke out survival in the richest kingdom in the world.

"It was a community of resilient people," Akbar told me. "Indi-viduals who packed their bags to travel to Saudi Arabia, not knowing the next time they would see their loved ones or experi-ence the sense of belonging of one's own language and culture. Every family in that complex moved to Saudi Arabia not just to support their nuclear members, but also to send money back home and create pathways for others in their family to migrate for work. The women were probably the strongest of them all—leaving the 'luxuries' of a familial community to arrive in a coun-try with only each other and their husbands to support."

One day, the Hossains saw a prominent American flag at a kiosk in a mall. It was an invitation to enter the US diversity visa lottery, with tiny odds. "Why not take a shot," Akbar told me. "But it wasn't like we actually thought we'd win."

Months after completing a form, an envelope addressed to Mir arrived at his parents' village in Bangladesh. The one person who knew a little English made out the words "congratulations" and "U.S. consulate" and contacted the Hossains. A short time later Mir gave up the welding job for which the family had left behind all they knew and loved in Bangladesh. It was like stepping through one of the magical portals in Mohsin Hamid's *Exit West*, transport-ing the Hossains into possibility.[5] Meticulously handling every de-tail, Mir found a Bangladeshi contact in the United States whom he paid to meet them at New York's Kennedy Airport and usher them through the rigors of resettlement.

On September 9, 2001, the Hossains and their three children passed through Customs and loaded all their possessions into a stretch limo. Akbar remembers that their contact brought them to a motel nearby in New Jersey. "Rest up here," he said, vanishing into the night . . . forever. The next day the family sat and waited in vain for him to return, worries mounting, and the day after that, September 11, brought global chaos.

They stood lost and terrified when the World Trade Center fell to the earth just across the Hudson River. Panic reigned everywhere. The streets emptied as most people hurried home and hunkered down with their families, glued to their TVs. The entire world was knocked off its axis. Now homeless and stateless, the Hossains only had each other. They were living in a nightmare. After a week of frozen time, at their wit's end, and all but out of cash, they resolved to get back to Saudi Arabia, when a sympathetic Indian restaurant owner in Newark learned of their plight and connected Mir to a mosque in Pennsylvania. The next day, a kindly stranger drove them to Norristown, where the community leaders gave them shelter, safety, and a start—"just because we were people and for the sake of humanity," Akbar told me.

Buffeted by these harsh winds of history, the Hossains' only option was to make it work in Norristown. The mosque helped them find a one-bedroom apartment, and Mir Hossain took on three minimum-wage jobs—at an In & Out Food Store by day, a light bulb factory at night, and a construction site on weekends. The children started elementary school, with all the culture shocks one can imagine, and some bullying because of their identity.

Resettlement required countless adjustments—to English, to America, to a secular society, and to a new legal system. The Norristown community was strapped by poverty but rich in character. Many neighbors welcomed them with meals, clothing, and furniture. Mir didn't even have enough extra money to take a bus to work, but he nevertheless insisted that the children focus on the open runways before them. They had a loving, modest life and were able to send money back home every month. Mir often told his children, "Never forget where you came from."

Then tragedy struck one sweltering August afternoon during Ramadan. Akbar was down the street playing basketball when his little sister appeared in a frenzy. Their father, who was fasting, had collapsed while cutting the grass. Akbar ran home and witnessed a frantic and futile CPR scene. His hero and protector died in his arms—literally working himself to death to provide for the family.

Again, the mosque (where they'd rarely worshipped) pitched in with help, inquiring if they'd prefer to return to Bangladesh. "The American dream was my father's dream for us," Akbar said to me. "After all his sacrifice, there's no way my mother was going to let us give up," and so *she* began working full time at the light bulb factory.

In eighth grade, Akbar went to work himself, securing a part-time job paying five dollars an hour in a gas station. He was industrious, just like his father, and brought sunlight into each customer's day. Counting his blessings rather than his wounds, he also excelled in school and later moved up to a 7-Eleven, where his diligence led the boss to promise him a ten dollar an hour position when he finished high school.

His mother wanted him to grab that job, which would help make ends meet, but a Norristown college advisor named Ernie Hadrick insisted it would be a bad move because he'd go farther and make more money with more education. College would open doors and widen his horizons, and he'd love the chance to learn something every single day and make lifelong friends. Akbar was wary about crossing with his mother, but he saw Hadrick's point. It had been drilled into his brain that America is a nation of immigrants, which meant that it was *his* nation and *his* destiny to rise . . . and college was the elevator.

As he weighed this choice—immediate family needs versus a longer-term investment—Hadrick arranged an overnight visit to Franklin & Marshall. That evening Akbar joined two dozen students from all around the country sharing their life stories and goals. Some were also newcomers who'd been strangers in this strange American land. Some also had lost heroic family members. Some also had ideas about wages or health care or policing birthed from tear-soaked times. For every single one, college was the avenue of their hopes and dreams.

Akbar felt completely in sync with this group of hopeful miners digging for educational diamonds. F&M would be the right place, he concluded—close to family, a bridge to success, and rich with resources. Something greater awaited him, he could taste it. This American life was there for him, as his parents promised, and so, with his mother's eventual blessing, he pledged himself to college.

"I always knew that America is the land of opportunity," he told me that day sophomore year when he let me in on his life story. "But until senior year of high school I hadn't realized the role college plays in *opening up* that opportunity. Now that I've made it to F&M, it's my responsibility to use this education to lower the barriers so that more families like mine can enjoy the benefits of this country."

In fact, Akbar was summarizing one of Ben Franklin's reasons for donating two hundred pounds to create Franklin College in 1787. He knew education was the best way to bring waves of newcomers (at that time, from Germany) into an American mainstream defined by pluralism and purpose—a collective becoming that will never not matter.

I saw Akbar often in his junior and senior years, constantly connecting and creating with faculty and peers. You'd have thought he was the son of doctors, not a refugee teenager whose life had been totally redirected because, just in time, he turned down 7-Eleven for college.

During his last two years, Akbar served as the elected president of Brooks College House and as an advisor to incoming students. He also led the creation of the Muslim Students Association, giving domestic and international students a place to worship and connect, and loved having his brother, Kabir, join him at F&M his final year. And he threw himself into classes, especially the Dicklitch-Nelson seminar mentioned in chapter 4, when a gritty team of undergraduates helped save a refugee named Aadam from deportation to Darfur.

Junior year, the college nominated him for a highly competitive Truman Scholarship, which has funded postgraduate studies for future public leaders like Susan Rice, Neil Gorsuch, and Stacey Abrams. Amazingly, this child of the Bangladeshi diaspora became Franklin & Marshall's first-ever winner. He joked that his mother was going to be mad when she figured out that public policy jobs don't pay too much. All the acclaim of being a "first" didn't change him one bit. He just kept on reaching and giving in the opportunity feast that was F&M. He made friends from across the social spectrum and met his now-wife, Lisa Yosevitz, who has become a highly accomplished young dentist. Really, he expressed all the mindsets this book describes; he learned, created, collaborated, and got and gave mentoring constantly, by choice and by habit, always his way, with a bottomless battery, in honor of his father and all who'd ever helped the family. He was a striver like his dad.

Senior year also brought that first competitive disappointment, a crucible for all used to winning gold, when he interviewed for Marshall and Rhodes Scholarships but wasn't selected. This, too, is part of social mobility in America, I told him when he got back from the Rhodes interview, which had been emotionally grueling: It's like elite mountaineering. The path gets steeper as we climb, but we can always double back and try another byway. No one wins every time. He was certainly buoyant enough to accept that.

With each new growth moment, Akbar felt and showed joy and gratitude. This was one of his gifts that drew people toward him. Yes, he'd suffered deprivation and grief, lived in hereditary societies where almost no one poor can rise, and felt the sting of being the Other after 9/11, but none of that defined him. Self-creation, bridging, and serving others did.

Which is to say, because of himself, because of his parents, because of his culture, because of his community, because of his professors, because of his college, and because of America, Akbar Hossain was becoming the person he yearned to be. Education was essential to the process. Whatever twists and turns he might face in the future, he would not carry the haunting feeling of having been held back by larger forces or his own failure to dream. As a representative of our college and our country, I felt so proud to hand him his diploma.

Well-educated at F&M, after graduation, he kept striving and achieving: Graduation from the University of Pennsylvania Law School in 2018. Recipient of the Paul & Daisy Soros Fellowship for New Americans. Positions in a law firm and then with the Pennsylvania Attorney General. Outside of work, he served on the Norristown Planning Commission and the mayor of Philadelphia's Millennial Advisory Commission. He advocated pro bono for vulnerable tenants in Philadelphia. Those intense first few years after law school added up to an incredible opportunity: In January 2023, he was sworn in as Pennsylvania's secretary of policy and planning with a mandate to help make sure that the commonwealth's economy, education systems, and government services work for all.

Through it all, Akbar continues to speak up to help break down prejudice against Muslims. For example, during law school, after a bigot shouted from a car, "Go back where you came from!" he published an op-ed piece in the *Philadelphia Inquirer* offering to have coffee with anyone who wanted to meet a Muslim and learn there's nothing to be afraid of.[6] Dozens of readers accepted the invitation.

Especially moving was a TEDx talk he gave right before law school, "Only in America," when he gave thanks for his American life, while pledging to help make a more perfect union.[7] Pacing across the stage, smiling while blinking back emotion, he said:

> My father passed away while believing in the American opportunity. And I'd say today—this very moment—is a testament to all of the sacrifices he has made and a testament to the American opportunity that if you work hard, you can achieve incredible things. Look at me now. I'm an underdog—I made it! . . .
>
> Yes, we need to fix our broken immigration system, but America still remains a country where a family like mine can come from nowhere and lead a life of dignity and respect. . . . While Washington has its problems . . . , America still remains a country where a community will come together to take care of a family in need.

Looking back, it seems so natural, so inevitable, that the winning sophomore I met in 2011 would animate his promise and become a rising policy leader who cares about other families in need. What if

Mir Hossain hadn't gone to work in the Saudi factory, or hadn't moved his family there, or hadn't applied for the visa lottery, or hadn't booked the September 9 flight but rather had chosen three days later? It seems like destiny . . . but, of course, a destiny must be made. Akbar could have been a cook in Bangladesh or a welder in Saudi Arabia. He could have been pumping gas in America. There's dignity in all forms of labor, but those careers wouldn't have deployed the abilities his parents protected, several "villages" of good people contributed to, and he then honed with his choice-powered growth mindset.

Only in America. Akbar Hossain will never stop striving and never stop serving. He knows that it's for this that he came. Ben Franklin would be proud.

Sheldon Ruby

Hailing from Artemas, Pennsylvania, a rural town best known for the Roadkill Cafe, Sheldon Ruby started at F&M when Akbar was a senior. People who haven't met them might assume they have nothing in common, but as strivers these two are a moral match.

Both were standout high school leaders for whom learning was life. Both worked part time to help with bills. Both came from working-class families that were dubious about college. And both used college to propel themselves into public service. Senior year, Sheldon won a prestigious Charles B. Rangel International Affairs Graduate Fellowship, which provided a scholarship to George-town for graduate school followed by a coveted job as a foreign service officer for the State Department.

This is quite the trajectory for a country boy who grew up learning practical skills like shooting deer, chasing away coyotes, and saving bales of hay from surprise thunderstorms. How did he do this? As a child, Sheldon became a fervent reader thanks to the library "book bus" that circled through Artemas every two weeks. As a teenager, he got the bug to venture beyond his town of 330 people and viewed education as a roadway. But it took an enterprising young college advisor at Everett Area High School to turn hope into a plan.

Stephanie Liederman Otis saw so much in this affable, soccer-playing, band member with a home-cut hairstyle. He was all-everything at the school and showed optimism when his family hit a financial landmine in the 2008 recession. It got so tough that they even allowed their son to live with a family near the school to save on the gas costs of the fifty-mile round trip, which stung his parents because it signaled that they needed a little help.

She saw one problem for this precocious Christian boy, though—his complete lack of exposure to the universe beyond Bedford County. What if the pluralism, the partying, or the sheer size of a college caused him to hightail it right back home? Yet, she believed he had the mind and the mettle to make it. So, to help him get ready, in 2012 she nominated him for our summer enrichment program, F&M College Prep, then going into its second year.

At sixteen, Sheldon showed up in Lancaster plenty eager if wide-eyed. Through the program, he didn't just meet students of color, immigrants, Muslims, and LGBTQ peers—the kinds of people he'd typecast as "other"—he lived with them. In workshops and in the suite at night, he'd swap stories with new friends like Anthony Thomas and Shawn Heyward, chatting about families and faiths, politics and values, trials and triumphs. None of them had money, but all had high hopes. They bantered a lot too, showing affection with their teasing.

He'd never made friends like this before. In this cohort of sixty teenagers, some had been wounded by people they loved. Some were old in their wisdom. Even the rural students weren't back-country kids like him (except for one poetic home-schooled girl whose parents did not allow her to take a full scholarship to F&M the next year). That said, they shared so much—honesty, respect for their teachers, community pride, and simple pleasures such as watching TV with family. He also enjoyed asking the F&M professors mischievous questions like whether evolution was an opinion, imagining how the answers would land back in Bedford County.

Three summer weeks at F&M whet his craving for the full-on college plunge—which he then took with gusto thirteen months later. Of course, starting out at F&M was like immigrating to a new country, given the campus culture and diversity. His family's vernacular—*y'ins, not a lick of sense, as useless as tits on a bull*—was as unfamiliar to his peers as academic jargon like *heteronormativity* and *intersectionality* was to him. To his Weis College House don, Joel Eigen, he initially seemed more foreign than an international student. Eigen advised him to take a six-month campus listening tour to learn how the world made sense to others who held very different beliefs.

Sure, he felt lost academically, but he trusted the faculty to help him. The eminent American studies professor Louise Stevenson sure did, right away, when she began the sacred work of showing him how to form and defend a thesis. Jennifer Kibbe's first-year seminar, Understanding Terrorism, might have been the linchpin of his entire education, because it forced him to accept that his sweeping opinions about Muslims were simply wrong. "I began to challenge myself to look at other cultures with an open, rather than condemning mind," he once wrote, and to avoid thinking about people as cleaved into fixed categories like rich and poor or Muslim and Christian.

And that's how he started to see his own identity—containing dualities. He longed to stand out and fit in. He hoped to transform and stay true. He yearned to be known for who he really was— neither a well-off white kid nor backwards "redneck." In some ways, he lived a double life—"F&M Sheldon" and "Bedford County Sheldon." The former, for example, wanted to explore potential gun safety policies, while the latter loved blasting tree limbs with his shotgun. Some days he felt frustrated by the intolerance of home, and some days by the intolerance *toward* home. However, in both cases, he tried not to judge others; it didn't seem right to sneer at people for having narrow apertures no one had helped them to widen. Plus, he knew his small-town values also gave him strengths some scions of privilege didn't even know that they lacked, like hard work, geniality, frugality, and compassion.

Balancing the gravitational pull of these two stars, home and college, his mindset was to explore growth actively, including making time for new activities that reflected his values. For example, he became one of the finest tour guides in the school, warmly engaging visiting teens about their interests while openly sharing his pride in being a first-gen undergrad. With a strong voice, he became a campus leader on sexual assault prevention. Later, he cofounded the First Generation Diplomats club. Making such choices, always authentically, Sheldon became more well-known and admired each semester. His fraternity even helped him cover the membership dues—another signal that he belonged, and, as I mentioned earlier, his brothers mentored him on what to wear to interviews. "They didn't care that I was weird, that I wore camouflage clothing, or that I didn't understand many of the cultural norms that define an institution like F&M," he told me, glowing. "Just being around them was enough to fill in a lot of gaps that I never would have gotten from professors because they were playing a very different role."

Academically, Monica Cable was the faculty member who jump-started his aspirations, for she recognized that he was a prodigious learner with a centered personal ethic. Seeing how intently he worked to learn about others' cultures, she nudged him to apply for a summer language fellowship after sophomore year. When he won, he got a passport and trekked to, of all places, Indonesia, living in Malang, on the island of Java, with a Muslim family. He was nineteen years old, dauntless, discovering the planet, and looking at America for the first time from beyond our borders.

He connected with his Indonesian host mother, bonded over soccer with guys his age, and learned the Bahasa Indonesia language. At night he would observe Ramadan with the family and ask about the tenets of Islam, realizing that his host mom's faith and his were equally about the devout love of God. Sitting in her small home, trying to describe Indonesia in messages to his family, it struck him that no one from his part of America had ever been where he was now, meaning he was authoring his own story, and that knowledge fed his soul. In her memoir, *In Other Words*, Jhumpa Lahiri recounts how she acted on her almost irrational yearning to master Italian, even moving to Italy to embrace that quest. She could have been writing about Sheldon's longing for exposure and experience: "The obstacles stimulate me. Every new construction seems a marvel. Every unknown word a jewel. . . . I find the process more demanding yet more satisfying, almost miraculous. I can't take for granted my ability to accomplish it. . . . The more I feel imperfect, the more I feel alive."[8]

After Indonesia, he became a travel gazelle, taking a semester in London followed by a study trip to China and India, all funded by

F&M. Then he made a mentor in Professor Nina Kollars, a rising star in cybersecurity and hacker cultures, who got him jazzed about global security and diplomacy. The doors of the world were opening wide before him and walking through them now felt as natural as helping his family at home. Like the writer Tara Westover, in college he came to hold "the conviction to live in your own mind, and not someone else's."[9]

As a senior he owned the college, just like Akbar before him. Besides winning the Rangel graduate fellowship, he also secured a Fulbright Scholarship to return to Indonesia to teach English. (It would take another chapter to describe his postgraduate experience in 2017–18 working with five hundred school students from five religions in a rural community.) Delving into the new fields of geology and environmental science, he found fascinating connections to global affairs, especially water security. His self-assigned capstone project was a twenty-five-page independent study paper he conceived with the advice of Professor Stephanie McNulty. It was ambitious. He'd planned to argue that decentralization in Indonesia led to reduced corruption, but a couple months of research and McNulty's mentoring brought him to the more nuanced view that as the central government devolved power, corruption gravitated to where the new power resided. He later called the paper "one of my proudest moments," for it proved that he'd worked his way to the top of the class:

> If F&M was the beginning of a one-mile race, I started in the red, one lap behind my peers. Despite this, with professors at my back, I not only made up the lap, but I was able to finish the race with the strongest runners at F&M. It was one of those moments that made me feel like I actually belonged at F&M and that I deserved to be there. No one could say that it was a fluke or F&M offering pity to a

poor kid from rural America—in that moment, I was just as good as the brightest kid from a wealthy suburb in New England.

And then some.

Sheldon Ruby earned that self-knowledge because he advanced his education by building growth upon growth upon growth, through discovery, collaborating, creating, and striving and by seeking out every mentor he could find. He's the one who took the initiative as a freshman to go to Louise Stevenson to say, "I want to learn how to write." He's the one who approached wealthy fraternity brothers to say, "I'd like to join." He's the one who teamed up with first-gen students of different races to say, "Let's make a club for students like us." He's the one who flew to the island of Java to say to each Indonesian he encountered, "I'm here to learn and share." It's as if Carol Dweck were describing him when she wrote:

> The fixed mindset limits achievement. It fills people's minds with interfering thoughts, it makes effort disagreeable, and it leads to inferior learning strategies. What's more, it makes other people into judges instead of allies. Whether we're talking about Darwin or college students, important achievements require a clear focus, all-out effort, and a bottomless trunk full of strategies. Plus allies in learning. This is what the growth mindset gives people, and that's why it helps their abilities grow and bear fruit.[10]

As graduation approached in 2017, I asked Sheldon if he could describe how much he'd grown and expanded his worldview since that first summer in F&M College Prep. He grinned softly and said those answers were still beyond him, just yet. As I thought about the green sixteen-year-old I'd met in July 2012—so heartfelt in his hopes for learning, so willing to test boundaries—I knew that he'd created from the college's involved faculty and abundant resources an education that would power his earnest striving for the rest of his life.

A few days later, however, he *had* to say something about the impact of college, because he was chosen to speak at a send-off reception for international and study-abroad students. Walking into International House for the event, I was delighted to see Sheldon's mom and dad, who had driven across the state for their son. We'd met four years before, on Accepted Students Day. Now their son had made his name at the school and opened doorways into many new vistas ahead.

I watched his parents as Sheldon spoke about some of the ways a college education helps students see, learn, and know feelingly the plain fact that almost all people everywhere live and love their cultures. The Rubys showed no sign of being cowed, resentful, or left behind. They looked proud at who their son was becoming.

Markera Jones

Markera Jones is a prodigiously gifted 2015 F&M graduate who I met at an icebreaker during her first week of college. Today, she's a newly minted clinical psychologist with a PhD from the University of Illinois Urbana-Champaign. She traveled just as far as Akbar and Sheldon, and like them showed up at F&M with hopes for growth that college life helped her ignite into a mindset. Again, it helps to know how she grew up to appreciate the difference a rigorous, personalized education made for her.

I first met her at an orientation event when my boring basic questions didn't break any ice. Clearly, this majority white campus was a new universe, and the school would have to earn her trust.

Then she pulled a 4.0 GPA in the first semester. Almost no one does that at F&M, so I invited her to my office to hear about her interests. When I praised her grades, she didn't respond with a prep school humble brag of hard work and helpful faculty. Instead, as if she were talking about having good penmanship, she said, "Oh, school isn't hard for me. I just read things and remember them."

She wasn't boasting. It's a fact that she's exceptional at learning—and at the harder work of coping with adversity and with grief. Growing up in Coatesville, Pennsylvania, she had a loving extended family but, with no stable income, her mom had to move often. One time she mentioned that she'd never had a bedroom until college. Her father was not in her life—a fact she'd had no choice but to accept. Before turning twelve, she taught herself to study and stay out of trouble. Even though good grades came easily, she never held herself above her peers. In fact, in sixth grade, at Horace S. Scott Middle School, she decided to leave the gifted program, because "I didn't have a sense of belonging with that advanced group."

In eighth grade, Markera was already taking Geometry. Based on her achievement, this placed her on a path to join the honors track at Coatesville High School—the academic program for students headed to Penn State, Villanova, or Ivy League UPenn. But she was the only Black student in Geometry, making her feel "terribly isolated." Her classmates all knew each other from middle school and swim teams, but she seemingly had nothing in common with anyone. She couldn't even start a conversation. Geometry wasn't challenging; it was distressing. She had no social friends in that class, and no psychic resting place. Who would talk to her? When it came time to finalize her ninth-grade schedule, she thought about if she wanted all this stress for high school. With the schedule card in her hand, she faced a question—advance to Algebra II for ninth grade, or retake Geometry? The comfort of having classmates who looked like her would simultaneously mean a step back academically.

At this critical juncture, Markera repeated her sixth-grade choice, which could have lowered the line of her life, by opting out of the honors track to join her friends on the regular track. Intuitively, she knew that stratified racial groupings were wrong, but it was also a relief to feel comfortable enough to focus on learning. Years later, she reflected, "I intentionally held myself back from opportunities because what was more important was fitting in and feeling safe to be me, and, by 'me,' I mean the stereotype I thought I should fit." It was a classic case of structural racism—turning segregation and lesser opportunity into a comforting norm.

A great deal of research has shown children and teens benefit from having a foundation of social and emotional security upon which to build academic success.[11] That's clearly what happened for Markera in high school. Learning with peers who could relate to her, and in classrooms where she never felt isolated, she earned top grades and took part in clubs and sports, while also working weekends and holidays at McDonald's to help her mom. This helped her feel that she was growing and advancing. It is also true that those classrooms were segregated, separate, and unequal.

A life-altering invitation came during her sophomore year, when a visionary educator named Michael Gardner recruited her to join his Upward Bound program. It was actually a repeat overture, because the year before she'd turned him down, apprehensive about all the extra academic commitments and summer study when she primarily "wanted to fit in and be popular." But, hearing two friends rave about the program, and sensing it could help her, she made "the most important decision of my life" and said yes.

Upward Bound gave her a chance to read Black scholarship for the first time. Weekend classes in history and social science compensated for the AP courses Coatesville High didn't offer her track. During the summers, she participated in the eight-week enrichment program at Lincoln University, one of the nation's first historically Black college and universities (HBCU), which not only expanded her understanding of college life, but also showed her a red carpet of learning unfurling at her feet. Being taught English, history, and foreign languages by professors of color gave her a new sense of hope and belonging. The summer before senior year, Gardner even sent her to the Upward Bound program at the University of the Virgin Islands—her first time out of the States. Through it all, her mind was expanding. She was taking in new ideas, new possibilities—and that felt natural.

Gardner took the students to visit colleges and taught them to fill out the FAFSA form for federal financial aid, requiring her, like Akbar and Sheldon, to initiate an awkward conversation at home about money. It was helpful for Markera that older peers in Upward Bound had figured out such things on their pilgrimages to college—including Sheena Crawley, a talented artist and track star who'd chosen F&M.

During these years, she often had to make sense of sadness—a girlfriend dropping out, a friend's brother getting hurt, unfair conditions holding down families just trying to rise—but at the same time, her confidence as a learner grew. Admittedly, she didn't really grasp all the educational opportunities that the Coatesville system denied to her and her friends. How could she see it all, from within the circle of poverty and systemic racism? Like Akbar and Sheldon, she grew up unaware of some of the realities of inequity, but she was by no means blind to her own talent for learning and value of playing out where that might take her. I remember asking her how she kept her motivation. "I don't really know," she replied. "I don't think I'm really that different from anyone else in my community. Except that sometimes I would step back and almost zone out, getting my space, finding inner peace. People have to accept that about me."

Perhaps this ability to withdraw allowed her to cocoon hope and keep focused on the long-term value of learning. Perhaps it allowed this teenager to *respond* to hardship rather than simply reacting—by recommitting to her studies, by loving her family, and by holding fast to a vision of educating herself to help others. "True resistance begins with people confronting pain—whether it is theirs or somebody else's," the social critic bell hooks once wrote, "and wanting to do something to change it."[12] By the time I met Markera, she was clearly confronting pain and wanting to make change, to save the children through education—for herself and for her community.

Senior year of high school, with stellar grades and sterling SAT scores, she stood in line for her one and only session with the school's college advisor, whose only idea was that she should immediately commit to a local open access university (without mentioning that it was graduating about one in ten enrollees). Four years after turning down the ninth-grade honors track, Markera had become Coatesville's invisible honor student. No one at the school saw her as a prospect for a top college—despite her record and her resilience and her growing pattern of pursuing opportunity. However, this time, through Upward Bound, Markera had fortified herself for the resister's path, and she said no to the counselor, telling her she was looking at colleges like Franklin & Marshall.

About fifteen months later, Markera had earned that first 4.0 at F&M. To some extent, all those early college A's came from natural brilliance. During her first two years, as she saw the menu of opportunities—so much more than she had enrolled knowing to want—she began to create her education. She learned the foundations of psychology. She excelled in French and sociology. She earned paid jobs mentoring at McCaskey High School and on campus. Markera had always known she could learn. For her, the change was that with each experience, her *vision* for herself expanded, prompting her to strive for more, and she picked up new learning techniques from writing to data analysis to research design. That's what activated her growth mindset. She was like the speaker in Elizabeth Alexander's timless lines:

> We cross dirt roads and highways that mark
> the will of some one and then others, who said
> I need to see what's on the other side.
>
> I know there's something better down the road.
> We need to find a place where we are safe.
> *We walk into that which we cannot yet see.* (my italics)[13]

Markera loved learning as an experience and knew that she was very good. But it could be disconcerting to hear privileged F&M students talk with authority about themes like homelessness or crime when in fact they'd never met the people about whom they were opining. A breakthrough came in Sociology 100 when some uninformed classmates debated the life choices and attitudes of the poor. "There are just some things textbooks and PowerPoint slides cannot teach," she reflected later. That was when she grasped that, yes, higher education could help her see causes and cures of the inequities she'd lived and, yes, she could draw on the details of her life to enhance scholarly understanding—a meaningful merging of her genius, her values, her past, her purpose, and her love for her community.

Hope also was seeded by mentors. Involved educators like Allison Troy, Michael Penn, Monica Cable, and Donnell Butler invited her into research and nudged her toward graduate school. Their support motivated her to envision working in education to knock down hurdles placed in front of low-income children. Markera was fortunate to have access to such mentors who, as Steven Mintz writes, believe they have the privilege and the duty to help their mentees "to consider their goals and dreams and work with them to craft a realistic path forward" in creating "their future selves."[14]

Still, straddling the starkly different worlds of home and school was a slippery balancing act for Markera, as it had been for Sheldon. How do you sustain hopes that your loved ones don't have? How do you choose optimism when some whom you love are being struck down by forces too distant to fight? These are perennial questions for anyone trying to break free from social strictures. Opt in, or sit out? True, higher education can foster the knowledge, training, skills, will, and mindsets that can be the electric currents of social mobility and political empowerment. But, long before college, we must instill in children the desire to learn and strive, the conviction they can, and the trust that society exists to help them. That's no small task given the injustices and inequities highlighting every chapter of the American story. Education at every level, including college, can and must prepare the young for lifelong growth and flourishing.

Which brings me to a time I saw firsthand the resilient hope that Markera bolstered in college, which America needs now. It was September 2013, in her junior year. We'd formed a warm relationship, and I knew she valued my mentoring and care. One afternoon, after we'd talked about her new idea to bring sociology classes to public schools, the internet blew up with bracing news from her alma mater, Coatesville High School. A local paper was reporting that two school employees had sent hundreds of racist text messages with their district-owned phones. Well, not just any two employees. It was the superintendent and the athletics director, who regularly called students and colleagues the nastiest of epithets, including the "n" word.[15]

I learned about this violation of trust and decency through my Facebook newsfeed, because Markera had posted her tormented reaction and linked to the news coverage. How could this happen at her high school, where her sister goes now, she lamented. How could this happen in her country?

I remember emailing her that night to express my concern. Meeting up the next day, she looked weary and drawn. Those abusive text messages brought back to the surface some facts of racial life she'd chosen not to dwell upon—the ninth-grade segregation, the police profiling, the decrepit public hospitals, the mainstream indifference toward the plight of Black Americans. Just talking, she grew more disgusted. The very people who are supposed to help her community—school leaders!—spewing ignorance and hatred.

My heart went out to this survivor of generational racial trauma. She was facing a crisis of double consciousness: This is how white America really sees us.

Would this be the blow that broke her hope? Would this melt her trust in F&M, or the white-dominated power structures into which her college education supposedly promised access?

The Coatesville outrage came to light during a semester, importantly, when Markera was trying out Arabic and nailing it. She also was talking with French professors about a bold goal to study overseas and live with a host family. I hoped, even as the reality of racism scratched her spirit, that she would also feel the moral weight of another reality, which was that some caring F&M educators were involved in her life and feeding her hopes, with actions based on seeing and caring for *her*, the person, without bias or a sense of superiority.

Happily, about a week after the Coatesville scandal quieted, Markera achieved her bold goal when she was chosen for a prestigious semester-away program in Aix-en-Provence, France. She immediately sent me a joyful email—I GOT IT!

Whew, I thought, glad that an uplift had arrived after all the anguish. Praise the day. She was again the striver, walking into that which she could not yet fully see. A few minutes after responding to her excited email, when scrolling again through the Facebook newsfeed, I came upon a brand-new post that she'd made to her friends. One little sentence, five words with wings:

I like who I'm becoming.

*

It's beautiful to see talent fly, especially among those who have taken to the air with a purity of heart and few advantages. Markera, Sheldon, and Akbar prove the possible for the unsung many who also have their gift for growth. Raised with love, propelled to F&M by sensational college advisors, they said yes to college opportunity every day they were there. They drove their growth as strivers and discoverers and collaborators and mentors with their choices and the good influences of college educators and the campus ecosystem. They're now promising leaders for our country—a psychologist, a diplomat, and a state secretary for policy, respectively. Each is flourishing and with a mindset for much more. How American is that?

I could say the same about Leo McFarland, the son of a New York City firefighter, a witness to 9/11 trauma, who went to F&M so that he could live his calling to fight terror on different battlefields than the one that chose his father.

Or Julie Song, who held dean's list grades and DACA papers with equal pride—a brave leader with an ardent mind devoted to standing up for the legions of unseen Dreamers who've earned a place in America with their guts and their goals and their records.

Or Donnell Bailey, one of the children left by the wayside in the wake of Hurricane Katrina, whose family ricocheted from New Orleans to Houston and back, and who learned in college that you can go home again, and thus did, equipped with the will and skill to help run the city someday.

Or Julia Ramsey, now working in national security; or Alec Hersh, still writing while also working in community development; or Eddie Alsina, who has just finished his doctorate; or Jeanette Berlanga, who earned her law degree; or Nadia Johnson and Allie Morey, now teaching school. The dancers and the dance. With their track records of learning, activated by college, they all know that today and tomorrow, come what may, they can do more and learn more and give more. Each has a growth mindset, ignited at F&M. Each looks forward to the future. Each is still becoming.

These are the faces of America's future. Their prospects, and this country's, are brighter because of their undergraduate formation. Some may argue that America doesn't need, can't afford, or isn't helped by the college system we've built—but that's counter to everything we know about people's need to keep developing in our weltering, knowledge-powered world. The core asset of a democracy is its young people, both as ends in themselves and as the engines of a more free, just, equitable, and inclusive country. They must be educated for lives of endless growth and supported in their originality. This is the calling and power of college. Kindle their fire. Involve them, and they will learn, and then they will keep learning, and as they do . . .

. . . *America will like who we're becoming.*

Chapter 6: Questions for Discussion

1. In the introduction, the author defines talent as the assets and potentialities people can tap to pursue their purposes, deal well with difficulties, and add value to the world. He believes that having a growth mindset is a form of talent predictive of college success (and more). Do you agree with this definition of talent and with the idea that growth mindsets are a form of talent?

2. The author believes that, at its best, college is more important and more relevant than ever for young people, and that America should prioritize investing in forms of education that enhance growth mindsets while reducing the cost of college for families. Do you agree?

3. The concluding chapter makes three interconnected arguments for college—the social case, the business case, and the human-centered case. Which speaks most strongly to you? Which do you think is most compelling to rebuild public support in an era of mounting skepticism about higher education?

4. The chapter profiles Akbar, Sheldon, and Markera, three young people from low-income Pennsylvania communities who easily could have missed out on college. Today, with college and graduate degrees under their belts, they are striving, highly promising young professionals serving the public good. Why do you think the author chose to end the book with these stories?

5. Now that you have finished the book, what questions do you have for the author? For higher education as a whole? If you work in higher education, does the book inspire you to do something differently? What about if you're a student?

ACKNOWLEDGMENTS

I'm grateful to the legions of people who made this book possible.

First and foremost, I'd like to thank the Franklin & Marshall College graduates who appear in these pages. As a group, they are talented, engaged, sincere, and appreciative. They were generous in sharing their stories of growth so that others could benefit from their experience. In a few cases, I have identified them with pseudonyms. My only regret is that I could not write about the learning of even more of students who attended F&M between 2011 and 2018.

Many F&M faculty and staff were equally generous with their time and perspectives. Caitlin Brust, now pursuing her PhD, helped me frame and structure the book and conducted insightful interviews with several students. I also would like to thank the extraordinary Michael Penn for reading the entire manuscript, and Ken Hess and Dan Wagner for discussing its themes with me. Pierce Buller, Donnell Butler, Alan Caniglia, Cristina Diez, Sonia Elliot, Bob Freund, Margaret Hazlett, Sam Houser, Shawn Jenkins, Julie Kerich, Daniel Lugo, Eric Maguire, Joel Martin, Keiran Miller, Robin Piggott, Ann Steiner, Beth Throne, Kent Trachte, and many others played pivotal roles in the development of F&M's Next Generation talent strategy and enhanced my understanding of the power of college to activate lifelong learning. Christian Hartranft advised me brilliantly on institutional strategy and the student experience, as did Ashley Christopherson, Robert Diggs, Kelseyleigh Hepler, and Katie Machen. I could easily thank dozens more F&M colleagues for their exceptional commitment to our students.

The same goes for the F&M Board of Trustees and alumni/parent community. My two board chairs, Larry Bonchek and Sue Washburn, devoted themselves to excellence, equity, and effective governance. I'm honored to have served as president immediately after Richard Kneedler and John Fry, and just before Barbara Altmann.

I would like to wholeheartedly thank Johns Hopkins University Press editor Greg Britton and his magnificent team, including Diem Bloom, Hilary Jacqmin, and Kris Lykke. I especially would like to acknowledge my superb copyeditor, Terri Lee Paulsen, and my indexer, Kathy Patterson. I'm grateful to a few friends who reviewed excerpts, including Emily Alden, Andy Delbanco, Deneen Howell, Jamie Merisotis, Rick Miller, Carol Quillen, Josh Wyner, and especially Peter Dougherty, who read the entire manuscript and set its publication in motion by introducing me to Greg Britton.

The book reflects insights gleaned from fourteen years teaching and working at Georgetown University. I'm indebted to many more colleagues than there's space to name, especially President Jack DeGioia; former board chair Paul Tagliabue; the late Timothy S. Healy, SJ; and the educators Tony Arend, John Glavin, Otto Hentz, SJ, and Todd Olson.

I want to thank the many scholars, practitioners, and journalists from whom I've learned, especially Carol Dweck, whose seminal research on growth mindsets is now a beacon for countless educators and in many fields. Others include Nick Anderson, Ken Bain, Douglas Belkin, Goldie Blumenstyk, Agnes Callard, Anthony Carnevale, Daniel Chambliss, Ron Daniels, Richard Detweiler, Michael Drake, Angela Duckworth, Chris Eisgruber, Joshua Eyler, Peter Felten, Mark Gearan, Kathleen Harring, the late bell hooks,

Cappy Hill, Freeman Hrabowski, Anthony Jack, Scott Jaschik, Brit Kirwan, Melissa Korn, Martin Kurzweil, Leo Lambert, James Lang, Tania LaViolet, Doug Lederman, David Leonhardt, Richard Light, Beth McMurtrie, Stephen Mintz, Ted Mitchell, Mary Murphy, Elizabeth Pisacreta, Song Richardson, Michael Roth, Jeff Selingo, Eric Spina, Christopher Takacs, Beverly Tatum, Paul Tough, Sara Weissman, and Richard Whitmire.

I'm also grateful to an array of precollege education leaders whose insights influenced F&M's Next Generation talent strategy, including Norman Atkins, Richard Barth, Elisa Villanueva Beard, Deborah Bial, David Coleman, John Foley, SJ, Kaya Henderson, Nicole Hurd, John King, Wendy Kopp, Dave Levin, and Joseph Parkes, SJ. We also learned a great deal from the nonprofit and philanthropic leaders Katherine Bradley, Doris Fisher, John Fisher, Don Graham, Patricia Harris, Jenny Kane, Julie Mikuta, Carrie Penner, Jon Schnur, and Howard Wolfson.

I drafted much of this book on weekends late in the COVID-19 pandemic. During this time, I was continuously inspired by my Aspen Institute colleagues, fellows, trustees, and partners, especially our current chair Margot Pritzker. With great sadness, I would like to acknowledge the passing of three public-spirited trustees who always supported education and young people: Ann Korologos, Jim Crown, and Madeleine Albright. May their reputations and reach continue to grow.

I come from a family of educators, including my late parents, Anne Butler and Gordon Porterfield, and my siblings, Kate Porterfield and Matthew Porterfield. Their influences run through everything I do.

Finally, my deepest gratitude goes to my spouse and partner, Karen Herrling, and our children, Lizzie, Caroline, and Sarah. For eight years we lived as a faculty family in a Georgetown residence hall—an almost idyllic experience—followed by seven years at Franklin & Marshall. Each of them has profound ideas about education. I admire the ways that Karen, Lizzie, Caroline, and Sarah have lived their lives and pursued their growth, and I thank them with all my love.

NOTES

Preface

1. Carol S. Dweck, *Mindset: The New Psychology of Success* (New York: Ballantine Books, 2006), 6–9.

2. See Paul Tough, "Americans Are Losing Faith in the Value of College. Whose Fault Is That?," *New York Times Magazine*, September 5, 2023.

3. Tough, "Americans Are Losing Faith."

Introduction

1. Zachary Schermele, "Public Trust in Higher Ed Has Plummeted. Yes, Again," *Chronicle of Higher Education*, July 11, 2023; Meghan Brink, "Public Opinion on Value of Higher Ed Remains Mixed," *Inside Higher Ed*, July 12, 2022; and Douglas Belkin, "Americans Are Losing Faith in College Education, WSJ-NORC Poll Finds," *Wall Street Journal*, March 31, 2023.

2. See "Educational Gag Orders: Legislative Restrictions on the Freedom to Read, Learn, and Teach," PEN America, 2023. https://pen.org/report/educational-gag-orders/.

3. David Leonhardt, "The Morning," *New York Times*, August 25, 2022. A 2023 study by the *Institute for Higher Education Policy* found that "nearly all public and private nonprofit institutions" give students "a meaningful increase in their financial well-being after attending college." See Kim Dancy, Genevieve Garcia-Kendrick, and Diane Cheng, "Rising Above the Threshold: How Expansions in Financial Aid Can Increase the Equitable Delivery of Postsecondary Value for More Students," *Institute for Higher Education Policy*, June 2023, 7.

4. The Lumina Foundation and Gallup, "Education for What?," Gallup, Inc., 2023.

5. Carol S. Dweck, *Mindset: The New Psychology of Success* (New York: Ballantine Books, 2006), 6–9.

6. Marshall College merged with Franklin College in 1853 to create F&M. Sally F. Griffith, *Liberalizing the Mind: Two Centuries of Liberal Learning at Franklin & Marshall College* (University Park, PA: Penn State University Press, 2010), 24.

7. In a 2021 study of the "educational ecology" of liberal arts education, Richard Detweiler documents the value of the *context, content*, and *purposes* of undergraduate learning, which are interlinked. The context includes an "authentic educational community" in which "students, faculty, and staff interact with each other in meaningful ways." Richard A. Detweiler, *The Evidence Liberal Arts*

Needs: Lives of Consequence, Inquiry, and Accomplishment (Cambridge, MA: MIT Press, 2021), 32.

8. Dweck, *Mindset: The New Psychology*, 6.

9. Dweck, *Mindset: The New Psychology*, 3–14.

10. Carol S. Dweck, "What Having a 'Growth Mindset' Actually Means," *Harvard Business Review*, January 13, 2016.

11. Dweck, *Mindset: The New Psychology*, 182.

12. Carol S. Dweck, *Mindset: Changing the Way You Think to Fulfill Your Potential*, revised ed. (London: Robinson, 2017), 7.

13. Agnes Callard, *Aspiration: The Agency of Becoming* (Oxford: Oxford University Press, 2018), 180.

14. See Paul Tough, "Who Gets to Graduate?," *New York Times Magazine*, May 15, 2014.

15. Jonathan Malesic, "My Students Are Not OK," *New York Times*, May 13, 2022; and Beth McMurtrie, "A 'Stunning' Level of Student Disconnection," *Chronicle of Higher Education*, April 5, 2022.

16. Julia Ramsey, "Convocation Remarks," August 30, 2016. https://www.fandm.edu/news/latest-news/2016/08/30/convocation-remarks-by-junior-julia-ramsey.

17. See Dani Blum, "The Other Side of Languishing Is Flourishing. Here's How to Get There," *New York Times*, May 6, 2021.

18. John Henry Newman, *The Idea of a University* (Notre Dame, IN: Notre Dame University Press, 1982), 91.

19. Private email conversation.

20. Danielle Allen, "Participatory Readiness," in *Education and Equality* (Chicago: University of Chicago Press, 2016), 50.

21. See the Coalition for Transformational Education, a consortium of colleges and universities innovating and learning together, at https://thecte.org. Wendy Fischman and Howard Gardner, *The Real World of College: What Higher Education Is and What It Can Be* (Cambridge, MA: MIT Press, 2022); and Edward Maloney and Joshua Kim, *Learning Innovation and the Future of College Education* (Baltimore: Johns Hopkins University Press, 2020).

22. For example, one could look to define and identify positive mindsets for friendship, spirituality, or industriousness, but it's not clear that college furthers them distinctively in comparison with other ecosystems. The same could be said of negative mindsets like selfishness or conformity. On the other hand, the five mindsets explored here clearly correlate with identifiable features of the undergraduate experience and have value for life after college.

23. James Baldwin, "The Creative Process," in *Creative America* (New York: Ridge Press, 1962).

24. Jeffrey J. Selingo, "What the Economy Needs, What Employers Want," in *There Is Life After College* (New York: HarperCollins, 2016), 29–60.

25. Ken Bain, "What Makes Great Teachers Great?," *Chronicle of Higher Education*, April 9, 2004.

26. Elizabeth A. Canning, Katherine Muenks, Dorainne J. Green, and Mary C. Murphy, "STEM Faculty Who Believe Ability Is Fixed Have Larger Racial Achievement Gaps and Inspire Less Student Motivation in Their Classes," *Science Advances* 5, no. 2 (2019). Also, Scott Jaschik, "The Impact of Faculty Attitudes about Intelligence," *Inside Higher Ed*, February 18, 2019.

27. Reyna Grande, *A Dream Called Home: A Memoir* (New York: Washington Square Press, 2018), 35–6.

28. Susan Magsamen and Ivy Ross document the benefits for learning, health, and relationships of "enriched environments," which they define as "Places that offer a variety of multisensory stimulation, which, in turn, triggers the neuroplasticity of your brain." Susan Magsamen and Ivy Ross, *Your Brain on Art: How the Arts Transforms Us* (New York: Random House, 2023), 182.

29. Twyla Tharp, *The Creative Habit: Learn It and Use It for Life* (New York: Simon and Schuster Paperbacks), 168.

30. "Who Mentored Gwen Ifill," *Who Mentored You?*, Harvard T. H. Chan School of Public Health (https://sites.sph.harvard.edu/wmy/celebrities/gwen-ifill/).

31. Keith Sawyer, *Group Genius: The Creative Power of Collaboration* (New York: Basic Books, 2017), 7.

32. Bendjhi Villiers, "Welcome Remarks, F&M New Student Convocation," September 1, 2015 (https://www.fandm.edu/news/latest-news/2015/09/01/class-of -2019-urged-to-pursue-their-big-hairy-audacious-goals).

33. See Elizabeth F. Barkley, Claire Howell Major, and K. Patricia Cross, *Collaborative Learning Techniques: A Handbook for College Faculty*, 2nd ed. (San Francisco: Jossey-Bass, 2014).

34. Callard, *Aspiration: The Agency*, 10.

35. Madeleine Albright, *Madame Secretary: A Memoir* (New York: Harper Perennial, 2013), 512.

36. Sujata Gupta, "QnAs with Carol S. Dweck," *Proceedings of the National Academy of Sciences of the United States of America* 110, no. 37 (August 16, 2013): 14818.

37. Paul Tough, *How Children Succeed: Grit, Curiosity and the Hidden Power of Character* (New York: Houghton Mifflin Harcourt, 2013), 49–104.

38. Claudia Goldin and Lawrence Katz, *The Race between Education and Technology* (Cambridge, MA: Belknap Press of Harvard University Press, 2008), 1–2.

39. Sir Ken Robinson, *Out of Our Minds: Learning to Be Creative*, fully revised and updated ed. (West Sussex, UK: Capstone Publishing, 2011), 19–47.

40. Erik Brynjolfsson and Andrew McAfee, *The Second Machine Age: Work, Progress, and Prosperity in a Time of Brilliant Technologies* (New York: W. W. Norton: 2016); and Klaus Schwab, *The Fourth Industrial Revolution* (New York: Crown Business, 2017).

41. See Jamie Merisotis, *Human Work in the Age of Smart Machines* (New York: RosettaBooks, 2020); and Peter Felten and Leo M. Lambert, *Relationship-Rich Education: How Human Connections Drive Success in College* (Baltimore: Johns Hopkins University Press, 2020).

42. Eduardo Briceño, *The Performance Paradox: Turning the Power of Mindset into Action* (New York: Ballantine Books, 2023), 16.

43. For a clear, practical review of strategies to optimize student agency and learning, see Sandra Yancy McGuire, *Teach Students How to Learn: Strategies You Can Incorporate into Any Course to Improve Student Metacognition, Study Skills and Motivation* (Sterling, VA: Stylus Publishing, 2015).

44. Daniel F. Chambliss and Christopher G. Takacs, *How College Works* (Cambridge, MA: Harvard University Press, 2014), 4.

45. See Felten and Lambert, *Relationship-Rich Education.*

46. See Sharon Daloz Parks, *Big Questions, Worthy Dreams: Mentoring Emerging Adults in Their Search for Meaning, Purpose and Faith*, rev. ed. (San Francisco: Jossey-Bass, 2000, 2011).

47. See James M. Lang, *Small Teaching: Everyday Lessons from the Science of Learning* (San Francisco: Jossey-Bass, 2016).

48. Sara Weissman, "New Analysis Finds Most Families Can't Cover College Costs," *Inside Higher Ed*, August 18, 2023.

49. See Anthony Abraham Jack, *The Privileged Poor: How Elite Colleges Are Failing Disadvantaged Students* (Cambridge, MA: Harvard University Press, 2019).

50. See "From a Nation at Risk to a Nation at Hope: Recommendations from the National Commission on Social, Emotional, and Academic Learning" (Washington, DC: The Aspen Institute, 2019).

51. Detweiler, *The Evidence*, 21.

52. Kevin Kiley, "Finding the 'Next Generation,'" *Inside Higher Ed*, December 14, 2012; Peg Tyre, "Improving Economic Diversity at the Better Colleges," *New York Times*, February 5, 2014; and Richard Whitmire, *The B.A. Breakthrough: How Ending Diploma Disparities Can Change the Face of America* (New York: The 74 Media, 2019), 126–139. Also, "Should Financial Aid Go Only to Students in Need?," *Newshour*, August 20, 2015. https://youtube.com/watch?v=BjxFookwIno&t=1s.

53. See Caroline M. Hoxby and Christopher Avery, "The Missing 'One-Offs': The Hidden Supply of High-Achieving, Low-Income Students" (Cambridge, MA: National Bureau of Economic Research, December 2012).

54. Daniel Porterfield, "Lower-Income Students to Top Colleges: A Little Help Here!," *The Hechinger Report*. July 2, 2015. https://hechingerreport.org/lower-income-students-to-top-colleges-a-little-help-here/.

55. See Angela Duckworth, *Grit: The Power and Passion of Perseverance* (New York: Scribner Book Company, 2016).

56. For a study of the benefits of wealth and class at 12 Ivy-Plus institutions, see Raj Chetty, David J. Deming, and John N. Friedman, "Diversifying Society's Leaders? The Determinants and Consequences of Admission to Highly Selective Colleges," *Opportunity Insights*, July 2023.

57. Nick Anderson, "Colleges Often Give Discounts to the Rich. But Here's One That Gave Up on 'Merit Aid,'" *Washington Post*, December 29, 2014.

58. For an explanation of the power of these interconnected self-beliefs, see Briceño, *Performance Paradox*, 200.

59. On the long-term benefits of a liberal arts education, see Detweiler. For a compendium of evidence-based findings on undergraduate learning and growth, see Matthew J. Mayhew et al., *How College Affects Students*, Vol. 3, (San Francisco: Jossey-Bass, 2016). On lifetime earnings, see Anthony Carnevale, "The College Payoff: Education, Occupations, and Lifetime Earnings" (Washington, DC: Georgetown University Center on Education and the Workforce, 2011). For alumni perceptions of college's value, see "Great Jobs, Great Lives: The 2014 Gallup-Purdue Alumni Report," Gallup, Inc., 2014."

60. Benjamin Franklin, "Proposals Relating to the Education of Youth in Pennsylvania," 1749; and Walter Isaacson, *A Benjamin Franklin Reader* (New York: Simon & Schuster, 2003) 140.

61. See Andrew Delbanco, *College: What It Was, Is, and Should Be*, 2nd ed. (Princeton, NJ: Princeton University Press, 2023).

62. See Michael Roth, *Beyond the University: Why Liberal Education Matters* (New Haven, CT: Yale University Press, 2015).

Chapter 1

1. Barbara K. Altmann, "Inauguration Address," October 27, 2018. https://www .youtube.com/watch?app=desktop&v=Demn9llFXMA.

2. John Dewey, *How We Think* (Boston: D. C. Heath & Co. Publishers, 1933), 6.

3. Carol S. Dweck, *Mindset: The New Psychology of Success* (New York: Ballantine Books, 2006), 48.

4. A 2014 survey of thirty thousand college alums found that "the three most potent elements linked to long-term success for college grads relate to *emotional support*: feeling that they had a professor who made them excited about learning, that the professors at their alma mater cared about them as a person, and that they had a mentor who encouraged them to pursue their goals and dreams. If graduates strongly agree with these three things, it doubles the odds that they are engaged in their work and thriving in their overall well-being." See Brandon Busteed, "The Biggest Blown Opportunity in Higher Ed History," *Gallup Business Journal*, October 7, 2014 (https://news.gallup.com/businessjournal/178082/biggest-blown -opportunity-higher-history.aspx).

5. Agnes Callard, *Aspiration: The Agency of Becoming* (Oxford: Oxford University Press, 2018), 61.

6. William Wordsworth, *The Prelude*, 1805–1806, Book XIII, 446–447 (New York: Penguin Books, 1972), 536.

7. JT Torres, "Four Questions to Ask to Promote Student Learning," *Inside Higher Ed*, March 8, 2023.

8. Beth McMurtrie emphasizes that it is important for faculty to carefully explain to students why particular academic techniques or skills required in a class will help them to learn. Beth McMurtrie, "Why the Science of Teaching Is Often Ignored," *Chronicle of Higher Education*, January 3, 2022.

9. Daniel F. Chambliss and Christopher G. Takacs, *How College Works* (Cambridge, MA: Harvard University Press, 2014), 155, 159.

10. Dweck, *Mindset: The New Psychology*, 67.

11. Frederick Douglass, *Narrative of the Life of Frederick Douglass, an American Slave* (New York: Penguin Books, 1982), 78–79.

12. Wendy Fischman and Howard Gardner, *The Real World of College: What Higher Education Is and What It Can Be* (Cambridge, MA: MIT Press, 2022), 246–47.

13. Joshua R. Eyler, *How Humans Learn: The Science and Stories Behind Effective College Teaching* (Morgantown: West Virginia University Press, 2018), 129. Also, see Chambliss and Takacs, *How College Works*, 53–59.

14. Maria Carrasco, "Survey: Most Students Self-Censor on Campus and Online," *Inside Higher Ed*, September 23, 2021.

15. Matthew J. Mayhew et al., *How College Affects Students*, Vol. 3 (San Francisco: Jossey-Bass, 2016), 384–86.

16. Louis Deslauriers, Logan S. McCarty, Kelly Miller, Kristina Callaghan, and Greg Kestin, "Measuring Actual Learning versus Feeling of Learning in Response to Being Actively Engaged in the Classroom," *PNAS* 116, no. 39 (2019): 19251–19257.

17. Beth McMurtrie, "Why the Science of Teaching is Often Ignored," *Chronicle of Higher Education*, January 3, 2022.

18. See https://pogil.org/.

19. Tara Parker-Pope, "The Growth Mind-Set: Why Friends, Family and Work Make a Difference," *Washington Post*, June 19, 2023.

20. Eyler, *How Humans Learn*, 161.

21. Agnes Callard, "Liberal Education and the Possibility of Valuational Progress," *Social Philosophy & Policy* 34, no. 2 (2017): 15.

22. Morgan Kincade, "Commencement Address," Franklin & Marshall College, 2016.

23. Hess was mentoring Eddie to value both *investing* himself in new experiences and *harvesting* the fruits of existing or acquired interests. See Richard Light and Allison Jegla, *Becoming Great Universities* (Princeton, NJ: Princeton University Press, 2022), 49–70.

24. A. Bartlett Giamatti, "The Earthly Use of a Liberal Education," in *A Free and Ordered Space: The Real World of the University* (New York: W. W. Norton, 1990), 119. Cited in Callard, "Liberal Education," 17.

25. Anthony Abraham Jack, *The Privileged Poor: How Elite Colleges Are Failing Disadvantaged Students* (Cambridge, MA: Harvard University Press, 2019). Also see Gregory M. Walton and Geoffrey L. Cohen, "A Question of Belonging: Race, Social Fit, and Achievement," *Journal of Personality and Social Psychology* 92, no. 1 (2007): 82–96.

26. Tara Westover, *Educated* (New York: Random House, 2018) and Ron Suskind, *A Hope in the Unseen: An American Odyssey from the Inner City to the Ivy League* (New York: Crown, 1999).

27. Anzia Yezierska, "Soap and Water," from *Hungry Hearts* (Cambridge: Riverside Press, 1920; reprinted in Research Triangle Park, NC: National Humanities Center, 2005), 11.

28. Ken Bain, "What Makes Great Teachers Great?," *Chronicle of Higher Education*, April 9, 2004.

29. Andrew Delbanco, *College: What It Was, Is, and Should Be*, 2nd ed. (Princeton, NJ: Princeton University Press, 2023), 35.

30. bell hooks, *Feminism Is for Everybody: Passionate Politics* (Boston: South End Press, 2000), 110.

31. Drew Gilpin Faust, "John Hope Franklin: Race & the Meaning of America," *New York Review of Books*, December 17, 2015.

32. Daniel Niederjohn, "Increasing Growth Mindset and Performance in the College Classroom," *American Psychological Association*, September 8, 2022.

33. Light and Jegla, *Becoming Great Universities*, 100–120.

34. Jeff Selingo, "It's Time to Ditch the Transcript, Diploma, and Résumé," *LinkedIn*, November 5, 2013.

35. Steven Mintz, "Teaching Matters," *Inside Higher Ed*, August 15, 2023. Mintz has written numerous insightful columns for *Inside Higher Ed* on the importance of high-impact practices, active learning, and more generally, a renewed focus on holistic undergraduate learning. For example, see "Raising the Quality of a College Education in Our Age of Diminished Expectations," August 4, 2023, and "Recapturing American Higher Education's Lost Promise," July 27, 2023.

Chapter 2

1. Kate Clifford Larson, *Rosemary: The Hidden Kennedy Daughter* (New York: Mariner Books, 2015).

2. Johann Hari summarizes three aspects of Mihaly Csikszentmihalyi's concept of flow that I've observed when undergraduates create: "First, flow takes all your mental energy deployed deliberately in one direction. Second, that goal needs to be meaningful to you—you can't flow into a goal that you don't care about. Third, it helps if what you are doing is at the edge of your abilities." Johann Hari, "Your Attention Didn't Collapse. It Was Stolen," *The Guardian*, January 2, 2022.

3. On creativity and growth mindsets, see Carol S. Dweck, *Mindset: The New Psychology of Success* (New York: Ballantine Books, 2006), 70.

4. Dean Hammer, "New Student Convocation Speech," September 2, 2014. https://www.fandm.edu/news/latest-news/2014/09/02/professor-of-government -dean-hammer-convocation-speech.

5. Beverly Daniel Tatum, *Why Are All the Black Kids Sitting Together in the Cafeteria?: And Other Conversations About Race*, revised and updated (New York: Basic Books, 2017), 339.

6. Hammer, "New Student Convocation Speech."

7. Martin Luther King Jr., "The Quest for Peace and Justice," Nobel Lecture, December 11, 1964. https://www.nobelprize.org/prizes/peace/1964/king/lecture/.

8. Dweck, *Mindset: The New Psychology*, 80.

9. Benjamin S. Selznick and Matthew J. Mayhew, "How Colleges Can Develop Innovators," *Inside Higher Ed*, June 2, 2022.

10. Lee Gardner, "Can Design Thinking Re-Design Higher Ed?," *Chronicle of Higher Education*, September 10, 2017.

11. The following semester, then-provost Joel Martin became the innovator and pitched a funder on a $400,000 grant to extend the class to a year-long format. More professors were recruited, from more departments, and the nature of the ventures was widened to include for-profit and campus-based work.

12. Tony Wagner, *Creating Innovators* (New York: Simon & Schuster, 2012), 4-5.

13. Wagner, *Creating Innovators*, 24-30.

14. Warren Glynn, "F&M Student Group Provides Solar Ovens to Guatemalan Families," *F&M News*, December 11, 2013.

15. Tim Stuhldreher, "Franklin & Marshall Debate Team Ranks among Nation's Best," *LNP/Lancaster Online*, February 28, 2016.

16. In 2022, the Mexican government arrested the former attorney general and at least thirty-two others in connection with the killings and their cover-up. See Oscar Lopez, "Mexico Says Disappearance of 43 Students Was a 'Crime of the State,'" *New York Times*, August 18, 2022.

17. Sir Ken Robinson, *Out of Our Minds: Learning to Be Creative*, fully rev. and updated ed. (West Sussex, UK: Capstone Publishing, 2011), 42.

18. Gloria E. Anzaldua, "Beyond Traditional Notions of Identity," *Chronicle of Higher Education*, October 11, 2002.

19. Clifford A. Pearson, "Winter Visual Arts Center at Franklin & Marshall College by Steven Holl Architects," *Architectural Record*, October 2, 2020.

20. Mary Oliver, "The Summer Day," in *Devotions* (New York: Penguin Press, 2017), 317.

21. Quoted in Maria Popova, "Nick Cave on Creativity, the Myth of Originality, and How to Find Your Voice," *Marginalian*, January 20, 2022. https://www.themarginalian .org/2022/01/20/nick-cave-creativity/.

Chapter 3

1. Peter Collier, "Why Peer Mentoring Is an Effective Approach for Promoting College Student Success," *Metropolitan Universities*, 28, no. 3 (2017).

2. Buffy Smith, *Mentoring At-Risk Students through the Hidden Curriculum of Higher Education* (Lanham, MD: Lexington Books, 2013), 47. Also, Rachel Gable, *The Hidden Curriculum: First Generation Students at Legacy Universities* (Princeton NJ: Princeton University Press, 2021).

3. See Peter Felten and Leo M. Lambert, *Relationship-Rich Education: How Human Connections Drive Success in College* (Baltimore: Johns Hopkins University Press, 2020), 135-146.

4. See Laurent Daloz, *Mentor: Guiding the Journeys of Adult Learners* (San Francisco: Jossey-Bass, 1999); Kathy Peno, Elaine M. Silva Mangiante, and Rita Kenehan, *Mentoring in Formal and Informal Contexts* (Charlotte, NC: Information Age Publishing, 2016).

5. To cite a few examples, see Toddi Gutner, "Finding Anchors in the Storm: Mentors," *Wall Street Journal*, January 27, 2009; Krithika Varagur, "To Gen Zers Working from Home, the Office Is a Remote Concept," *Wall Street Journal*, August 21, 2021.

For an excellent series of practical guides, see Lois J. Zachary, *Creating a Mentoring Culture: The Organization's Guide* (San Francisco: Jossey-Bass, 2005); Lois J. Zachary with Lory A. Fischler, *The Mentee's Guide: Making Mentoring Work for You* (San Francisco: Jossey-Bass, 2009); and Lois J. Zachary, *The Mentor's Guide: Facilitating Effective Learning Relationships* (San Francisco: Jossey-Bass, 2000).

6. See W. Brad Johnson, *On Being a Mentor*, 2nd ed. (New York: Routledge, 2016); and Maria Lamonaca Wisdom, "Why Don't We Teach PhDs to Be Mentors," *Chronicle of Higher Education*, September 21, 2021.

7. Zachary, *Creating a Mentoring Culture*, xxi.

8. Felten and Lambert, *Relationship-Rich Education*, 132–34.

9. Christa Rodriguez, "LIFT Hosts Voices, Performers Focus on Violence, Injustice," *College Reporter*, December 6, 2015.

10. Carol S. Dweck, *Mindset: The New Psychology of Success* (New York: Ballantine Books, 2006), 215.

11. Melissa Ezarik, "Students Need Mentors, and More Help in Making Those Connections," *Inside Higher Ed*, October 28, 2021.

12. Smith, *Mentoring At-Risk Students*, 89–141; Richard Detweiler, *The Evidence Liberal Arts Needs* (Cambridge, MA: MIT Press, 2021); Johnson, *On Being a Mentor*, 137–146; and Alexander C. Kafka, "For Mentorships to Work, Colleges Have to Commit," *Chronicle of Higher Education*, November 18, 2018.

13. See Peter J. Collier, *Developing Effective Student Peer Mentoring Programs: A Practitioner's Guide to Program Design, Delivery, Evaluation and Training* (Sterling, VA: Stylus Publishing, 2015); Jenepher Lennox Terrion, Ruth Philion, and Dominique Leonard, "An Evaluation of a University Peer-Mentoring Training Programme," *International Journal of Evidence Based Coaching and Mentoring* 5, no. 1 (February 2007).

14. Felten and Lambert, *Relationship-Rich Education*.

15. See Dan Barry, "A Joyful Bustle to Get Ready for Guests: Syrian Refugees," *New York Times*, December 24, 2016; "Lancaster, Pennsylvania: America's Refugee Capital," *BBC News*, January 27, 2017.

16. Bennett Helm, "Friendship," *Stanford Encyclopedia of Philosophy* (Fall 2021 ed.), Edward N. Zalta (ed.), https://plato.stanford.edu/archives/fall2021/entries/friendship/; Dean Cocking and Jeanette Kennett, "Friendship and the Self," *Ethics* 108 (1998): 502–27.

17. David Whyte, *Consolations: The Solace, Nourishment and Underlying Meaning of Everyday Words* (Langley, WA: Many Rivers Press, 2015).

18. Douglas Belkin, "A Generation of American Men Give Up on College: 'I Just Feel Lost,'" *Wall Street Journal*, September 6, 2021; Derek Thompson, "Colleges Have a Guy Problem," *Atlantic*, September 14, 2021.

19. Maria Carrasco, "Students Embrace Peer Mental Health Counseling," *Inside Higher Ed*, January 23, 2022.

Chapter 4

1. Sir Ken Robinson, *Out of Our Minds: Learning to Be Creative*, fully revised and updated ed. (West Sussex, UK: Capstone Publishing, 2011), 235.

2. Jon R. Katzenbach and Douglas K. Smith, "The Discipline of Teams," *Harvard Business Review* (March–April 1993). https://hbr.org/1993/03/the-discipline-of -teams-2#:~:text=A%20working%20group's%20performance%20is,interviews%2 C%20surveys%2C%20or%20experiments.

3. Eduardo Briceño has written thoughtfully about how and why learning cultures improve team performance. See Eduardo Briceño, *The Performance Paradox: Turning the Power of Mindset into Action* (New York: Ballantine Books, 2023), 16, 157–193.

4. Rob Cross, Reb Rebele, and Adam Grant, "Collaborative Overload," *Harvard Business Review* (January–February 2016). https://hbr.org/2016/01/collaborative -overload.

5. Robert D. Putnam with Shaylyn Romney Garrett, *The Upswing: How America Came Together a Century Ago and How We Can Do It Again* (New York: Simon & Schuster, 2020), 288.

6. Wendy Fischman and Howard Gardner, *The Real World of College: What Higher Education Is and What It Can Be* (Cambridge, MA: MIT Press, 2022), 171–233; Colleen Walsh, "Young Adults Hardest Hit by Loneliness during Pandemic," *The Harvard Gazette*, February 21, 2021; Anemona Hartocollis, "Another Surge in the Virus Has Colleges Fearing a Mental Health Crisis," *New York Times*, December 22, 2021; and Marisa Iati, "A New National Crisis," *Washington Post*, December 24, 2021.

7. See https://standnow.org/about/history/.

8. See https://lgbtq.georgetown.edu/history/outforchange/.

9. A temporary security officer at F&M falsely reported that an anonymous Black male had shot him when he was leaving campus after a shift. It came out that he had accidentally wounded himself.

10. Daniel F. Chambliss and Christopher G. Takacs, *How College Works* (Cambridge, MA: Harvard University Press, 2014), 78–103.

11. https://inside.fandm.edu/roschel-college-house/roschel-house-government /roschel-college-house-constitution.php.

12. https://inside.fandm.edu/_resources/pdfs/Roschel-houserules.pdf.

13. Ronald J. Daniels with Grant Shreve and Phillip Spector, *What Universities Owe Democracy* (Baltimore: Johns Hopkins University Press, 2021), 93–94.

14. A well-documented success story is the Meyerhoff Scholars Program at the University of Maryland, Baltimore County. See Kenneth Maton, Shauna Pollard, Tatiana McDougall Weise, and Freeman Hrabowski III, "Meyerhoff Scholars Program: A Strengths-Based, Institution-Wide Approach to Increasing Diversity in Science, Technology, Engineering, and Mathematics," *Mount Sinai Journal of Medicine* 79, no. 5 (2012): 610–623.

15. See Nicole M. Stephens, Stephanie A. Fryberg, Hazel Rose Markus, Camille S. Johnson, and Rebecca Covarrubias, "Unseen Disadvantage: How American

Universities' Focus on Independence Undermines the Academic Performance of First-Generation College Students," *Journal of Personal and Social Psychology* 102, no. 6 (2012): 1178–1197.

16. Stephen E. Ambrose, *Band of Brothers: E Company, 506th Regiment, 101st Airborne from Normandy to Hitler's Eagle's Nest* (New York: Simon & Schuster, reissue ed., 2017).

17. Larry Alexander, *Biggest Brother: The Life of Major Dick Winters, the Man Who Led the Band of Brothers* (New York: Dutton Caliber, 2006), 27.

18. https://www.youtube.com/watch?v=5gRZhSlEoGI.

19. Jeré Longman, "Mandela Embraced the Power of Sports for Resistance and Unity," *New York Times*, December 5, 2013.

20. Jane S. Halonen and Dana S. Dunn, "Why and How to Teach Teamwork," *Chronicle of Higher Education*, November 15, 2021. The article offers excellent suggestions for the design of effective group learning. Also see Neil Garg and Kevin D. Dougherty, "Education Surges When Students Learn Together," *Inside Higher Ed*, May 25, 2022.

21. https://drive.google.com/file/d/1xIuBbC3kTf2BDgM9yXLwbcqgn_e5aeq8 /view, 8.

22. Eric Schoeniger, "Change Agents: The Transformational Effects of Community-Based Learning," *Franklin & Marshall Magazine*, June 5, 2012.

23. Carol Quillen and Elisa Villanueva Beard, "Education at an Inflection Point," an unpublished dialogue (Aspen Institute: July 22, 2021).

Chapter 5

1. Susan Hay, "From Child Soldier in Uganda to Documentary Filmmaker: Dominic Akena Shares Story of Survival," *Global News*, July 25, 2019. As a child, Dominic was featured in the 2007 documentary *War Dance* by Sean Fine and Andrea Nix Fine.

2. Dave Sheinin, "This Deaf-Blind Paralympian Was Told to Navigate Tokyo Alone. So She Quit Team USA," *Washington Post*, July 19, 2021. Also, see https:// usopm.org/swimmer-becca-meyers-found-her-happy-place-in-the-pool/.

3. Mike Andrelczyk, "F&M Senior Jonny Teklit Declared Most Promising Young Poet by Academy of American Poets," *LNP/Lancaster Online*, November 29, 2019.

4. Angela Duckworth, *Grit: The Power and Passion of Perseverance* (New York: Scribner Book Company, 2016), 8.

5. Agnes Callard, *Aspiration: The Agency of Becoming* (Oxford: Oxford University Press, 2018), 61.

6. W. B. Yeats, "To a Shade," in *Collected Poems* (London: Macmillan, 1977), 123.

7. Gwendolyn Brooks, "Life for My Child Is Simple, and Is Good," in *Selected Poems* (New York: Harper & Row Publishers, 1963), 55.

8. Agnes Callard, *Aspiration*, 24.

9. Anindya Kundu, *The Power of Student Agency: Looking Beyond Grit to Close the Opportunity Gap* (New York: Teachers College Press, 2020), 21.

10. For example, the scholar Gene Brody has found that African Americans with "unrelenting determination to succeed" are more likely to suffer compromised immune systems, diabetes, hypertension, and heart problems. See James Hamblin,

"Why Succeeding Against the Odds Can Make You Sick," *New York Times*, January 27, 2017.

11. Kundu, *Power of Student Agency*, 21.

12. For a riveting discussion of these themes, see Jennifer M. Morton, *Moving Up Without Losing Your Way* (Princeton, NJ: Princeton University Press, 2019), especially 98–119.

13. James Martin, SJ, *The Jesuit Guide to (Almost) Everything: A Spirituality for Real Life* (New York: HarperOne, 2012), 7–8.

14. Colleen Flaherty, "Measuring and Promoting Thriving in College," *Inside Higher Ed*, July 13, 2023.

Chapter 6

1. See Brian Rosenberg, *"Whatever It Is, I'm Against It": Resistance to Change in Higher Education* (Cambridge, MA: Harvard University Press, 2023).

2. Quoted in Thomas B. Edsall, "There Are Two Americas Now: One with a B.A. and One Without," *New York Times*, October 10, 2022.

3. Gerard Manley Hopkins, "As Kingfishers Catch Fire," in *Poems and Prose of Gerard Manley Hopkins*, ed. W. H. Gardner (New York, Penguin Books, 1953), 51.

4. Michelle Obama, *Becoming* (New York: Crown, 2018), 419.

5. Mohsin Hamid, *Exit West* (New York: Riverhead Books, 2017).

6. Akbar Hossain, "Commentary: A Muslim Immigrant Is Standing His Ground," *Philadelphia Inquirer*, December 4, 2016.

7. Akbar Hossain, "Only in America," TEDx Franklin & Marshall College, May 20, 2014. Video, https://www.youtube.com/watch?v=9B1-jsx-qhg.

8. Jhumpa Lahiri, *In Other Words* (New York: Vintage, 2017), 37, 113.

9. Tara Westover, *Educated* (New York: Random House Books, 2018), 197.

10. Carol S. Dweck, *Mindset: The New Psychology of Success* (New York: Ballantine Books, 2006), 67.

11. See *From a Nation at Risk to a Nation at Hope: Recommendations from the National Commission on Social, Emotional, & Academic Development* (Washington, DC: Aspen Institute, 2019).

12. See Andrea Juno and Vivian Vale, *Angry Women* (San Francisco: RE/Search Publications, 1991), 78.

13. Elizabeth Alexander, *Praise Song for the Day* (Minneapolis, MN: Graywolf Press, 2009).

14. Steven Mintz, "Our Future Self," *Inside Higher Ed*, April 18, 2023.

15. Michael Rubinkam, "DA: Racist Texts on Pa. School Officials' Phones, Parents Demand Firings," *New Pittsburgh Courier*, September 24, 2013. https://newpittsburgh courier.com/2013/09/24/da-racist-texts-on-pa-school-officials-phones-parents -demand-firings/.

INDEX

housing/dormitories, 50; College House model, 63, 184–89; housing insecurity, 43–44, 123

Howard Hughes Medical Institute, 68–69

How College Works (Chambliss and Takacs), 35

humanism, 15–16, 38, 91–92

human rights, 83–84, 145, 218

Human Rights Initiative, The (THRI), 145–46, 147–48

Hungry Hearts (Yezierska), 77

identity: culture and, 183; dual, 31, 274; emotions and, 218; growth mindsets-based, 15, 17, 20, 125, 142, 178, 218; intersectional, 239; loss of, 236; mentorship as, 131; racial, 80; relation to learning, 42, 43–44; teaching as expression of, 82

Ifill, Gwen, 22

imagination, 18, 60, 85, 87, 107, 213; immigrants and refugees: community service projects for, 218, 219, 263; education-based social integration, 267–68; political asylum, 218, 219; US diversity visa lottery, 264–66, 270–71

immigrant students, 28–31, 145, 148, 191; collaboration mindset, 191, 192; colleges serving, 37–38; creation mindset, 103–7; DACA/"Dreamers" program, 160–63, 287; mentorship mindset, 156–63; Mexican American, 85, 116–23; Muslim, 30–31, 262–71; recruitment, 38; striving mindset, 157–62, 222–23, 225–29, 243–57

I.M.P.A.C.T, 22–24, 128, 137–38, 140, 171, 172, 180–82, 200, 254

imposter syndrome, 43

inclusivity, 25–26, 40, 82–83, 107, 131, 188, 192, 287

independence, 3, 6, 32, 74, 88, 159, 226

initiative, 27, 39, 43, 83, 255, 277

innovation and invention, 20, 33, 97, 102–3; as "creative construction," 123–24; The Ideas Class seminar on, 112–15. *See also* creation mindset; entrepreneurship

In Other Words (Lahiri), 275

integrity, 51, 62, 118, 154, 171, 175, 187, 188, 201, 210–11, 230

international students, 38, 64, 130, 179, 268, 273, 278

internships, 30, 61, 68–69, 82, 89, 110–11, 145, 166, 255

Islamic studies, 64, 65

isolation, 178, 236

Jack, Anthony, 77

Jesuits, approaches to education, 71–72, 132, 248

Katz, Lawrence, 33–34

Katzenbach, Jon R., 176–77

Keller, Helen, 8

Kennedy family, portrayed in *Domestic Animals*, 21, 97–99

Kennett, Jeanette, 151–52

King, Martin Luther, Jr., 107

KIPP public charter schools, 79, 136, 239–40

knowledge, 3, 17–18, 21, 36, 42–44, 51, 66, 91; connectedness, 63; data-based, 52; economy of, 261

Kundu, Anindya, 237, 239, 257

Lambert, Leo M., 143

Lancaster County (PA) Career and Technology Center, 165

language(s): English as second language, 157, 158; language studies, 75–76, 87, 200–201, 276; sexist or homophobic, 181; summer language fellowships, 275

Latino students, 37–38; mentorship mindset, 156–63, 171; Mexican American, 85, 116–23; recruitment, 38

law school education, 242, 262, 269–70

leadership, 37; peer leadership, 37, 200, 201, 214, 232, 234; response to change, 224–25; servant, 22, 205–6, 230; striving mindset-based, 224–25, 271

learning: active, 5, 43, 53, 54, 55, 59, 60–61, 62, 83, 87, 88, 93; campus-based model, 45–46; culture of, 45; disorientation aspect, 66–67, 70, 88; ecosystems, 34, 37, 48, 68, 88, 95, 101, 116, 130, 295n7; emotional and social barriers, 91; evidence-based peer-learning, 61; experiential, 37, 146; faculty-student relationship in, 35, 43, 51, 56, 57–58; fixed

learning (*cont.*)
mindset in, 277; how to learn, 32; humanistic, 38; journeys, 7; lifelong, 3, 7–8, 9, 16, 19, 37, 90–91; motivation for, 5–6, 44; natural critical environments for, 18–20, 81; "on-boarding process," 59–72; opportunities for, 8, 39; passive, 52–53, 60; personalization of, 31, 39, 48, 50–51, 58–59, 88–89, 90, 161–62, 227–28, 236, 260; project-based, 37; relation to identity, 42, 43–44; self-propelled, 56; sequential nature of, 51; skills, 51; striving mindset approach to, 235–37; team-enabled, 37
Leonhardt, David, 3
LGBTQ students/community, 78, 96–97, 179, 182–83, 218, 272
liberal arts education, 64, 100, 109, 195, 295n7, 299n59; in innovation, 112–13; for STEM students, 54
liberal education, 15–16, 70
Lincoln University, 281
Lorde, Audre, 123

Malcolm X, 8
Mandela, Nelson, 208, 211
marginalized/low-income students, 36; recruitment, 38–40; in rural communities, 163–72; sense of purpose and meaning, 77–86; undermatching, 78, 169–70. *See also* Black students and students of color; immigrant students
Marshall College, 5, 295n6
meaning, sense of, 53, 63, 67; discovery mindset-based, 53, 63, 67, 71–86; *eudaimonia* concept of, 261; mentorship mindset-based, 132, 170, 172; striving mindset-based, 230, 255
meaningful relationships, 35, 68, 295n7; among cohort group members, 189–202; among sports team members, 241, 242, 245–46; creation mindset-based, 96–103; mentorship mindset-based, 132, 143–51
medical education, 61, 147, 152, 154, 189, 192, 206, 222, 225, 247, 255–56
mental health, 36, 261
mentorship, 4–5, 8, 9, 42–45, 58–59, 236, 262–63, 277, 284; in the arts, 97, 100–101,

119, 120–21, 130, 215–18, 223–24, 248–49, 251–53; of athletes, 41, 73, 158, 203–13, 209, 214, 229, 230, 232–35, 241; availability of mentors, 19–20, 63, 142, 163–64; for collaboration mindset development, 215–18; for creation mindset development, 111, 112–13, 114–15, 119, 120–21, 125, 130; for cultural diversity, 273–74, 275, 276; of DACA/"Dreamer" students, 160–63; definition, 22; for discovery mindset development, 43, 52, 54, 55–58, 59, 64–71, 88, 92; in F&M College Prep program, 23, 135–37, 153, 156, 164, 172, 197, 200, 201; of high school and middle school students, 163–72, 171, 281–82, 283; institutional policies for, 163–64, 173; interracial, 82–83; for invention and innovation, 111, 112–13, 114–15; need for, 46, 142; origin, 128–29; personalized, 54; in Posse program, 56, 67–68, 133–34, 189–90, 247, 248; prioritization of teaching in, 18–20; in STEM education, 67, 129, 189, 193, 194–95, 196–97, 198, 199–200, 201, 202, 228, 244–45, 246, 248, 251, 300n23; for striving mindset development, 13–14, 28, 243–45, 246, 248, 251, 254, 277–78; of students of color, 22–25, 82–83, 133–35, 136–37, 180, 181; training in, 35, 131, 142, 163–64, 303n9
mentorship mindset, 4–5, 10–11, 16–17, 32, 127–74; among Black students, 22–25, 128, 137–38, 140, 171, 172, 180–82; as basis for meaningful relationships, 6, 143–55, 163; collaboration mindset-based, 125; ethical or moral resonance of, 155–63, 173; flywheel analogy, 129–30, 137–38, 173; group mentorship, 137–43, 173–74, 181; influence of mentoring on, 22–25, 142, 163–64, 168–69; lifelong advantages, 131–32, 143, 144; motivations for, 130–31; mutual mentorship, 150–55, 163, 180; peer mentors, 39, 125, 128–31, 134–50, 159, 160–62, 163–64, 200; as personal fulfillment, 163–73; reciprocal nature of, 22–25, 129–30, 132, 137, 143–55; as response to trauma, 132, 156–63; striving mindset-based, 14
meta-cognitive qualities, 32

Mexican American students: creation mindset, 85, 116–23; LGBTQ, 182–83; mutual mentorship of, 150–55; striving mindset, 238–42

Mexico, Ayotzinapa college student massacre, 117–20, 302n16

Miami Posse One cohort, 54, 56, 190–202, 222, 244, 246, 247, 248

military institutions, 38, 206

military service, 41, 55, 166, 167, 170, 189, 203–5, 253; child soldiers, 223, 305n1

Miller, Richard K., 16

Miller-Muro, Layli, 145

Millersville University, 167, 230

mindset: definition, 7–8. *See also* growth mindsets

Mintz, Steven, 90, 284, 301n35

moral development, 36; mentorship mindset-based, 155–63

motivation, 9, 32, 35, 44, 89, 90–91, 131, 134, 152, 281–82

multiculturalism, 29, 30–31, 76, 191

multidisciplinary studies, 112

Murphy, Mary, 61

Murtrie, Beth, 60–61

Muslims, 275; prejudice toward, 270, 273–74

Muslim students, 30–31, 64, 262–71, 272

mutuality, 26, 244; in mentorship, 150–55, 159, 163, 180

National College Athletics Association (NCAA), 204, 207, 234

Newman, John Henry (Cardinal), 15

North Star Academy, 79, 86

Obama, Michelle, 261

Odyssey, The, 128–29, 157

opportunity: as American dream, 6, 267, 270; collaboration mindset toward, 180, 187, 189, 193–94, 212; creation mindset toward, 109; discovery mindset toward, 83, 90; ecosystems, 7, 34; equity/inequity of, 36, 280; lost, 8; mentorship mindset toward, 22, 127, 151, 152, 154, 160–61, 162, 180; openness to, 196, 268, 282, 286; striving mindset toward, 31, 224, 228, 229, 238, 240

optimism, 8, 32, 169, 204, 272, 284

orientation programs, 50, 62, 77–78, 144–45, 183–84, 200, 278

out-of-class growth experiences, 37, 39, 68–69, 83, 260. *See also* community service projects; student clubs and organizations

Oxx, Gerry, 159

Paralympic Games, 223

parents: death of, 72, 76, 77, 98, 99, 105, 239–42, 246–49, 256, 266, 270, 286–87; immigrant, 115–18, 122, 191, 225–29, 242, 256, 263–67, 269, 270–71; opposition to children's aspirations, 29, 30, 41; role in growth mindset formation, 9–10, 154; role in striving mindset formation, 225–29

"pedagogy of involvement," 35, 43, 54, 57, 87, 90, 93, 101, 110, 124

peer leadership, 37, 200, 201, 214, 232, 234

Penn Medicine Lancaster General Health, 114

Pennsylvania College Advising Corps (PCAC) program, 164–72

Philadelphia College of Osteopathic Medicine, 225

pluralism, 219–20, 267–68

poetry, 133, 138–43, 172, 175, 192, 194, 200

portfolios, 214; e-portfolios, 90

Posse Foundation, 54, 56, 67, 103, 133–34, 189–90, 254; Miami Posse One cohort, 190–202, 222, 228–29, 244, 246, 247, 248; partnership with F&M College, 189–202

Prendergast, John, 145

problem solving, 42, 61, 260–61; collaboration mindset approach, 25–26, 61, 176–77, 198, 200; creation mindset approach, 21–22, 96, 108–15; discovery mindset approach, 18, 52–53; mentors' encouragement of, 42–44, 200; seminar model, 215, 218–19

Process Oriented Guided Inquiry Learning (POGIL), 61

Public Safety Committee, 201, 231, 232

public service, growth mindsets for, 262–78

purpose, sense of, 17, 39, 53, 67, 71–86, 115, 163, 255

Putnam, Robert, 177

Quillen, Carol, 219–20
Quinnipiac University, Center for Teaching and Learning, 56

racism, 58, 81, 84, 87; apartheid, 208, 210–11; Black students' responses to, 103–7, 108, 122, 123, 200, 237, 279–86
Ramadan, Tariq, 65
Rauch, Frederick, 5
recruitment, of students: DACA/"Dreamers" students, 160–61; Next Generation talent strategy, 38–40, 41, 118; student athletes, 72
reflection, relation to action, 244–53, 254
religion: campus religious life, 64; religious beliefs, 30–31; religious institutions, 38; religious studies, 64, 65, 87; spirituality, 13, 255. *See also specific religious denominations*
research, 223; about growth mindset, 34; about mentorship, 131, 142–43; creativity mindset approach, 21; discovery mindset approach, 56–58, 61, 62, 65–66, 68–71, 74–75, 88, 92; in innovation and invention, 113–14; in learning ecosystems, 37; peer leadership, 200; postgraduate employment in, 202; with primary sources, 74; striving mindset approach, 247, 251
residential higher education, 17, 219; American model, 2–3, 6; human energy system of, 94–97, 127–28
resilience, 4, 11, 13–14, 39, 41, 51, 160, 205, 238, 255, 264, 282, 284
Robinson, Ken, 119, 176
role models, 23, 24, 27, 66, 81, 241–42, 251
Roosevelt, Theodore, 21, 98–99
Rotaract program, 68
rural students, 163–72, 38, 272–78

Sandy Hook massacre, Newton, CT, 102
Sawyer, Keith, 25
scholarship, 20–21, 56–58, 64, 85, 142, 167, 172, 188, 210, 281
scholarships, 30, 31, 41, 54, 56, 67, 103, 117, 147, 159, 172, 188, 190, 191, 210, 229, 262, 268, 271, 273, 276
Schreiner, Laurie, 255
science, 16, 34

self-knowledge, 44, 67–68
self-reliance, 158, 224, 251
September 11 terrorist attacks, 265, 269, 271, 287
sexual misconduct, 214, 232, 274
Shapiro, Josh, 262
shared governance committees, 176, 183–89
S.I.S.T.E.R.S, 83, 180, 181, 182–83, 201
Smith, Douglas K., 176–77
social mobility, 260–61, 269, 284
sociology, 78–79, 85, 237, 283–85
"solutions culture," 113
sororities, 188, 201, 231, 232, 233
South Africa, 73, 208–11
sports. *See* athletes
Stanford University, Hasso Plattner Institute of Design, 112
STEM (science, technology, engineering, and math) education, 54, 68, 170, 228; active learning in, 60–61; cohort streams, 189–202; growth mindsets-based approaches, 60–61, 68–71, 87, 195, 228–29, 243–53, 256; mentorship in, 56–58, 67, 129–30, 189, 193, 194–95, 196–97, 198, 199–200, 201, 202, 228, 244–45, 246, 248, 300n23
stress management, 114, 130, 238, 239, 245
striving mindset, 10–11, 16–17, 26–31, 45, 46, 222–57, 262–78; action and reflection in, 244–53, 254; of artists and writers, 223–24, 251–53; of athletes, 223–24, 239–42; in cohort groups, 198, 254; definition, 256–57; friendship-enhanced, 163; grit and agency in, 238–39; of immigrant students, 157–62, 222–23, 225–29, 243–57, 271; new pursuits-based, 229–35; as response to trauma, 11–15, 26–27, 223, 225–29, 235–50; social benefits, 224–25, 255; supportive strategies, 253–55
student clubs and organizations, 22–24, 129, 131, 145–46, 153, 175; all-student organization model, 176, 179–83, 213, 214; guidelines for success, 213–14, 221
student government, 63, 116, 153, 176, 183–89, 214, 221
study-away programs, 71, 83–84, 286
study habits and skills, 42, 57, 79–80, 196, 236, 237, 244–45, 279, 299n8

talent, 21, 39, 47, 96, 141, 191, 260–61, 281, 286; as college admission basis, 38–40, 41, 118; for collaboration, 177, 182, 211; definition, 32, 288; development, 32–33, 35, 36, 51, 67, 223, 229; for mentorship, 141, 160–61; for striving, 224, 229

Tatum, Beverly, 106

Teach For America, 85, 202, 237

teaching: as citizenship, 47; for discovery mindset development, 59–63; excellence, 19–20, 90–91

team experience. *See* collaboration mindset

technical and vocational education, 37, 167, 170, 172

technology: learning-supportive, 89–90; transformational, 3–5, 33–34, 47, 224–25

Temple University Medical School, 61

testing and test scores, 58, 150, 282

Thaddeus Stevens College of Technology, 172

Tharp, Twyla, 21

theses, 20–21, 43–44, 51, 65–66, 70, 71, 122, 123, 273

thinking/thought: critical, 19, 51, 52, 62–63, 91, 96, 111, 188, 237; dialogue-based, 59–60; discovery mindset-based, 87–88; ethical, 17; freedom of, 51, 52; leadership, 131; new paradigms, 52; passive, 52–53

thriving, in undergraduates, 255

Torres, JT, 56

transfer students, 59, 73–74, 76

trauma, students' responses to: collaboration mindset-based, 182–83; creation mindset-based, 101–3, 116–23; discovery mindset-based, 72, 76, 77, 88–89, 91; immigrant resettlement, 263–67, 269; mentorship mindset-based, 132, 156–63; racial trauma, 281–86; striving mindset-based, 223, 225–29, 235–44, 246–48, 256, 257

trust, 26, 44, 78, 104, 134, 155, 157, 177, 178, 186, 189, 191, 192, 193, 205, 215–16, 278, 285

Tufts Medical School, 247

undermatching, 78, 169–70

Uniformed Services University, 206

Universidad EAFIT, 226

University of: Alabama, 154; Chicago, 66; Colorado, 68–69; Illinois, 278; Maryland, 40, 69; Miami, 246, Michigan, 30, 45; Missouri, 103–4; Nevada, 41; Pennsylvania, 251, 262, 269; Rochester, 147; South Florida, 189; Virgin Islands, 281

Upward Bound, 117, 280–81, 282

Ursinus College, 234

values, 4–5, 32, 36; of athletes, 73, 204–14, 230, 233, 239–43, 250; communal, 189; growth mindsets-related, 26–27, 33; 51, 224, 225, 229, 235–40, 255, 256–57

virtual technology, 89–90, 143

Walker, Susan, 41

Washburn, Sue, 38

Westover, Tara, 276

What Universities Owe Democracies (Daniels), 188

white privilege or supremacy, 58, 237, 240, 285–86

Whyte, David, 154–55

Winter, Ben and Susan, 122

Winters, Dick, 31, 203–5

writing skills, 55–56, 62–63, 65, 134, 207–8, 223; poetry, 138–43, 223–24; theses, 20–21, 43, 51, 122, 273, 277

Yik Yak app, 104, 200, 237

Zachary, Lois J., 131–32

ABOUT THE AUTHOR

In 2018, Daniel R. Porterfield became the fourteenth president and CEO of the Aspen Institute.

Before that, he served as the president of Franklin & Marshall College from 2011 to 2018 and as an English professor and senior vice president for strategic development at Georgetown University from 1996 to 2011.

At F&M, he was recognized as a 2016 White House Champion of Change, the creator of the college's Next Generation talent strategy, and a cofounder of the American Talent Initiative, through which more than one hundred of the finest institutions in the United States are teaming up to increase the enrollment and graduation rates of Pell Grant students.

At Georgetown University, while leading multiple strategic initiatives, he was an award-winning professor and lived for eight years with his family in a residence hall.

Porterfield is a Rhodes scholar and a Mellon fellow in the humanities, and a graduate of Georgetown University, Oxford University, and The City of New York Graduate Center. In 2022, he was inducted into the American Academy of Arts & Sciences.